Ice Bear

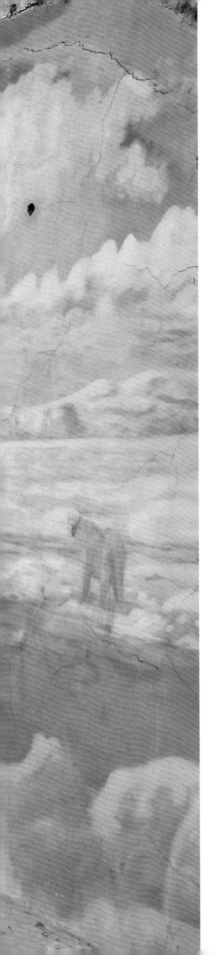

Ice Bear

The
CULTURAL
HISTORY
of an
ARCTIC
ICON

Michael Engelhard

UNIVERSITY OF WASHINGTON PRESS
Seattle and London

© 2017 by the University of Washington Press
Printed and bound in China
Design by Thomas Eykemans
Composed in Warnock, typeface designed by Robert Slimbach
21 20 19 18 17   5 4 3 2 1

FRONTISPIECE: "Taco" in Santiago de Chile's Metropolitan Zoo.
Photo by Aldo Fontana.

IMAGE ON PAGE V: Postcard after a lithograph by the Norwegian
painter and illustrator Thorolf Holmboe, 1915. Author's collection.

IMAGE ON PAGE VI: With its "chiseled" silhouette, the polar bear
lends itself to abstraction in sculptures or logos. In his acrylic
painting and serigraph *Scary Scenario*, the American modernist
Charley Harper (1922–2007) reduced to their essentials two species whose ranges could soon overlap. Courtesy of Charley Harper
Art Studio.

IMAGE ON PAGE VIII: Echoes of Goya: this untitled oil-on-wood
portrait by Miguel Macaya (born 1964) asserts the bear's individuality. Photo by Inés Mazuela.

"The Polar Bear," by William Carlos Williams, from *The Collected
Poems: Volume II, 1939–1962*, copyright © 1962 by William Carlos
Williams. Excerpt by permission of New Directions Publishing
Corp.

UNIVERSITY OF WASHINGTON PRESS
www.washington.edu/uwpress

Cataloging data is on file with the Library of Congress
ISBN 978-0-295-99922-7

The paper used in this publication is acid-free and meets the min-
imum requirements of American National Standard for Information Sciences—Permanence of Paper for Printed Library Materials,
ANSI Z39.48–1984. ∞

The land is very sterile. There are in it many white bears . . .

—LEGEND BY SEBASTIAN CABOT ON A MAP OF NORTH AMERICA (1544)

They appeared to be very fat and prosperous, and very much at home, as if the country had belonged to them always. They are the unrivaled master-existences of this ice-bound solitude.

—JOHN MUIR, *THE CRUISE OF THE CORWIN* (1917)

CONTENTS

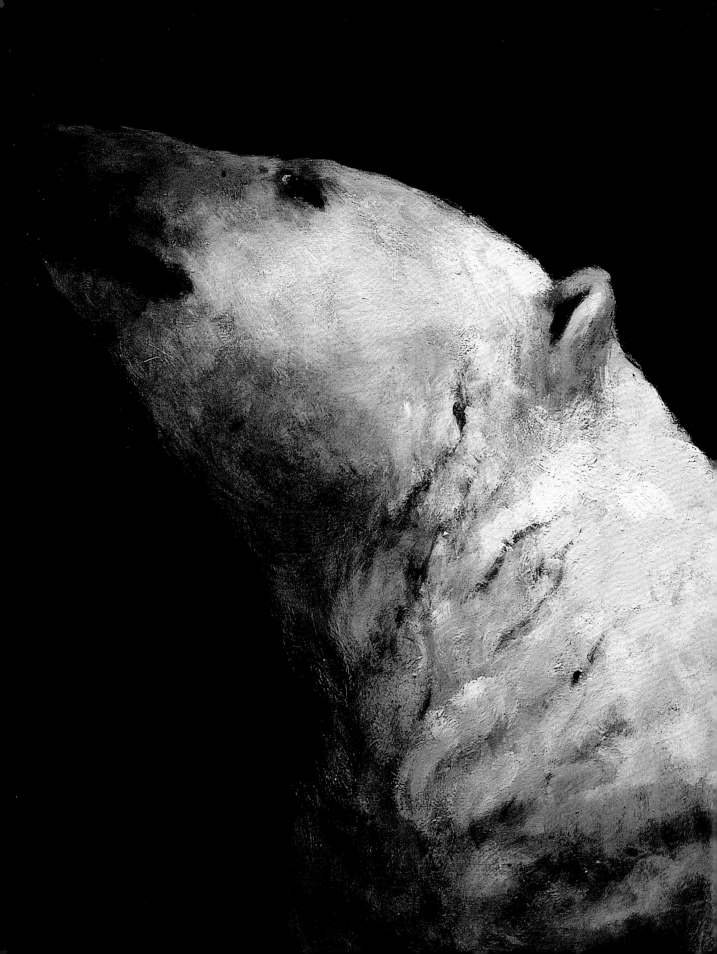

ACKNOWLEDGMENTS

It has been a pleasure, in the course of writing this book, to meet fellow polar bear buffs and other specialists (and that's putting it mildly), even if only online. I appreciate their time, expertise, and patience with endless follow-up questions. Thank you, Valerie Abbott, Naja Abelsen, Silke Adam, Sigurður Ægisson, Eric Ames, Martin Appelt, Allison Athens, Ronald Broglio, Bernd Brunner, Victoria Buckley, Joel Castanza, Jack Coogan, Ekaterina Devlet, Alexander Dolitsky, Kelsey Eliasson, Richard Ellis, Klaus Gille, Patty Gray, Lynn Hetlet, Linda Honey, J. Donald Hughes, Larry Kaplan, Anatoly Kochnev and Svetlana Kochneva, Janis Kozlowski, Lisa LaPoint, Raynald Harvey Lemelin, Martha MacDonald, Garry Marvin, John McKay, Sean Mooney, Georg Nyegaard, Ævar Petersen, Rachel Poliquin, Russell Potter, Tanyo Ravicz, William Reaves, Richard Reynolds, France Rivet, Mette Rønsager, Bernard Saladin d'Anglure, Michael Schimek, Dennis Sears, Bryndís Snæbjörnsdóttir, Rhonda Sparks, Amy Dee Stephens, Ann Sylph, Chris Trott, Zac Unger, Glen Vaudrey, Haijo Westra, and Mark Wilson. Unsurprisingly, this polyglot lineup testifies to a far-flung fascination with all things polar bear, an attraction that draws people of all stripes to each other and to the North.

Special thanks go to Jonathan Burt, editor of Reaktion Book's Animal series, for helping me "find" this animal, as intriguing a writing subject as it is face to face. Winfried Dallmann at the Norwegian Polar Institute compiled and kindly provided the map, Indigenous Peoples of the Arctic, which we adapted to include the White Bear's range. Thanks go to Wolfgang and Mechtild Opel and to Hartmut Jäcksch of Mana Verlag for a copy of their fine book, *Eisbären*. Wolfgang also generously shared information and images. Andrew Derocher, one of the world's leading polar bear biologists, made useful suggestions and caught errors and oddities in his close reading of the manuscript.

The University of Washington Press saw the potential, perhaps even need, for another polar bear book in the slew of already published titles, one that deals exclusively with the animal's cultural aspects. For that, I am grateful.

Caroline Knapp streamlined my thinking and prose, and I enjoyed our exchanges in parentheses as well as learning about "scare quotes."

I cannot acknowledge here individually all those who contributed images, often free of charge or at a reduced fee. Others pledged money, which allowed me to obtain even more high-quality illustrations. The generosity of these contributors added color and nuance to this work. I do have to single out Walton Ford and the Paul Kasmin Gallery. Walton's goose bump–producing *Novaya Zemlya Still Life*, which Tom Eykemans turned into an exquisite cover, perfectly resonates with this book's tone. As always, my wife and adventurous companion, Melissa Guy, advised me patiently about images and good design and has been a sounding board for my sometimes outlandish ideas.

Mistakes are bound to sneak into any attempt to summarize and interpret eight thousand years of interaction between an animal species and us. I apologize in advance. I'd also like readers to indulge a certain amount of guesswork and digression, which always should be evident in the text; some of the leads, even seemingly disparate ones, were simply too tempting not to follow and try to connect.

No animals were mistreated or hurt in the making of this book, "only" trees. I sincerely hope their sacrifice at the altar of knowledge was worth the sap spilled.

POLAR BEAR–HUMAN TIME LINE

CA. 8,000 BP — In northeastern Siberia's De Long Archipelago, people hunt polar bears, predominantly females, perhaps in or near dens.

FIRST CENTURY CE — A female shaman is buried at Ekven, Chukotka. Her grave goods include a decorated ivory paddle for pottery, which shows a shaman whose outstretched legs and hands are transforming into the paws of a polar bear spirit helper.

CA. 500 CE — Indigenous artists incise polar bear images on rock faces in the Pegtymel' River valley on the Chukchi Peninsula. Hunters of the Middle Dorset culture, in what is today Canada, carve ivory "flying" polar bear effigies.

894 — Ingimundur the Old, a Norse settler in Iceland, captures two polar bear cubs and sends them to King Harald of Norway.

1234 — Holy Roman Emperor Frederick II gifts a white bear to King Mohammad Al Kamil of Egypt. (Al Kamil, years later, allegedly reciprocates with a giraffe.)

1492 — German mariner-astronomer Martin Behaim adds polar bears, in the vicinity of Greenland, to his famous painted globe.

1534 — During Jacques Cartier's exploration of Newfoundland, on an island offshore, Cartier's men find a bear "as big as a calf and as white as a swan"—the first polar bear described in its native environment.

1544 — The first image of a polar bear on a map of North America appears on a world map usually ascribed to Sebastian Cabot. It shows the Arctic Circle at the correct latitude and two bears south of it, around present-day Quebec.

1585 — Approaching Baffin Island, John Davis spots four white "beares of a monstruous bignesse."

1609 — Captain Jonas Poole transports two polar bear cubs from Svalbard to London, where they are kept in the Beargarden and possibly appear in pit fights and three Shakespeare productions.

1733	The first polar bear is exhibited in North America, in Boston.
1774	Captain Constantine J. Phipps names the polar bear *Ursus maritimus.*
1859	The first zoo in the United States is established in Philadelphia, with a polar bear as the first North American "zoo bear."
1864	Sir Edwin Henry Landseer exhibits *Man Proposes, God Disposes*, his painting of the Franklin Expedition's remains.
1894 TO 1897	Wintering on the Russian Arctic's Franz Josef Land in the Barents Sea, members of the Jackson-Harmsworth Expedition kill seventy-three polar bears; the crew gets rewards for spotting bears for the gentleman hunters.
1909	Seventy-five polar bears, trained by Wilhelm Hagenbeck, perform in a 100,000-gallon water tank at the London Hippodrome.
1917	Trainer "Captain" Jack Bonavita is killed while working with a group of polar bears.
1918	Woodrow Wilson sends an intervention force to Arkhangelsk to fight the Red Army in the Russian Civil War, an operation known as the Polar Bear Expedition.
1922	The French sculptor François Pompon—assistant to Auguste Rodin—finishes *L'Ours Blanc*, also known as *Polar Bear in Stride.*
1939	After his zoo visit, a writer for *The Jack Benny Show* invents the character of Carmichael the pet polar bear, which lived in Benny's basement, was rumored to have eaten the gasman, and was impersonated by Mel Blanc—the voice of *The Flintstones'* Barney Rubble.
1951	Marilyn Monroe poses for a studio portrait on a polar bear rug. By this time, polar bear sport hunters in Alaska mostly use fixed-wing aircraft on skis to locate their prey.
1956	The Soviet Union bans all polar bear hunting in its territories; the year before, it detonated the first of more than ninety nuclear weapons on Novaya Zemlya, a polar bear denning area in the Kara Sea.
1961	One of the largest polar bears on record is shot near Kotzebue, Alaska. It weighs 2,210 pounds.
1973	All five nations with territory inhabited by polar bears—Canada, Denmark, Norway, the United States, and the Soviet Union—sign an international

conservation agreement. The treaty allows hunting "by local people using traditional methods."

1980s   Modern methods of tracking polar bear populations are implemented to determine ranges and subpopulations.

1988   The twin polar bears "Hidy" and "Howdy" are the official mascots for the Winter Olympics in Calgary.

1990s   More than thirty years after *Silent Spring*, biologists detect a number of toxic chemicals in Svalbard's polar bears.

2006   A trophy hunter kills a grizzly bear–polar bear hybrid near Banks Island, Canada.

2008   The U.S. Fish and Wildlife Service determines that polar bears should be listed under the Endangered Species Act; Debby, the oldest polar bear on record, dies at age forty-two in Winnipeg's zoo.

2009   In Copenhagen, the Ice Bear Project showcases a polar bear statue made of ice that, in melting, exposes a bronze skeleton; in Berlin, a woman attempts suicide by jumping into the zoo's polar bear enclosure.

2011   In an attempt to forestall poaching, Russia approves quotas allowing indigenous people in the Chukotka region to hunt polar bears for the first time since the 1950s.

2013   A U.S. appeals court upholds the 2008 decision to list the polar bear as threatened. It is the first species ever listed solely because of expected future trends.

2014   A filmmaker and a biologist attach "crittercams" to four Bering Sea polar bears, trying to see what the bears see and to learn how they spend their days.

2015   A study shows that some polar bears have shifted their ranges to include Canada's Arctic archipelagos, where annual sea ice lasts longer; another finds that Knut, the Berlin Zoo's famous polar bear, drowned in 2011 due to auto-immune disease of the brain.

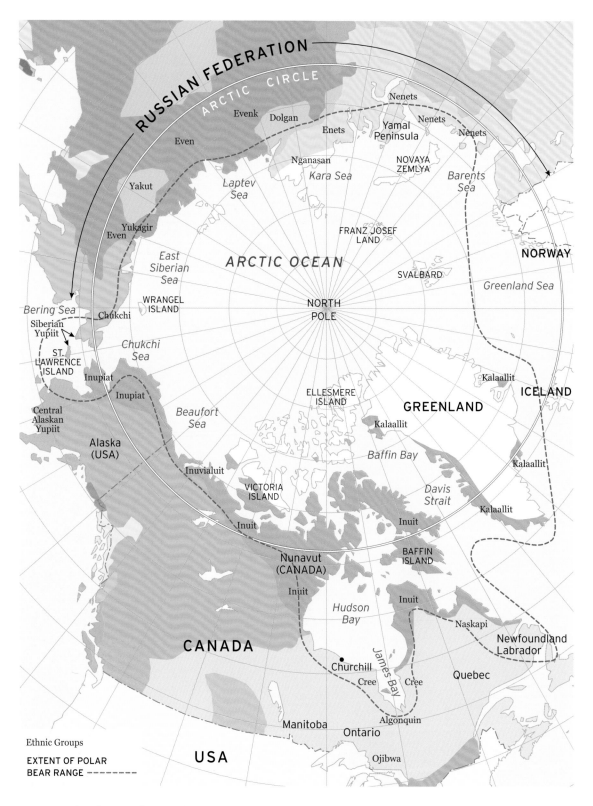

Territories of northern peoples and polar bear range

Ice
Bear

The polar bear as political
subject, in a 2006 *Le Temps*
cartoon by Patrick Chapatte.
Polar bears play the role
that whales played in the
conservation movement in
the 1980s, though updated
with the additional twist of
climate change. Courtesy of
Patrick Chapatte.

A Beast for the Ages

Stories . . . can separate us from animals as easily as they can connect us. And the best stories are likely to complicate our relationships, not simplify them.

—CHRISTOPHER R. BEHA, *ANIMAL ATTRACTION* (2011)

T HESE DAYS, NO ANIMAL EXCEPT PERHAPS THE WOLF DIVIDES opinions as strongly as does the polar bear, top predator and sentinel species of the Arctic. But while wolf protests are largely a North American and European phenomenon, polar bears unite conservationists—and their detractors—worldwide.

In 2008, in preparation for the presidential election, the Republican Party's vice-presidential candidate, the governor of Alaska, ventured to my then hometown, Fairbanks, to rally the troops. Outside the building in which she was scheduled to speak, a small mob of Democrats, radicals, tree-huggers, anti-lobbyists, feminists, gays and lesbians, and other "misfits" had assembled in a demonstration vastly outnumbered by the governor's supporters. As governor, the "pro-life" vice-presidential candidate and self-styled "Mama grizzly" had just announced that the state of Alaska would legally challenge the decision of the U.S. Fish and Wildlife Service to list the polar bear as threatened under the Endangered Species Act. Listing it would block development and thereby endanger jobs, the worn argument went.

Regularly guiding wilderness trips in Alaska's Arctic and feeling that my livelihood as well as my sanity depended upon the continued existence of the White Bears and their home ground, I, who normally shun crowds, had shown up with a crude homemade sign: *Polar Bears want babies, too. Stop our addiction to oil!* I was protesting recurring attempts to open the Arctic National Wildlife Refuge, the area with the highest concentration of polar bear dens in Alaska, to drilling. From the top of my sign a plush polar bear toy dangled, a bear toddler in effigy. Though wary of anthropomorphizing animals, I was not above playing that card.

As we were marching and chanting, I checked the responses of passersby. A rattletrap truck driving down Airport Way caught my eye. The driver, a stereotypical crusty Alaskan, showed me the finger. Unbeknownst to him, his passenger—a curly haired, grandmotherly Native woman, perhaps his wife—gave me a big, cheery thumbs-up.

The incident framed opposing worldviews within a single snapshot but did not surprise me. My home state has long been contested ground, and the bear a cartoonish, incendiary character. Already in 1867, when Secretary of State William H. Seward purchased Alaska from Russia, the Republican press mocked the new territory as "[President] Johnson's polar bear garden"—where little else grows.

In those days, polar bears were at best seen as a nuisance and at worst as a practice target. Sealers killed them because they competed for seals. Their flesh fed explorers and whalers. Their hides carpeted the homes of wealthy burghers and industrialists. One commercial hunter alone could make a big dent in polar bear numbers. The Norwegian trapper Henry Rudi, a man with a twinkle in his eye, earned the sobriquet "Polar Bear King" for killing a total of 713 polar bears on Norway's Arctic Svalbard and Jan Mayen Islands and in Greenland between 1907 and 1947. Scottish whalers from Dundee shot as many bears in a single season. They and Rudi, a Norwegian Medal of Merit recipient, together wiped out the equivalent of the estimated current population of polar bears in Canada's Baffin Bay. Losses through live capture also were severe. Between 1871 and 1973, two thousand polar bears went to zoos, carnivals, and vaudeville theaters all over the world.[1]

As awareness of declining numbers grew, conservation measures seemed necessary, if only for economic reasons. The Danish East Greenland Nanok Company, a hunting and trapping outfit, from 1937 onward proscribed the hunting of polar bears in designated months and forbade killing the slowly reproducing females and their cubs. Government regulations quickly followed, first in Greenland in 1950. They protected females with cubs year-round and all bears in the summer. In 1956, the USSR closed its polar bear hunt, concerned with the bear's possible extinction from overhunting. In Canada, after 1967, bears could no longer be killed in their dens, a method especially popular before the advent of firearms. By 1973, poison, foot traps, and "spring guns"—self-killing guns with a string to the trigger attached to bait—as well as hunting by aircraft or snowmobile, had been banned throughout Greenland.[2]

During the winter of 1964–65, two Norwegian trappers killed 144 polar bears on Halvmåneøya (Halfmoon Island) in the Svalbard archipelago. They used strychnine and blubber-baited "self-shot" gun traps like this replica in Tromsø's Polarmuseet. Photo by Erlend Bjørtvedt, courtesy of Wikimedia Commons.

The same year, after similar developments in other "polar bear nations," Canada, Denmark, Norway, the United States, and the USSR signed the International Agreement on the Conservation of Polar Bears and Their Habitat, which regulated commercial hunting and forbade the capture of bears for circuses and zoos. (The agreement does not mention it, but zoos still can adopt orphaned cubs.) Polar bears could henceforth be killed only for scientific reasons, or in self-defense, or by Native peoples who had traditionally done so. Inuit were allowed a quota based on the numbers and health of Canadian polar bear populations. Their communities could also sell some of these permits to non-Native trophy hunters for much-needed revenue.[3]

In 2005, the International Union for Conservation of Nature (IUCN)—also known as the "Red Cross of the conservation movement"—upgraded the polar bear's status from a "species of least concern" to "vulnerable." The U.S. government, under the Endangered Species Act, in 2008 declared the bear "threatened." As climate change and resource extraction in the Arctic became a more serious threat, the five signatories of the 1973 agreement reconvened in 2009 and 2013 to discuss additional, or further-reaching, measures of polar bear conservation. An attempt to outlaw all trade in polar bear parts under the international Convention on the Trade in Endangered Species (CITES) failed in 2010. Too many traditions collided. Too many interests intervened at the bargaining table. But some form of regulation is badly needed. In the curio market, polar bear parts yield a nice chunk of

change: twenty dollars for a hind claw; fifty for a front claw; two hundred for a canine; a thousand for a skull; and ten thousand to twenty-four thousand for a pelt.[4]

Polar bear killing a young bearded seal on Svalbard, a sight that makes some people uncomfortable and challenges ideas about the bear's "purity," "cuteness," or "nobility." At zoos, viewers are spared such messiness, because there the animals have a different diet, or the meat has already bled out. Photo by Marion Jonchères.

• • •

The White Bear looms large in human history and not just because of its size. In part, our fascination with it springs from the charisma all carnivores share: their quickness, intensity, and acuity, magnified by their strength. It is the idea of their unfettered existence, their calm in the crucial moments, that attract us. We see ourselves in them. "Their courage is in their breast, their resolution in their head," the anonymous scribe of the thirteenth-century Aberdeen *Liber de bestiarum natura* explained. "They are called 'beasts' from the force with which they rage. . . . They are called 'wild' because they enjoy their natural liberty and are borne along by their desires. They are free of will, and wander

A truly immersive experience at the Detroit Zoo. Modern zoos try to give visitors an understanding of the bear in its home environment, while also considering the animals' well-being. Photo by Lon Horwedel.

here and there, and where their instinct takes them, there they are borne."[5] Nine hundred years later, a children's book author reprised the theme, enthusing about bears that roam "over sea made solid, knowing nothing of false borders and boundaries, caring nothing for the concerns of man."[6] Unlike us, polar bears are not very gregarious. Neither am I, and that, as well as their nomadism, partly explain why they so appeal to me.

Deeply held preconceptions keep us from seeing the true nature of some animals. The polar bear is a prime example. Over the past eight thousand years, we have regarded it as food, toy, pet, trophy, status symbol, commodity, man-eating monster, spirit familiar, circus act, zoo superstar, and political cause célèbre. We have feared, venerated, locked up, coveted, butchered, sold, pitied, and emulated this large carnivore. It has left few emotions unstirred. Where the bears' negative image prevailed, as so often, a perceived competition for resources or a threat to our dominion were the cause.

But in and with this book, I do not intend to take sides. I also don't think the

White Bear—despite its bulk, charisma, and relative rarity—more worthy of conservation than the "unattractive" and obscure naked mole rat, or any other page in life's ledger. My main purpose here is to examine attitudes toward, interactions with, and beliefs about polar bears across cultures and time, the history of their symbolic representations and physical presence in our midst and ours in theirs.

The vibrant, interdisciplinary field of anthrozoology, or animal studies, in whose footprints I seek to tread, charts our place in the world of living things. Unlike ecology, anthrozoology engages in this endeavor by investigating ideas, not biological relationships, drawing on disciplines as varied as history, anthropology, psychology, art history, ethology, comparative literature, and zoology.[7] A drive to identify with animals marks all levels of culture, from the individual to the state. For reasons that will become clear, the polar bear makes a great vehicle for such self-identification.

Bears, and in particular polar bears, might not dwell in our neighborhoods but they do live in the collective consciousness. I have turned to this creature as *other* "in a world where otherness of all kinds is in danger, and in which otherness is essential to the discovery of the true self."[8] Animals, which we have hunted, worshipped, and observed for tens of thousands of years, have made us who we are. An attitude that accepts them as separate and different yet also as fully formed equals is rare and found mostly among tribal peoples and a few select naturalist-authors—Aldo Leopold, Loren Eiseley, Edward Abbey, Georg Schaller, Bernd Heinrich, E. O. Wilson, Ellen Meloy, Jane Goodall, and Konrad Lorenz among them. None of them, to my knowledge, has written a single sentence about polar bears. But Ellen Meloy shed light on the mystery of glances across species boundaries, the tenuous connection that also hooked me: "Each time I look into the eye of an animal, one as 'wild' as I can find in its own element—or maybe peering through zoo bars will have to do—and if I get over the mess of 'Do I eat it, or vice versa?' . . . I find myself staring into a mirror of my own imagination. . . . There is in that animal eye something both alien and familiar."[9]

Championing this elusive species that is native to where I live, I've attempted to fill the gap in other writers' work, to peel back layers of meaning and find the creature underneath.

· · ·

"Take a walk on the wild side and see polar bears in their natural habitat before they are gone," a small Alaska airline hawks in its brand of extinction tourism, an overnight packaged trip to the shores of the Arctic Ocean. You put the White Bears on your bucket list and make sure you see them before you—or they—kick it.

I did too. And the rush of my first polar bear sighting still affects me.

After years of trying to break into a highly competitive job market (competitive not because of the wages but because of the fringe benefits, which include fitness, wildlife, and some of the world's most addictive scenery), I was finally guiding a rafting trip on the Marsh Fork of the Canning, a Brooks Range river flowing north to the Beaufort Sea. Its course marks the western boundary of Alaska's Arctic National Wildlife Refuge, and from our trip's take-out point—a rough tundra airstrip—you can see gas flares in Prudhoe Bay's oilfields. We never expected to see a polar bear: we were thirty miles from the coast.

Sipping coffee in the morning's quiet, looking south from the top of the bluff where we had pitched our tents, I noticed a white lump on the bench below muscling toward camp. I could not believe my eyes. The clients popped from their nylon cocoons like ground squirrels from their burrows when I alerted them, one clad in nothing but boxer shorts and a down jacket.

I pretty much knew my way around grizzlies but was a polar bear novice.

With no natural enemies except humans, polar bears often take naps in the open. Their clean lines and flowing form enchanted the English sculptor and painter John Macallan Swan in 1903, as they have artists before and since. Courtesy of Rijksmuseum Amsterdam.

The bear's wedge of a head swung on its pendulous neck, snakelike, gauging god-knows-what. This far from the coast, radiant against heather and willows, the bear looked more out of place than it would have in a zoo. Without a care in the world, it then lay down for a nap halfway up the bluff's slope, a quarter mile from us. What was there for it to fear?

We sat and kept our binoculars trained on the white pile, which could easily have been mistaken for a limestone boulder. Occasionally, the bear lifted its head to sample the air. We crouched downwind from it, and it remained unaware of our presence. In the next hour or so, a golden eagle flew past, a wolf sauntered by, and gulls kept mobbing it—but the bear never stirred.

When we shoved into the current a few hours after the initial sighting, the bear was up and moving again, sniffing and pawing through bushes on the bench. We stole away like thieves, trying to avoid its attention.

As low-key as the episode had been, we all agreed it had been a highlight of our outdoor lives. Without moats, steel bars, gunwales, rifles, or expectations between the bear and us, anything could have happened. Real contact, physical, life-changing contact, had been a possibility.

I have long been aware of some ironies, such as the fact that setting out to meet polar bears in the wild is largely a privilege for the financially—if not always physically—sound, while locals who live with the bears often struggle to make ends meet. If I did not work as a guide, having my way paid and burning fossil fuels to reach the job site, I would have to visit a zoo to come face to face with live polar bears.

What draws me, my clients, and many other people toward these wanderers of the ice as if they were long-lost kin? One explanation lies in biological contact points, the physical and behavioral similarities between them and us. In the Arctic, only humans and bears hunt sea mammals, and bears are the only creatures to sometimes kill humans. Among the polar bear's humanlike characteristics, the upright posture of fighting males or inquisitive bears might be the most impressive trait. In the northern hemisphere, where apes were unknown, bipedalism is otherwise found only in lemmings, ermines, ground squirrels, marmots, and owls, to which Native peoples also ascribed human qualities. In both species the sexes differ in size: adult male polar bears weigh twice as much as breeding females, while in *Homo sapiens*, the difference is normally less pronounced. For a long time, people even believed that bears have sex

"Dancing bear" stone carving by the Inuit artist Noo Atsiaq from Cape Dorset, Nunavut. Polar bears only occasionally stand upright. Anthropomorphizing, we ascribe motives and emotions to them that resemble our own. Courtesy of Canadian Arctic Gallery, Switzerland.

Polar bears purse their lips, flatten their ears, and twist their noses or muzzles. Circus trainers thought their "poker faces" unreadable; their alleged "smiles" most likely are human projection. Art Deco lithograph by the French illustrator and designer Auguste Jean-Baptiste Roubille, ca. 1925. Courtesy of Sotheby's.

in the missionary position. "The female is said to be more lustful than the male," wrote the eighteenth-century French naturalist Georges-Louis Leclerc, Comte de Buffon. "Some claim that, in order to receive him, she lies on her back, embraces him, holds him fast, etc."[10]

The bear is a plantigrade walker, placing its entire sole on the ground, as humans do, and prints from its hind feet in particular resemble barefoot human tracks. Its eyes are aligned in a nearly frontal plane. Visual acuity, a keen sense of hearing and smell, dexterity, and a broad variety of vocalizations further strengthen the resemblance. Native people think that polar bears, like people, differ in personality; some are aggressive, others are timid. By observing them, the Inuit supposedly learned seal hunting techniques: stalking seals hauled out on the ice, or waiting at their breathing holes, sometimes scratching the ice nearby to lure these curious animals. Like ravens, polar bears are thought to possess what the Inuit call *isuma*—the ability to reason—and like ravens, they ceaselessly investigate their surroundings. As seaworthy terrestrial creatures, polar bears conceptually connect animals of the sea and those of the land. (Modern science proves that the bears' closest non-ursine relatives are in fact doglike animals and seals, a genetic underpinning to their position between land and sea.) In Native minds, they also mediate between this world and the spirit world, between nature and culture.

Like *Homo sapiens*, *Ursus maritimus* can be an opportunistic feeder with an appetite that rivals its curiosity, though it thrives on a largely seal-based diet. It moves seasonally between summer and winter grounds, as the Inuit used to. And while polar bears, unlike people, are not very social, they occasionally share a kill with another bear and feed in large numbers on dead, stranded whales.

The polar bear's maternal dedication impresses us as much as its fitness as a hunter. Pregnant females den in the winter, and the interior shape and material of their shelter recalls the igloo. The den is very clean, as the female stops eating and defecating before giving birth. The newborns—pink, helpless, and thinly haired—suggest our babies, just as a skinned adult bear resembles a

Ours polaire.   Polar Bear.   Eisbär.   Orso bianco.   Ijsbeer.
Uitg. P. OUT — KOOG a/d ZAAN.   No. 766

"Ice bear," "white bear," "polar bear"—a beast with many names. Here, it is shown with its preferred prey, spotted seal, in a late nineteenth-century Dutch school wall chart. Courtesy of Nationaal Onderwijsmuseum, Dordrecht, the Netherlands.

A polar bear at the Nuremberg zoo nurses her cubs. Suggestive of human breastfeeding, this pose represents only one of many aspects in which the bear resembles us. Photo by Christophe Dayer.

Polar bear hunting has become controversial and strictly regulated. To be recognized as a skilled hunter, young men in some northern communities are still expected to kill a polar bear. Here, an Inuk from Kangiqsualujjuaq in northern Quebec misses one on the eastern shore of Ungava Bay. Photo by Scott Heyes.

naked adult human. Polar bear mothers strongly bond with their offspring but sometimes also discipline them with a growl or cuff. They generally nurse in a sitting posture, with one or two cubs on their chest. The young slide down snowy slopes, wrestle, and play tug of war.

For Siberia's Chukchi people, the resemblance between humans and bears exceeded biological traits, extending to the cultural. They believed that a tribe of polar bears with human faces and gentle customs lived somewhere on North America's shores, hunting walrus and seals, building snow dens lit with oil lamps, and engaging in long expeditions.[11] (This mythic tribe could well have been the bearskin-clad Inuit of the Central Canadian Arctic.) Lastly, like us, polar bears are blessed with a relatively long life span—more than twenty years in the wild and close to forty in captivity.[12]

Complementing these similarities, some of the bear's more "exotic" traits fuel our imagination. Foremost perhaps are its whiteness, its relative rareness, and the remoteness of its home—the far northern reaches, long unknown to Europeans, where danger, dragons, and mystery dwelled.

Far from being entwined exclusively with its Arctic indigenous neighbors, the polar bear has lately assumed iconic status in the dominant culture. With the wholesale domestication or destruction of wildness that marks industrial civilization, the polar bear has become a focus of our self-awareness, contentious as

no other animal is. Its ascent from food to coveted curiosity to pampered celebrity may seem incremental, inconsequential even, but it speaks volumes about our relations with nature. Transferring polar bears—or their body parts or representations—into highly charged cultural contexts, we share in their essence and employ them for our own purposes. In the wake of its first importation into Europe, the bear triggered scientific curiosity and inspired artworks and nationalistic myth building; it enlivened heraldic devices and Shakespeare's plays; in naval paintings, it defined the self-image of a nation. On the eve of industrial revolution, Britain turned bear slaying into a symbol of manhood and expansionist drives. With the waning of Arctic exploration, the bear's economic and even symbolic importance diminished. It was relegated to advertising, trophy hunting, or popular culture until, starting in the 1980s, conservationists promoted it as both an indicator of environmental degradation and also a symbol of hope. (Ironically, oil companies co-funded some of that period's polar bear research, fulfilling government stipulations.) Where wildness is threatened the

Donald Gialanella's *Spirit of the North*, concept for a sixty-foot sculpture welded from scrap automobiles for a downtown park in Fairbanks, Alaska. The artist sees his bear as projecting "a confident attitude; intelligent, regal, and powerful." Courtesy of Donald Gialanella.

A BEAST FOR THE AGES

In the consumer society the polar bear helps to sell products associated with coolness, freshness, vigor, or purity. This sexualized Art Deco liquor ad poster also puns on the brand's name, which means "of the bear." From A Polar Bear's Tale, www.polarbearstale .blogspot.com (site discontinued).

bear has been elevated. Its revived economic clout boosts films, fund-raising campaigns, eco-merchandise sales, and high-end wildlife tourism.

The traditions of northern Native peoples regarding polar bears frequently intersect with this "Western" trajectory, contradicting as well as enriching our knowledge of the animal. Indigenous concepts of kinship and transformation force us to reassess mechanistic, Cartesian views of the animate world.

My biggest surprise in researching this book has been the longevity of attitudes involving the polar bear, which is particularly striking in fast-changing countries such as ours. The bear is sometimes still a sexual predator or a "stud"; it still is protector, is killer, is idol; it can still serve as the embodiment of a nation, as figurehead for a group of people.

I have tried to outline these broader currents, these patterns of practice and thought that pertain to an animal still unfamiliar to modern observers. In assaying the stories and myths, the ideas and perceptions of many societies— including our own—I seek to highlight the interplay of external and internal landscapes and the bear's place in both. For the lore and awe it inspires, for the diversity and the sheer life force it adds to the world, I hope that the Great White Bear will continue to prowl both our internal and external landscapes for thousands of years to come.

• • •

A few closing words should clarify linguistic usage, exclusions, and the book's flow. After an introductory chapter that touches upon contemporary settings with which readers will likely be familiar, I loosely follow a historical chronology. Beginning with the bear's place in Norse culture and medieval Europe, I move on to Jacobean and Elizabethan England and the Dutch early modern period. I then consider the heydays of enlightenment and exploration, when European or American missionaries and explorer-naturalists often were also the first (amateur) ethnographers. The Western "discovery" of the White Bear on its home ground went hand in hand with the West's initial in-depth contacts with Arctic peoples; that chapter examines how the early scientific knowledge generated by those contacts shaped the polar bear's place in contemporary societies. A discussion of our deep-seated fear of becoming food and of the enigma of whiteness follows, set in the context of exploration literature. I continue with two relatively modern institutions, the circus and zoo, which now seem almost obsolete. The next chapter shifts to deal exclusively with indigenous uses of the bear—and their ceremonial framework—and is succeeded by a cross-cultural examination of eating polar bear. The remaining chapters analyze not only Native customs and perceptions, but also trophy hunting, taxidermy, polar bear–watching, and political activism. As the distinction between Native and non-Native worlds has grown more complicated since the late nineteenth century, these final sections—focusing on the bear's roles rather than chronology—draw on both perspectives to show contrasts and congruencies.

I've not delved deeply into polar bear biology and ecology here, because other books already do. I have also disregarded sources about "white bears," such as the Norwegian folktale "White Bear-King Valemon" or its American-English counterpart "Whitebear Whittington" (in which the bear appears deep in the woods), as well as accounts of them in a Roman arena and King

(*Above*) War as a male pissing contest, in a French postcard on the subject of the Russo-Japanese War of 1904–5. While canines claim space through scent marking, polar bears are not territorial, because their sea-ice environment constantly changes. Courtesy of the Boston Museum of Fine Arts.

(*Right*) From early modern to Victorian times, the White Bear was the most popular visual representation of the High Arctic's dangers. Adrien Marie, illustration for Jules Verne's short story "A Winter amid the Ice" from *Le Docteur Ox*, 1879. Courtesy of Staats- und Universitäts-bibliothek Bremen.

Ptolemy II's menagerie—unless I could rule with certainty that the animals mentioned were not light-colored Syrian brown bears, or "symbolically white," or the white variety of Kermode bears, a black bear subspecies native to British Columbia. Whether or not polar bears could have survived in the Mediterranean is disputable. An early nineteenth-century naturalist noted that even "under the heat of Britain" the polar bear "suffers the most painful sensations," and while one survived twenty years in an Argentinian zoo, another died there from heat stroke. The famous animal dealer and circus entrepreneur Carl Hagenbeck, who, it was said, caught animals in nearly every country in the world, thought all animals could be acclimatized to live in any part of the world. Their health and longevity seem indeed to depend largely on the quality of the care they receive.[13] So there could well have been a polar bear in the pharaoh's keep. That said, the first unequivocally identifiable polar bears came to Europe by way of Greenlandic Norse traders and from Iceland, where sea currents still sometimes maroon them.

Throughout this book, I have used "Inupiat" for Alaska's speakers of Inupiaq and "Yupiit" for speakers of Yup'ik—both groups call themselves "Eskimo," but that term is no longer acceptable for Greenland's Kalaallit and Canada's Inuit and has become controversial in Alaska. (*Inuk* or "person" is the singular noun of Inuit, *kalaaleq* that of Kalaallit.) Culturally and linguistically, these peoples are closely related, forming one branch of the Eskimo-Aleut family. That family inhabits the North from the Siberian mainland to Greenland, including the Aleutian Islands and the western Gulf of Alaska. Siberian Yupiit are a group formerly divided by Cold War politics. Some live on St. Lawrence Island, a sliver of the United States adrift in the Bering Strait, and some on the Russian mainland's Chukchi Peninsula, or Chukotka. Those Yupiit should not be confused with the Chukchi, reindeer-herding speakers of a Palaeosiberian language, who also live in Chukotka and encounter polar bears. Lastly, I have distinguished non-Native ancient Greenlanders, mostly Danes, as "Greenlandic Norse," where necessary. The book's map of the polar bear's range and northern indigenous peoples' territories should help readers to locate ethnic groups and places mentioned in the text.

Some readers no doubt will object to my ranking the polar bear as the Arctic's top predator. Indeed, with current climate changes, it's become more common to find orcas patrolling high-latitude waters, and these sleek, torpedo-like mammals rival the bear in speed, size, strength, and intelligence. But for me the quadruped still takes the prize, because it lives up north more consistently and in greater numbers and sometimes preys even on us.

The Life and Death
of a Superstar

I don't know which criteria an animal has to fulfill to become a
personality, but there has to be a story behind it. It is not sufficient
to be a nice-looking polar bear or hippo to become a personality.

—CHRISTOPH SCHEUERMANN, *DER SPIEGEL* (2013)

EVEN IN DEATH, KNUT ARGUABLY HAS THE DISTINCTION OF BEING
the world's most prominent polar bear. "It cannot be that the little
Knut is completely forgotten," said a woman who spent five thousand
dollars on a public Knut memorial marker—one of several in Berlin, a city that
teems with monuments commemorating two World Wars, the Holocaust, and
the Iron Curtain.[1]

Knut's short career at the Berlin Zoo and his "afterlife" as a taxidermy exhibit at the city's Museum of Natural History highlight both our obsession with
this species and the cultural status it has gained. His story is representative,
touching upon issues of captivity and commercialization, upon concerns about
the appropriation and preservation of animals, upon history, psychology, economics, belief, and ecology—the very bones of contention and meat of this
book, so to speak. The story of Knut can also be read as a footnote to the thousands of polar bears that have lived and died anonymously, but that nevertheless shaped—and were affected by—human culture and consciousness.

Knut was a zoo polar bear born in 2006 in Berlin, a city that centuries
before had chosen a bear as its emblem. Knut's story is worth telling in some
detail, as it illuminates our troubled and troubling relations with nature. This
bear had a rough start. His birthmother Tosca—afflicted, perhaps, by her former circus career—rejected the little *Eisbär* and his twin brother, which four
days later succumbed to an infection.

Controversy surrounded Knut as soon as he came out of the incubator. His caregiver, Thomas Dörflein, bathed, bottle-fed, played with, slept next to, put baby oil on, and strummed lullabies on his guitar for the cub. Animal rights activists and even one zoo director argued that it would be better to let the cub die or to euthanize it than to raise it like a human infant, which would lead to neuroses or turn it into an outsider among the zoo's other bears. On these grounds, People for the Ethical Treatment of Animals (PETA) sued the zoo for "extreme animal mistreatment." Thousands of Knut supporters in turn wrote e-mails and letters pleading with the zoo to keep the cub alive and with its "foster dad." Children protested in front of the zoo, which stayed its course. (Financial interests could also have influenced the decision.) Knut's first public appearance, like that of famous debutantes, was a media event, with hundreds of journalists from as far away as Uzbekistan vying to snap his picture. A bear of the digital era, Knut had his own blog with first-person entries in several languages and a webcam inside his enclosure. The celebration of his first birthday was broadcast live on German television. The media covered

Ernest Griset, *Some Late Arrivals at the Zoo*. Zoos have changed much since the nineteenth century, though some bear enclosures similar to the one shown here still exist. From *The Boy's Own Paper* (1895). Author's collection.

THE LIFE AND DEATH OF A SUPERSTAR

The "world's most famous polar bear," Knut, with treats on his fourth birthday in 2010. The infantilizing of animals is a hallmark of captivity—they are fed and restricted—but is also evident in other forms in which they are represented in our society, such as advertising and children's books. Photo by Karl Bröseke, courtesy of Zoo Berlin.

each aspect of Knut's existence as if he were royalty—from teething pains and a craving for croissants and hammocks to the alleged moment of his conception, caught by a zoo visitor on a blurred photo.

He did have a first-rate pedigree—his dam, Tosca, had starred in East German circus acts under the prominent trainer Ursula Böttcher. Visitation to the Berlin Zoo during Knut's first year soared to a high unequaled in the zoo's 163-year history.[2] The appearances of Knut and his keeper became a twice-daily ritual. Not everyone was taken with Knut; "Kill Knut" graffiti marred Berlin walls, and he received a death threat at the zoo, which led to police security measures. At the height of the craze, 30 percent of Germans surveyed admitted they had already had enough of Knut.

The trim, bearded Dörflein, who simply by proximity or for his paternal image attracted a female following of his own, commented on less endearing behavior shown by the nation's sweetheart: "He started to be threatening at a very early stage. Creeping up from behind and pouncing on his prey, he likes to do that with us [handlers]." Dörflein, to whom Berlin's mayor awarded a medal, admitted having ambivalent feelings about Knut, feelings that will sound familiar to any guardian of infants: "When he's shat on everything and then bites me because he's unsettled, it's enough to [make me] blow a fuse sometimes."[3]

Whether or not the public was willing to acknowledge its nature, the bear was a bear after all, and it behaved like one. When Knut was just over one year old, animal welfare campaigners criticized the zoo again, this time for allowing Knut to kill and eat ten carp from the moat around his enclosure.[4]

The drama ("farce" some would call it) continued. First, the Berlin zoo settled with a zoo that owned Knut's sire and claimed profits from Knut's success. Then PETA demanded that the zoo castrate Knut to avoid inbreeding, which could threaten the genetic diversity of the German polar bear population. Eventually, Knut had a seizure and drowned at the age of four while facing an audience of hundreds. An autopsy revealed the cause of death to be encephalitis from an autoimmune disease. Despite his diminishing cuteness (and therefore, marketability), the adolescent bear still had a following. The resulting outpouring of grief turned vitriolic when the city's Museum of Natural History presented to the Berliners a life-size polar bear "sculpture" wearing their beloved Knut's pelt. A spokeswoman stressed its artistic and educational value. "It's important to make clear we haven't had Knut stuffed," she tried to appease the public.[5]

Man and beast in harmony. The roughly six-month-old Knut with his caregiver, Thomas Dörflein, at the Berlin Zoo. The public commissioned adjacent gravestones for both, after their deaths, which occurred less than three years apart. Photo by Simone Reinhardt.

Putting final touches on the taxidermic mount of Germany's beloved zoo bear. Some people saw Knut's preservation for posterity as disrespectful, but the embalming of remains also gave an "afterlife" to famous humans (such as Mao and Lenin). Courtesy of Museum für Naturkunde Berlin.

Long before Knut became a facsimile of himself, he had become first an asset and then an industry. The formerly nonprofit Berlin Zoo registered him as a trademark and at the Berlin stock exchange, shares in Zoologischer Garten Berlin AG promptly doubled their worth. The zoo announced that most of its proceeds would go toward nature conservation and research. (It also pointed out the importance of captive breeding programs for endangered species, one justification for present-day zoos.) Knut merchandise invaded stores and people's lives. There were Knut ringtones and cuddly toys, commemorative coins and candies, pop music hits and a weekly television show. There were DVDs, magazine stories, children's books, posters, T-shirts, and several films. There were Knut porcelain figurines, packaged hotel tours, and bank credit cards to pay for all of this. There were mock products even, such as the Knutburger—white fur between slices of cheese on a bun. Hollywood called. Taiwan, Japan, and China called. Knut product knock-offs began flooding the market.[6] The zoo's coffers overflowed. During

Easter weekend in his first year, management had to limit the time each visitor could look at Knut to seven minutes.

The German government jumped on the media-circus bandwagon, issuing a stamp featuring year-old Knut that urged people to preserve nature worldwide. Ironically, this bear out of its element had been promoted to eco-ambassador, representative of an endangered place. And since he was generating a fortune, he was "a symbol of the economic potential of ecology." The media had at last put a face to the climate crisis, one more photogenic than Gore's. It was a predator's, but fluffy: Nature defanged. A member of the zoo board praised Knut for his ability to draw attention to the environment "in a nice way. Not in a threatening, scolding way."[7] The German minister for the environment met with Knut, became his godfather, and adopted him as the mascot for a biodiversity conference and the logo for an anti–global warming campaign. Tellingly, media coverage of Knut's 2007 debut drowned out the simultaneous launch of the International Polar Year in Berlin, which sought to educate the public about climate change. The megastar overwhelmed the message. Meanwhile, Knut posed for the celebrity photographer Annie Leibovitz. Her pictures of him became covers for *Vanity Fair*; for the U.S. edition, the actor and climate activist Leonardo DiCaprio (in crampons on an Icelandic glacier) was photoshopped onto the page with Knut.

Other polar bears have had time in the limelight. There was Binky, at the Anchorage Zoo, who in 1994 mauled two careless visitors in separate incidents but supposedly cried in the evenings, when his laughing, applauding audience had left for the day. (Alaskans loved him not for his cuteness but for his rebelliousness, and Binky T-shirts sported the slogan *Send another tourist, this one got away.*) There was Gus, at the Central Park Zoo, who swam obsessively and was diagnosed by a therapist, which resulted in his being treated with Prozac and made to work harder for his food. (As the "bipolar" bear, he became a symbol for neurotic New Yorkers.) There was Carmichael, who came to the Oklahoma Zoo after Kaiser Wilhelm of Germany had him sent to the St. Louis World's Fair and who lived into his forties. And there was Velox, a massive female polar bear, who in 1941 retired at the Denver Zoo after nine years of touring with the American Ringling Brothers' circus, and who enchanted generations of visitors until her death in 1961. It was said she had killed two African lions during her time at the circus. Velox made an appearance in a prize-winning short story, and, as "a fighter" who had endured hardship, was chosen as the mascot of the U.S. Army's 31st Infantry Regiment.[8]

These zoo bears were each famous in their own way. But they could not compete with the cub that had first the Germans and then the rest of the world gushing like teenagers, the bear that caused a collective fever: Knut-mania. Many who mourned Knut's premature death on that bleak March day in 2011 felt a personal bond with him, regarding him as a family member and comparing their feelings for him to those for their pets. But Knut's significance was multifaceted. He embodied a yearning to see harmony between people and beasts restored, a new Utopia, Eden, Noah's Ark—a world where we're all in it together. What's more, Knut had been Berlin's first *Eisbär* in over thirty years to survive infancy, overcoming adversity and slim odds, a tale universal in its appeal. The bear's troubled existence somehow stood for that of his entire tribe. It reminded us of our own perils, shared fates, our own flesh-and-blood mortality. It also reminded us of childhood's innocence and of the innocence, which, as a species, we think we have lost—and here the bear's whiteness, its "purity," mattered. Many who had seen Knut had felt seen by him in return and, thereby, that they existed as part of a larger-than-human world. "When an animal looks at you like that, it changes everything," his caregiver, Dörflein, said after the cub opened its eyes for the first time. Dörflein died two years before Knut, at age forty-four, from a heart attack, as if their fates were connected.[9]

This reciprocity of glances and the understanding that we attribute to it, some critics are quick to point out, could be merely projected desire: "The public purpose of zoos is to offer visitors the opportunity of looking at animals. Yet nowhere in a zoo can a stranger encounter the look of an animal. At the most, the animal's gaze flickers and passes on. They look sideways.

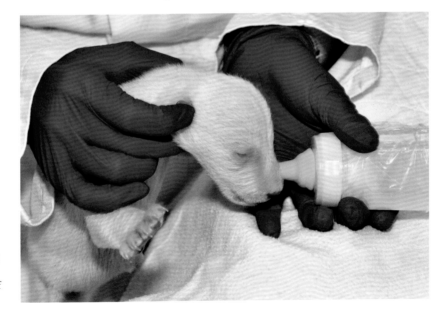

A five-day-old polar bear is bottle-fed at the Toronto Zoo. As wild-capture is no longer possible due to conservation regulations, many zoos run their own breeding programs, in part to satisfy visitor demands. Courtesy of Toronto Zoo.

They look blindly beyond. They scan mechanically. They have been immunized to encounter, because nothing can anymore occupy a *central* place in their attention."[10] There is an obvious downside to the empathy zoo polar bears evoke. Like domestication, captivity is an infantilizing situation. It takes the animal's freedom, depriving it of choices and causing dependency on an appointed custodian.

The continuing frenzy over zoo polar bears, stoked by the media, has sociocultural roots also. Exposure to polar bears and bear-related issues increase the demand for more of the same. Before climate change and its effects upon wild polar bears caught the public's attention, interest in the bears had waned, and many zoos had downsized or discontinued their polar bear breeding programs and exhibits. With intensive press coverage of the issue in the new millennium, visitor demand for the animals rose, and some zoos struggled to fill their vacancies, as wild-capture is no longer an option. When field biologists affiliated with the IUCN suggested that captive polar bears might play a key

Bronze monument, *Knut the Dreamer*, by Josef Tabachnyk, in the Berlin Zoological Garden. The statue freezes the idealized, four-month-old Knut in cubhood instead of portraying the gangly adolescent he was at the time of his death. Tokens left by his fans four years later, on his eighth "birthday," include Knut's favorite food, croissants. Photo by Anke Zeschmann.

role in boosting wild populations, the bear became a "focus species" for some zoos, and captive bears more acceptable to conservation-minded audiences. But zoos have to make choices about how to spend limited conservation funds and therefore choose threatened species they consider most likely to rebound in the wild. For some, that excludes the polar bear.[11]

Ultimately, the key to understanding Knutmania—and the appeal of polar bear cubs in children's books and eco-campaigns—can be found in "the cute factor." Who, really, is immune to the charms of these tots, their cuffing and wrestling matches, their tipsy-sailor gait, their mewling, stub-nosed, button-eyed somersaulting or nipping at mom's heels? Who would want them to lose their sea-ice home? In this context it is revealing that the committee in charge of selecting the design for a Knut statue for the Berlin Zoo decided it had to show the cuddly Knut, not Knut as a delinquent adolescent. (The material posed a further challenge. It was difficult to capture the cub's fuzz and playfulness in bronze.)[12]

The Austrian, Nobel-Prize-winning researcher of animal behavior, Konrad Lorenz, first surmised in 1949 that we strongly respond to physical features and behavior of many mammalian young, not just those of our own species. A shortened nose, big eyes, a disproportionately large head, and round and soft body features paired with playfulness or curiosity turn us all gooey inside. It has since been proven that cuteness triggers nurturing instincts in adults, and the urge to protect. Recent research suggests that pictures of puppies or babies stimulate pleasure centers of the brain that are also aroused by sex,

Cuddly carnivores—cubs feeding on a ringed seal pup their mother has killed. Ironically, in the 1970s, pictures of baby seals boosted a successful anti-sealing campaign. Photo by Jon Aars, courtesy of Norwegian Polar Institute.

Perhaps polar bear cubs remind us of our own, idealized childhoods. Children's alphabet plate, circa 1880, Brownhills Pottery Co., Staffordshire, England. Photo by Nancy Barshter, courtesy of Childhood Antiques.

drugs, or a good dinner. As an evolutionary adaptation, this preference for immature traits makes parents care for their offspring. These paternal and maternal feelings, elicited by cubs like Knut, now could affect the survival of polar bears as a species.

Walt Disney's documentary *White Wilderness* (1958)—known for its staged lemming "suicide" scenes—delighted Baby Boomers with a polar bear cub tumbling down an icy slope (also possibly staged), one of the earliest cinematic examples of exploiting the polar bear's cuteness. The theme can be traced from that scene to the BBC's 2011 mini-series *Frozen Planet*, narrated by Sir Richard Attenborough. Its episodes are structured according to the seasonal round of polar bears, with a bombastic soundtrack and subtly anthropomorphized treatment of the bears, with the requisite shots of cub antics. (The cuteness of cubs notwithstanding, occasional lapses in image-building occur. On its website, Polar Bears International describes the nearly hairless, blind newborn as looking "like a big white rat." But, it assures readers, feeding on milk with the same fat content as whipping cream, cubs quickly morph into "22 to 26 pounds of pure adorableness.")

. . .

As nature documentaries and similar artifacts show, popular culture largely confines polar bears to limited scripts, to parts subordinate to our own. The bear can be roly-poly and immature, maternal, or else a combative male. These of course are stereotypical roles in the modern Western nuclear family. In a socioeconomic context, the bear functions as marketing tool and political rallying point. Yet beyond these dominant tropes, undercurrents and traditions exist, which this book will explore.

Even years after his death, people continue to leave flowers at a memorial statue of Germany's most famous, most treasured bear. To understand Knut's hold on us, it will help to know how his kind came to live in our midst and our minds.

The Bear as
Early Commodity

To the west lies the Island of White Falcons. . . . And in their
country is the white bear, which goes out into the sea and catches
fish, and these falcons seize what is left over by it, or what it has
let alone. . . . The skin of these bears is soft, and it is brought to the
Egyptian lands as a gift.

—IBN SAID AL-MAGHRIBI, *THE EXTENT OF THE EARTH IN*
ITS LENGTH AND BREADTH (THIRTEENTH CENTURY CE)

T HE FIRST DOCUMENTED "WHITE BEARS" ARE NOT, AS I HAD EX-
pected, found in sources from Europe but rather in those from Japan,
which in the seventh century CE already described them as a valued
commodity. Almost 350 years before they appear in Icelandic Norse records,
"white bears" feature in the *Nihongi*, a chronicle of Japan's emperors. In 658,
after campaigning in the North, the governor of Koshi Province presented two
live white bears to Empress Kōgyoku. The following year, envoys from Korea
tried to sell a white bearskin for sixty pounds of floss silk, the price a good
indicator of its rarity.[1]

I cannot establish the identity of these bears with absolute certainty. Polar
bears have sometimes drifted south from the Bering Sea as far as Japan's sec-
ond-largest island, Hokkaido. There is also a chance that these could have
been Ininkari bears, a genetic mutation like British Columbia's "spirit bear,"
a variety within the local black bear population. The Ininkari, however, is a
brown bear. It occurs on the two southernmost Kuril Islands, stepping-stone
extensions of Siberia's Kamchatka Peninsula that rise from the sea northeast
of Hokkaido. The bear's color pattern is unique: the upper half of its body—
head, forelegs, chest, and part of the back—is yellowish white, the lower half,

Japanese polar bear embroidered in silk, ca. 1900. During the heyday of polar exploration, Arctic subjects became fashionable even in Asia. Though we don't normally associate polar bears with Japan, a chronicle mentions two live ones given as gifts in 658 CE—one of the earliest verifiable written records of them. Courtesy of Mallett.

grayish-brown. I think Japanese court scribes were discerning enough not to call such animals "white," but the truth remains shrouded. No other early Japanese sources speak of white bears.

To better understand the origins of our current obsession with polar bears, I therefore must turn to first-contact situations in Northern and Western Europe. Unencumbered by sentimental ballast, medieval and Renaissance adventurer-entrepreneurs sought polar bear cubs to trade or gift them to potentates, for profit or political influence. They coveted the bear because it was rare, and cubs foremost because they were more tractable than adults. Profits made the man, then as now. As a form of live currency, polar bears quickly became embedded in the mercantile exchange systems of early modern capitalism—but medieval Norse sources already mentioned them as property and objects of trade.

Before the bear became *isbjørn*—"ice-bear"—Norse poets and scribes called it *hvítabjørn,* "white-bear." Young polar bears were common enough in Icelandic households to warrant their own designation: *alibjørn*, "house-bear." A penal code held an owner liable for his bear, just as he was for his dog. The punishment for unleashing either one on a neighbor was exile, even if nobody got hurt. The first documented capture occurred in 894 CE, when Ingimundur the Old, a Norse settler in Iceland, trapped two cubs stranded by an ice floe that had drifted in from East Greenland. (Such strandings were recorded surprisingly often and still happen today.) After keeping the cubs at his homestead, Ingimundur sent them to King Harald of Norway aboard a timber cargo ship. The event was remarkable enough for the locals to name the nearest municipality Húnavatnssýsla, after the "Cub Lake" where the bears had been caught.[2]

The Icelanders, however, did not always spare the lives of marooned bears, which, ravenous with hunger, attacked the first herds they encountered. Those ravages did not last long, as neighbors quickly took up arms and killed these bears. One eighteenth-century hunter killed more than twenty polar bear–drifters by spear, long after firearms had become widespread in Europe. He had to turn in their skins to the local justice of peace, in exchange for a reward, because they belonged to the king.[3]

The *Morkinskinna* (literally, "rotten parchment"), a chronicle of medieval Norwegian kings, tells how another Icelander traded everything he owned for a bear to present to a king. In the story, Auðun, a lowborn man from West-fjord, sails to Greenland to obtain a polar bear, which he plans to give to King Sveinn Estridson of Denmark to make his fortune from the king's subsequent generosity. A Greenlandic Norse settler sells a bear to Auðun. Though the *Morkinskinna* does not specify this, the bear, which Auðun led on a leash or chain, could have been a sub-adult, hence more manageable. The winds of opportunity then blow Auðun and his bear to southern Norway, where King Harald Hardradi of Norway—a stern ruler—tests Auðun's willingness to offer the bear to him, as a gift or for payment at twice its value. Auðun declines, likely hoping for better remuneration from the Danish king, and grudgingly King Harald sends Auðun on his way.

William Ian Miller, the author of a study of the legal and economic aspects of this little-known story, remarks that the scarcity of polar bears in the medieval Scandinavian world that drives the plot arose from rather different reasons than that of our own times. Polar bears were rarely seen not because they were endangered but because their home was remote. Their worth remains high: as I will show in the chapter on polar bear watching and trophy hunting, nowadays the bears' predicted decline translates hand-somely into cash.

Abraham Anghik Ruben, *Thor 900 AD*, bronze, 2009. Traders from the Norse colonies of Iceland and Greenland first introduced polar bears to Europe's nobility, which kept them as status objects in menageries. Courtesy of Kipling Gallery Collection.

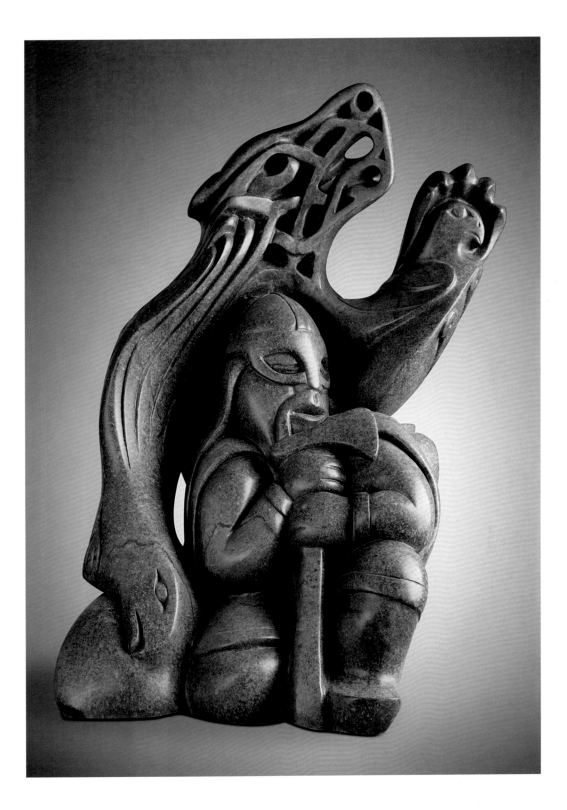

In the end, Auðun's investment and daring pay off. Impressed by the gift, King Sveinn of Denmark retains Auðun and later rewards him with a fully loaded ship, a purse of silver, and a gold bracelet.[4] Some have questioned the truth of Auðun's story as history, but this distinction does not matter to the student of polar bear lore, a historian of world-views. Like depictions of it in "high art" and in "kitsch," both fictional and factual accounts speak of our attitudes toward the bear. In fact, I believe that invented attributes or incidents reveal our values and psychological needs even more clearly than purely historical records, because they re-quire so much creative effort.

Six hundred years after Auðun's adventure, Scandinavians still talked of this country boy who had done well for himself. In a nineteenth-cen-tury Norwegian fairytale version, the bear and his owner stay at an inn plagued by trolls. The bear chases away the trolls, who mistake it for a big white cat.[5] Even today, Auðun and his bear entice people: a Finnish fan adapted the story into an an-imated film, and several retellings for young adults have been published.

This H. L. Brœkstad engrav-ing, from *Peer Gynt and the Trolls*, a folktale in Peter Christen Asbjørnsen, *Round the Yule-Log: Christmas in Norway*, 1895, may be a later variant of Viking trader Auðun and his bear. In oral traditions, some tales survive, often reworked until the source has become obscure. Courtesy of Adams State University, Nielsen Library.

For those distrustful of the sagas, the archaeological record adds hard-won, substantial details to our knowledge of Norse uses of polar bears, if only in parts of Greenland. Most Norse settlement sites where a large number of an-imal bones have been preserved include a few polar bear bones, typically ca-nines or other teeth. Sometimes there only are finger and toe bones, indicating that skins with paws rather than whole carcasses were brought to settlements. In general, few fragments from other polar bear bones are found at each site. These could have come from stray bears killed near the farms or from a few bears killed on hunting grounds to the north, which also yielded walrus.

Far from being self-sufficient, the Greenlandic Norse depended on trading goods from the Scandinavian homelands—timber, iron, and whatever was not available or could not be substituted locally. To attract merchants to Green-land, the settlers offered trade items valued in Europe, such as walrus tusks, walrus skin, narwhal ("unicorn") teeth, and polar bear hides—and sometimes, live cubs.[6]

After their conversion to Christianity, the Norse also offered some of their most precious possessions to the Church as tokens of their devotion. Given the risk and privation under which polar bear skins were obtained, these counted for as much as silver or gold. In 1032, King Canute, who ruled over a North Sea empire that comprised Denmark, England, Norway, and parts of Sweden, gifted twelve white bearskins to Brithmer, the abbot of Croyland Monastery. The skins were laid out in front of the chapel's altar for the congregation to see.

Rare walrus-ivory figurine from a Norse archaeological site in South Greenland. It is unclear if a Norseman carved it or if he obtained it from the so-called *skræling-jar*, the proto-Inuit Thule people who also lived on the island. Photo by Georg Nyegaard, courtesy of Greenland National Museum and Archives.

Polar bear skin and walrus ivory, two kinds of luxury goods that Norse traders exported from Greenland. The objects in this image were confiscated from modern-day illegal traffickers in Alaska. Courtesy of U.S. Fish and Wildlife Service.

The sixteenth-century scholar and archbishop of Uppsala, Olaus Magnus, in his travel guide *Description of the Northern Peoples*, provides details about this custom: "Hunters give these white bear skins to the high altar of their cathedral or parish church, so that during the season of terrible cold, the feet of the priest celebrating mass are not affected by frost. In the church of Trondheim, the main city of Norway, each year such white skins can be found. The hunters faithfully offer them whenever they take them—and even wolf skins—to pay for candles burned in honor of the saints."[7]

Magnus was also justly famous for his *Carta Marina*, a splendid map of northern Europe published in Venice in 1539. Quite often, Renaissance maps—printed in black and white—were hand-colored by their owners, not their publishers, and different copies can therefore have different color schemes. Though Magnus clearly labeled the bears that appear in "Islandia" as "white bears" *(ursi albi),* those who finished the extant copies of the *Carta Marina* colored them according to their own fancy, sometimes in the more familiar brown. The *Carta Marina*'s three ornamental bears are the earliest unmistakable polar bears on any map. The inland bear is shown inside a cave or den, although polar bears most likely never hibernated in Iceland.

A 1590 map of the island by the Flemish cartographer Abraham Ortelius (who was also the first to intuit continental drift) explains how polar bears get there: on sea ice floating southward and eastward from Greenland and the Davis Strait. The map's legend gives details: "Huge and marvailous great heaps of ice brought hither with the tide from the frozen sea, making a great and terrible noise; some pieces of which oft times are fourty cubites bigge; upon these in some places white beares do fitte closely."[8]

Further documentation comes from the Venetian Pietro Querini, who, perhaps lacking good maps or just good luck, in 1432 shipwrecked on an island in Norway's Lofoten archipelago. Traveling homeward from the wreck, he reports having seen a perfectly white bearskin at the foot of the metropolitan's chair in Trondheim's Nidaros Cathedral. Greenland then was under the jurisdiction of the Archbishop of Trondheim, and this skin could have been a gift from pious Greenlandic Norsemen, or a tithe.[9]

Trade between the island colonies—Greenland and Iceland—and the Norse homelands was spo-

Detail of Ortelius's *Islandia* map (ca. 1608), showing polar bears on ice floes off the northeastern Icelandic coast. Ocean currents flowing from Greenland have stranded polar bears in Iceland from the Middle Ages to the present. Courtesy of alteagallery.com.

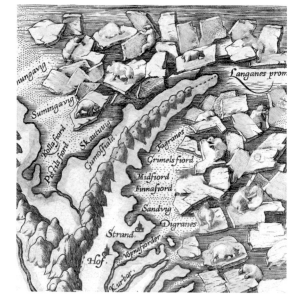

radic but lucrative. Bergen, on the west coast of Norway, functioned as an economic hub for this trade. To Bergen came Greenland's polar bear skins and the white gyrfalcons that Europe's hunting elite especially valued. Together with Trondheim, Bergen supplied medieval England, Flanders, and Germany with bearskins both brown and white. It is also possible that the white-bear skins that Querini and others described in Norway could have come from Norwegians seal hunting in the Arctic Ocean or bartering with Siberian Natives along the Barents Sea coast.[10]

As mentioned, Norse colonial trade in polar bears was not restricted to their pelts. It is remarkable that as early as circa 1060, the monk Adam of Bremen reported having seen a live polar bear—not just a pelt—in the retinue of the Danish king Sveinn Estridson. Conceivably, this could have been the bear Auðun had given to Sveinn. And around 1075, Adam even reported *wild* white bears occurring in Norway, which might have inspired the folktale "White Bear-King Valemon." "Norway is the only place," Adam wrote, "that has black foxes [silver foxes] and hares, white marten [ermine] and bears of the same color, who live in the water."[11] Statements about white bears in northern Norway also appear on Angelino de Dalorto's 1339 portolan—a type of navigational map used in the late Middle Ages that showed only ports and coasts in any significant detail—and on several later maps: "Here are the white bears

and they eat raw fish." Polar bear fossils have been discovered at several sites in southern Norway, outside the bear's current range. Possibly, during Europe's Little Ice Age, polar bears routinely crossed the ice pack or drifted ashore on the continental mainland as they did in Iceland. Whether these bears were stranded individuals or whether they were a resident population, it appears that the great demand for polar bears and their skins quickly led to their extermination in Norway.

Presented as gifts, polar bears greased diplomatic gears and careers. In 1056, Isleiv, the bishop of Iceland, brought a white bear from Greenland for the emperor of Germany, Henry III, as "the most costly and remarkable present possible." Einar, the envoy of Greenland, gave a white bear to King Sigurd of Norway, whose help he needed in the appointment of a bishop of Greenland.[12]

The practice continued. Word spread about these rare imports from the North. The bears circulated farther south. In the thirteenth century, King Haakon Haakonsson (Haakon IV) of Norway gave a "pale" bear to Henry III of England and "a gigantic bear white as snow" to the Holy Roman emperor and king of Sicily, Frederick II, an expert on falconry, who kept it at his Palermo menagerie for many years.[13] Black and brown bears were still rather common in Western Europe, and any bear different enough to be considered a worthy

Situated on the west coast of Norway, the town of Bergen benefitted from Arctic trade and long remained a hub for supplying Europe with polar bears. This photo shows one that escaped from its crate in 1953 but was caught again. It had been on its way to a German zoo. Courtesy of Bergen Byarkiv.

gift for a king was probably a polar bear. Light-colored Syrian brown bears are a possibility but would not have been all that special to the Emperor Frederick, given his location in Sicily.

Henry sequestered his gift in the Tower of London's menagerie (one of Europe's oldest and longest-operating zoos), where its appointed keeper sometimes led the king's status symbol around the grounds. In a royal decree of 1252, the sheriffs of London were commanded to pay four pence a day for the bear's maintenance, and, in the following year, "to provide a chain and muzzle to hold the said bear while [it was] fishing, or washing himself, in the river Thames." The bear was important enough for His Highness to take special interest in its well-being. Tower of London records thirty-five years after the arrival of Henry's Norwegian bear also show payment for the transport of a white bear, "Lynn," which presumably had been shipped from a place with the same name—the fifty-mile Lyngen Fjord near Tromsø, perhaps. It could have been caught about five hundred miles north of Norway, in Svalbard, the birth-

Kendra Haste, *Polar Bear*, a steel and galvanized wire representation of Henry III's bear of 1252, commemorating the Royal Menagerie at the Tower of London. Commissioned by Historic Royal Palaces for the Tower of London, 2010–11. Courtesy of Patrick Davies, Contemporary Art, and the Tower of London.

Detail from Johan Axel Gustav Acke's 1881 painting *King Gustav I Vasa (ca. 1496–1560) of Sweden and King Hans (1483–1513)* [of Norway] on a bear skin rug. A symbol of privilege and wealth, polar bear skins initially decorated only churches and the households of Europe's nobility. Courtesy of Nationalmuseum, Stockholm.

place of some bears then traded, and once it arrived in London, likely served as a replacement for Henry's original bear.[14]

With the ascendancy of the English and Dutch as sea powers at the beginning of the age of exploration, the center of polar bear business shifted from northern to Western Europe. Still, during the reign of Queen Mary I of England (1553–58) a polar bear hide presented at the English court by either the explorer Sebastian Cabot or the duke of Muscovy was uncommon enough to dazzle courtiers, "on account of its size and whiteness." And when, in 1599, "The Virgin Queen" Elizabeth I paraded through Spitalfields escorted by one thousand men-at-arms, the real excitement for the thronging crowds was a cart in the procession with two polar bears riding in it.[15]

Londoners would soon get to see more of the strange bears from the North. Newly returned from the American colony Jamestown, Jonas Poole, master of *Lioness,* reported precious cargo. On May 30, 1609, this pioneer of the English whaling trade had logged that, at Bear Island near Svalbard (then called "Spitsbergen"), a party from his ship "slue 26 Seales, and espied three white Beares: wee went aboard for Shot and Powder, and coming to the Ice again, we should see a shee-Beare and two young ones: Master Thomas Welden shot and killed her: after shee was slayne, wee got the young ones, and brought them home into England, where they are still alive in Paris Garden."[16]

"Paris Garden" was not the bucolic refuge the reader might expect—I will explain its significance in a moment. Likewise, bringing the young bears "home" was not a gesture of kindness after killing their mother. Showbiz—and profit—motivated Renaissance seal hunters and sailors in the Arctic to capture polar bears. Already fifty years earlier, the Dutch navigator Willem Barentsz, on his search for a sea route to India, had tried to capture a female polar bear for display. He "thought to have carried her alive in the shippe, and to have shewed her for a strange wonder in Holland." Roped from a rowboat, the wounded bear proved too intractable and had to be killed with a pike.[17]

Commercial sealing and whaling by the Dutch and English off Svalbard and Greenland during the early seventeenth century quickly delivered more polar bears to Western Europe's port towns. Often these were orphaned cubs, more manageable than adults—crews normally killed grown bears on sight. Consequently, by zoological trickle-down the White Bear ceased to be the exclusive privilege of royals and their entourages and could now be admired by commoners.

You could find plenty of commoners at Bankside, a marshy south London district, beyond the pale, across the Thames, outside the city's jurisdic-

Sailors led by the Dutch explorer Willem Barentsz rope a polar bear near Spitsbergen (now Svalbard), in a drawing by crewmember Gerrit de Veer, 1598. The Dutch planned to send the bear to the Netherlands alive. From de Veer's *The Three Voyages of William Barents to the Arctic Regions*. Courtesy of Rijksmuseum, Amsterdam.

tion. During Shakespeare's time, buildings topped the "bank," a raised dyke: inns, bullrings, taverns, bear pits (euphemistically called "bear gardens" or "Paris Gardens"), a prison ("the Clink"), a graveyard for paupers ("the Cross Bones"), and playhouses, such as the Rose, the Hope, and the Globe. The suburb was a sore on a pastoral landscape, a place of brothels and bards, of gibbets and knives in the dark.

Social anthropologists remark that by removing wild animals from their own worlds and transplanting them to the human, the cultural realm, we transform and reduce them.[18] This is not only true in the physical sense—through confinement and coercion—but also and perhaps more devastatingly, at the conceptual level. Simply to be looked at, to be put up as a spectacle and denied an agenda of their own, turned the polar bears into mere objects. Their transformation began aboard the ships, with their capture. Whaling captain William Scoresby's "sovereign of the arctic countries . . . powerful and courageous; savage and sagacious" quickly became "Poole's bears"—mere possessions.

The bear cubs that Poole had captured near Svalbard now were property, to keep or dispose of as he wished. They resurface two years later, in a 1611 royal decree that warrants theater impresario Philip Henslowe and his son-in-law, actor Edward Alleyn, to keep two white bears and a young lion. Henslowe and Alleyn had purchased the office of Keeper of the Royal Game (namely, bulls, bears, and mastiffs), early during King James I's reign, and Henslowe sometimes arranged animal fights for James at the Tower of London.

Henslowe and Alleyn were both shareholders in the Fortune Playhouse, and Henslowe also managed the Hope, built at Bankside over a former bearbaiting arena. The Hope had a removable stage so that fights could take place between plays, and the stink of animals lingered during theatrical performances.[19]

In the modern theater, performers are fitted to the script, but in Shakespeare's time, the script was tailored to the performers. Shakespeare might have taken advantage of animal actors available to the cast. In the 1610–11 theatrical season, polar bears could have starred in three Shakespeare productions: the old play *Mucedorus*, revived, with scenes added for a bear; *Oberon*; and his own *The Winter's Tale*.[20]

In *Oberon the Faery Prince*, a showpiece of scenic techniques and set design that had premiered at Whitehall Palace, a large moonlit crag split open to reveal a palatial hall, furnished with a throne lit by multicolored lights. The "Knights Masquers" then magically appeared, and the prince of Wales, son of James I, entered in a chariot drawn by two white bears. For *The Winter's Tale*, Shakespeare wrote a true showstopper, one of theater's most famous stage directions, for Antigonus, a minor character: "Exit pursued by a Beare."

In the wake of explorers. A young male bear investigates a tourist ship in Svalbard's Hornsund fjord. Whaling captain Jonas Poole, who in 1609 brought two polar bear cubs to London, named the fjord after reindeer antlers his men found there. Photo by Leif Sylvan.

Scholars formerly thought—and some still think—that this "Beare" (and those featured in the other two plays) was a man in costume. However, some later allowed that it could have been a real animal that Shakespeare wrote into the scene to cash in on the popularity of bear fights at the Paris Garden—and on the novelty of a bear onstage. A few historians even insist that it could have been a polar bear, perhaps one of the two in Henslowe and Alleyn's keep. Skeptics averred that bears are "dangerous and unreliable beasts," though circus trainers proved this to be untrue. Fence sitters thought it possible, though very difficult, to train polar bears but considered that brown bears painted white could have filled in for their Arctic cousins, "being less dangerous and less difficult to control."[21]

Modern polar bear trainers agree about the fickleness of their charges but not about the impossibility of training them. It therefore would have been unnecessary to paint a brown bear—Henslowe and Alleyn's bears *could* have been tame enough at the time of the plays to participate. As far as the hypothetically more docile nature of captive brown bears is concerned, the 1990 mauling death of the Kodiak bear trainer Manfred Horn speaks volumes. We detect here a view, unsupported by statistics, of the polar bear as a superkiller.

Part of this reputation without doubt springs from our lack of familiarity with polar bears. Early modern Europeans were familiar with brown bears as dancing bears at fairs and denizens of their woods and knew how to handle them—but polar bears were still pretty new. For a cash magnet, Shakespeare could have hardly done better.

Polar bears become dangerously moody in adolescence, however, and these two therefore could have been sent to an even tougher stage soon after their premiere. The poet John Taylor, on his roster of animals kept at Bankside's Paris Garden, includes two white bears that might have been Shakespeare's bit players: Will Tookey and Mad Bess.[22] Already in Roman antiquity, fighting bears had personal names; the three brown bears in Duke Jean de Berry's late fourteenth-century menagerie were called Chapelin, Martin, and Valentin. "Mad Bess," as a character description, certainly could explain a transfer from the stage to the bear pit. If Captain Poole caught the two bears as cubs—the common practice—they would have been about thirty years old when Taylor's list was published, well within the life span of captive polar bears. They would have been too old to stand any chance against mastiffs or bulls in the rings.

Exit Poole's bears. The curtain falls. Nothing more is known of their fate.

The blood sport at Bankside, unsettling as it may seem today, needs to be seen in its historical context. Actors were not treated more kindly than the bears in the fighting pits: if a play was considered seditious or libelous, they and the author could be fined, jailed, or even mutilated by branding or ear- or nose-cropping. Visits to London's Bedlam asylum to laugh at the mentally ill were a popular entertainment. "A naturall propension to crueltie" was accepted in the paragon of all creation.[23]

Though historians generally consider him a serious and thoughtful monarch, James I, who had issued the warrant providing for the two orphan bears, was himself a lover of baiting and maintained the Tower of London menagerie in part for that purpose. Under James, the spectacle became very popular; he had a platform built over the Tower's dens so that he and his courtiers could watch lions, bears, and dogs set to fight each other to the death.

The valet of a visiting Spanish nobleman left a vivid description of this grisly London pastime:

> In another part of the city we saw seven bears, some of them of great size. They were led out every day to an enclosure, where being tied with a long rope, large and intrepid dogs are thrown to them, in order that they may bite and make them furious. It is no bad sport to see them fight, and the

assaults they give each other. To each of the large bears are matched three or four dogs, which sometimes get the better and sometimes are worsted, for besides the fierceness and great strength of the bears to defend themselves with their teeth, they hug the dogs with their paws so tightly, that, unless the masters came to assist them, they would be strangled by such soft embraces.[24]

The fights served not only as entertainment for nobles but also as catharsis for a powerless underclass—the classic imperial strategy of keeping proletarians pacified through "bread and games." But not everybody thrilled at the violence. "I went with some friends to the Bear Garden," the cultivated and wealthy John Evelyn confessed to his diary, "where was cock-fighting, dog-fighting, bear and bull-baiting, it being a famous day for all these butcherly sports, or rather barbarous cruelties . . . . I most heartily weary of the rude and dirty pastime."[25]

In the catalogue of callous exploitation, one searches in vain for further twinges of empathy, for stirrings of enlightenment. In this scene from Poole's Arctic journal, economic motives most likely stayed the sealer's hand: "There came a Beare with two young ones as big as Lambes of a moneth old: they skipped about their dams necke, and played with one another very wantonly. The dame came so neere that I shot at her, and being loth to hurt the young ones, being playing about her fore-parts, I shot her through the top of the shoulder; then she went away."[26]

◆　◆　◆

Another link between Shakespeare and bearbaiting is worth exploring. The bard's birthplace was Warwickshire, and in *Henry VI*, there is much talk of the sport. In Part 2, Act 5, Scene 1, Warwick proclaims

> *Now, by my Fathers badge, old Neuils Crest*
> *The rampant Beare chain'd to the ragged staffe*
> *This day I'll weare aloft my Burgonet* [helmet]

According to legend, the first earl of Warwick killed a bear by strangling it. The second slew a giant with a ragged staff, which he then added to his family coat of arms. A bear chained to a stout pole—the "bear rampant and ragged staff"—is still the heraldic sign of the earls of Warwick, and often the bear is white.

The Warwick bear's color may be the result of heraldic conventions, but white bears crop up elsewhere in London at that time. In 1603, King James I knighted Baptist Hicks, a wealthy silk mercer whose business was at the sign of the White Bear. A stone sculpture was discovered in 1882 during renovations at the site of the merchant's house—a bear in chains. An inn called the White Bear existed in Piccadilly as early as 1685. Its large central courtyard was called the Fleece Yard and the whole complex the White Bear and Fleece Inn. Ye Olde White Bear, in Hampstead, opened its doors around 1700.[27] The connection between bears, commerce, and entertainment in Elizabethan London was pervasive and polar bears fit right in.

Flag of Warwickshire County, birthplace of Shakespeare. The sign of the earls of Warwick is a bear "rampant" with a "ragged staff." The bear could be white or "argent" simply because of a heraldic rule that forbids placing color upon color, but polar bears did live in Jacobean England. Courtesy of Warwickshire County Council.

Displaying a host of foreign creatures in a feudal menagerie—or displaying their body parts, strewn across marble halls and cathedrals—showed that a sovereign's influence spanned the globe, at least its known quarters. Animals perceived as regal or powerful—lions, bears, gyrfalcons, or elephants—yielded metaphors for self-definition, especially if they were rare or exotic. In this context, the appearance of white bears in the Bear Garden's rings and perhaps on Shakespeare's stage heralded the gradual dissolution of aristocratic monopolies on the luxurious, an idea with explosive political implications. During King James's reign, regicide was in the air, gunpowder mingled with the stench of bulls and bears.

A last scene to end this strange, eventful history: the Puritans, after they'd come to power in the English Civil War, temporarily banned Bankside dog-fighting and bearbaiting—not because such bouts caused suffering for the animals, but because they gave pleasure to the spectators. In 1656, a company of Cromwell's soldiers shot to death the Bear Garden's seven remaining bears, together with all of its dogs and cocks. Supposedly, "one white cub was spared, saved by its youth and rare color, and the association with innocence."[28] One cannot help but wonder if financial motives played a role in this act of mercy as well.

The menagerie at the Tower underwent a similar transformation, one summed up (and sanitized) by Edward Turner Bennett, an English zoologist, in 1829. Originally, he records, the Tower had been intended "merely for the safe-keeping of those ferocious beasts, which were, until within the last century, considered as appertaining exclusively to the royal prerogative; it has occasionally been converted into a theatre for their contests, and has termi-

Detail from Bonaventura
Peeters the Elder's painting
*Hunting Polar Bears on the
Coast of Norway* (1635–52).
Polar bears likely coexisted
with humans in coastal Nor-
way for a time. Fossils have
been found in that country's
southwestern parts, beyond
the animal's modern range.
Courtesy of Wikimedia
Commons.

nated by adapting itself to the present condition of society as a source of ra-
tional amusement and a school of zoological science."[29] In short, modernity
had arrived. But while people's urban amusements became less bloody, their
dealings with wild animals did not.

As the following chapters show, Europeans—and soon after, Americans—
combined exploration with the pursuit of economic interests in the Arctic for
three hundred years after Shakespeare's death. This brought them increasingly into contact with polar bears on the animals' home grounds. The titillation that spectators felt at staged fights and theatrical plays gave way to
the fear of encountering the bear face-to-face—and of becoming its prey. A
new narrative pitted explorers against the forces of Arctic nature, battling the
most daunting representative of a hostile environment. The same explorers
often acted as amateur scientists or provided naturalists back home with both
information and dead or living specimens. A parallel story therefore evolved,
in which the bear found its place in the Enlightenment's reasoned ordering of
the world.

Object of
Scientific
Curiosity

I can see no difficulty in a race of bears being rendered, by natural
selection, more and more aquatic in their structure and habits.

—CHARLES DARWIN, *THE ORIGIN OF SPECIES* (1859)

LTHOUGH DARWIN'S WORDS REFER TO THE POSSIBILITY THAT
black bears, by means of pursuing insect prey in the water, could
evolve to be as big as whales, they perfectly sum up our beast's origins and nature. From the very first encounters to the turn of the twentieth century, European whalers and explorers commented on the polar bear's
feats and fitness in the water, its main habitat, which eventually inspired its
official name, *Ursus maritimus,* "sea bear," and led to its inclusion in the Marine Mammal Protection Act. The earliest attempts of travelers to the Arctic
to understand this new creature reflect personal and cultural attitudes and
are thereby of interest to the scholar of animal-human relationships. Strictly
speaking, the endeavor was "pre-scientific." They were working in a field more
commonly known as "natural history"; "science," as defined in our present understanding, was still developing. Scientists in those days were naturalists and
often amateurs, not formally trained.

In Europe, the connection between bears and the North goes back to antiquity. The Greek *arktos,* or "bear," gave us *Arctic,* the land that, from the Greeks'
perspective, lies under Ursa Minor; it also denotes the fearsome subspecies of
(brown) bear, *Ursus arctos horribilis,* that wanders there. The Indo-European
root of the Greek word means "harm" or "injury" and first referred to the
bear, possibly as a taboo or avoidance name. Such "circumlocutions" honor

Arctic marine mammals, including a "sea unicorn" (narwhal) and a "sea horse" (walrus) illustrate Henry Ellis's *A voyage to Hudson's-Bay*, 1748. Compared to the fantastical rendering of the walrus, the "White Bear" here appears fairly realistic. Courtesy of Library and Archives Canada.

the bear's spiritual power. A "bear" called just that might take offense and seek revenge, a belief I'll explore in a different chapter. Alternatively, Indo-Europeans may have named the bear for its most notable *physical* impact on them.

Non-Scandinavian Europeans of the medieval period at first believed that the polar bear was simply a rare variety of brown bear with very light-colored fur. Early modern European writers still had limited access to live polar bears and therefore often based their descriptions—and engravers, their images—on body parts or on anecdotes that professional travelers brought home. Naturalists also copied and glossed accounts written by their predecessors or peers. "Many scholars, many student naturalists," complained Charles-Lucien Bonaparte, a biologist and nephew of the emperor, "occupy themselves in building the systems, and in turning and returning in every sense the few facts (of which some are unfortunately even false) that others have brought to their notice."[1]

This in part explains distortions that can strike us moderns as comical, or even absurd: walruses with lion paws, White Bears with ferret heads, and whales looking friendlier than they should. Such depictions may seem only slightly more truthful than medieval manuscript miniatures that show she-bears licking their unformed, lumpy cubs into shape, but they did increasingly draw on direct observation rather than hearsay. Still, some illustrators continued to lift images such as the *ours blanc de mer* or "white sea bear" straight from the Comte de Buffon's *Histoire Naturelle* (published serially between 1749 and 1788) and to place them in different contexts, a form of Enlightenment photoshopping or recycling.

Naturalists also learned directly from animals displayed at fairs and from their exhibitors or caregivers. At an arena near the Paris boulevards, from the late sixteenth through the early nineteenth century, wild animals were pitted against dogs in staged fights similar to those in Elizabethan London. They included at least one polar bear, before the French Revolution. Buffon himself gleaned a great deal of knowledge from such fairs and *combats d'an-*

imaux, where bodies could be obtained for dissections. Before it was sent to the arena, the Paris polar bear was exhibited at the 1776 Saint Germain fair, with this verse attached to its cage:

> *I am always dressed in white*
> *My suit is all I own*
> *I please both small and great.*[2]

Watching exotic beasts no longer was for the privileged only. Dangerous ideas such as égalité were bandied about.

In the *Histoire Naturelle*'s chapter about bears, Buffon clearly distinguished a "land-bear" from a "sea-bear." But his land-bear category was still muddled: it included a "white bear of the forest" as well as a white sea-bear. The count would have likely become aware of polar bears in the forests of Hudson Bay by 1782, when France occupied Prince of Wales Fort at the mouth of the Churchill River. His classifying of animals by region or habitat—as in the case of the two "different" white bears—prompted later naturalists to speculate about their origins.

Buffon's writing rivaled that of Rousseau, Montesquieu, and Voltaire in stylishness and popularity, but taxonomy was his bête noire. He criticized Carl Linnaeus's binomial system, the Latin names now commonly used, without devising a good alternative.[3] In a 1785 German edition, Buffon's white land-bear looks different from his sea-bear, clearly showing the shorter neck and snout characteristic of brown bears and black bears. Perhaps the count knew about British Columbia's white black bears or "spirit bears," which could have confused him. He could have heard of them through the work of the English explorer James Cook, who had briefly landed on that mist-shrouded coast in 1778, years before the *Histoire Naturelle*'s publication. At Nootka Sound, Vancouver Island, Captain Cook reported seeing evidence of a "white bear, of whose skin the natives brought several pieces, and some entire skins of cubs." Cook's account also mentions true polar bears near Icy Cape in Alaska, where his men chased two with HMS *Resolution*'s jolly boat. These bears afforded the crew with a few excellent meals of fresh meat that tasted strongly of fish but was "in every respect infinitely superior to that of the sea-horse [walrus]."[4] They also afforded the ship's draftsman an opportunity. John Webber, later the official artist on Cook's fateful, third voyage, drew one of the Icy Cape bears, and the British Admiralty included his image in the 1784 report of the expedition.

The naturalist and antiquarian Thomas Pennant had, before Cook's depar-

L'ours de mer, the Comte de Buffon's "sea-bear," from his *Histoire naturelle, générale et particulière,* 1776. The eminent French polymath paved the way for theories about speciation. His bear categories, however, were muddled, including a "white bear of the forest" also. Courtesy of Université de Bordeaux.

ture, sent him a zoological inventory of Kamchatka, a Siberian stopover on this voyage. It listed the White Bear as at home "in the frozen sea only." Pennant, who never left his native Wales, published *Arctic Zoology* in the same year that Cook's report appeared. "They seem to give a preference to human blood," the learned man wrote apropos of polar bears, though his book also contains much that is true.[5]

With the dawning of the Enlightenment the young discipline of biology flourished. Scientist-explorers who accompanied expeditions returned with more accurate information about polar bears, as well as with dead or living specimens. Facts firmly emplaced the animal in its home environment and filled in the blanks that so held the public in thrall. What was known about polar bears was collated laboriously and interpreted and revised throughout centuries.

Despite this blossoming knowledge, unverified and perhaps unverifiable observations about polar bear behavior—asserting their handedness, use of weapons or tools, and practice of covering their nose while stalking seals—persisted. The Danish missionary and ethnographer Otto Fabricius observed in *Fauna Groenlandica* (1780) that in fights between polar bears and walruses, bears often win by "taking large masses of ice and dashing them against the heads of their opponents."[6] Tool use is commonly seen as a sign of higher intelligence, and such tales served as further evidence of the bear's "cunning." Paired with its reclusive lifestyle, they situated the bear close to the realm of mystery where it still resides, more so than many other creatures alive.

Dutch title page of Pierre-Martin de la Martinière's *Voyage des Pais Septentrionaux*, 1671. King Frederick III of Denmark ordered the expedition to secure biological specimens. It captured four Natives in Novaya Zemlya and, if the engraving is accurate, a walrus and polar bear. Courtesy of Rijksmuseum, Amsterdam.

One of the earliest descriptions of polar bear behavior comes from *The King's Mirror*, a Norse Baedeker for ambitious young men, written around 1245 by an unknown Norwegian. When it first appeared, it was also the most detailed work on northern animals to have been published. In the section about Greenland, the author states, "There are bears, too, in that region; they are white, and people think they are native to the country, for they differ very much in their habits from the black bears that roam the forests. These kill horses, cattle, and other beasts to feed upon; but the white bear of Greenland wanders most of the time about on the ice in the sea, hunting seals and whales and feeding upon them. It is also as skillful a swimmer as any seal or whale."[7]

The Swedish cleric, scholar, and mapmaker Olaus Magnus, in the aforementioned *Description of the Northern Peoples* (1555), provided additional information about the bear's aquatic lifestyle, although he misidentified its main prey as fish—an idea that lingers in the popular imagination today: "White bears are the greatest and strongest. As is so often mentioned, they are found in Iceland. They break holes in the ice with their claws. They plunge into the sea through these holes and catch fish under the ice, which they carry to the shore where they live. They repeat this as often as necessary to sustain themselves and their young who, in turn, know how to fish by natural instinct."[8]

Edward Topsell, with his doorstopper, *The History of Four-footed Beasts* (1609), further disseminated the fishy bit throughout the English-speaking world: "There are Beares which are called Amphibia, because they live both on the land and in the sea, hunting and catching fish like an Otter or Beaver, and these are white coloured"—but then, his illustrated bestiary also has entries on the unicorn and the ram-headed, faunlike "aegopithecus."[9]

Despite many accounts of their piscine diet, polar bears generally turn to fish only when other food sources are scarce. The eighteenth-century English naval officer John Cartwright watched them paw salmon from southern Labrador streams repeatedly, once, near the White Bear River, at "a most beautiful cataract" that fed a deep pool: "It was so full of salmon, that a ball could not have been fired into the water without striking some of them. The shores were strewed with the remains of thousands of salmon which had been killed by the white-bears, many of them quite fresh." The country all around, Cartwright reported, was veined with bear-paths leading to the falls. Cartwright was an accomplished polar bear hunter and once shot six in a day. He would have shot more that time, but he ran out of ammunition.[10]

The bear's swimming prowess also drew the attention of sea captains, with their keen eye for marine performances. William Scoresby, a whaling clergyman who also took time to write about snow crystals and ocean

Polar bear skull in a Norwegian museum. The bear's bite impressed nineteenth-century naturalists. It was known to sever iron lances half an inch in diameter. Skulls and teeth still are coveted trophies and collector's items. Photo by Genevieve Anderson.

waves, clocked the bear's speed in the water. "He can swim with the velocity of three miles an hour," the skipper reported, and can "accomplish some leagues without much inconvenience. He dives to a considerable distance, though not very frequently." Scoresby was equally impressed by the bear's bite: "Having an amazing strength of jaw, he has been known to bite a lance in two, though made of iron, half an inch in diameter."[11] Others, too, considered the polar bear an adept swimmer, but not so fast that it could outdistance men rowing.

These early observers concluded that the polar bear is no slouch on sea ice either. "He runs clumsily, but even deep snow cannot stop him," wrote a Russian explorer. And, "It is strangely moving to see a female loping across thin, fresh ice with her cubs. She practically crawls on her stomach with her legs widespread, and the cubs jump along behind her like frogs."[12] Scoresby calculated that, upon a large, snow-covered ice sheet, propelling itself with extended paws, a polar bear can "travel with twice the speed of a man, who, perhaps, sinks to the knees at every step."[13] As the English naturalist and surgeon Frank Buckland noted, the bear's agility in part results from its gait, an efficient shuffle, in which it lifts its feet only a little off the ground. Also, Buckland fancifully asserts, "as an old woman ties a bit of list [cloth strip] on the bottom of her shoes to prevent slipping in frosty weather, so we find a somewhat similar provision in the bear, the sole of whose foot is nearly as hairy as the top of his head, only the hairs on the foot are thinner and longer."[14]

Buckland credited the bear's white hair with bad conductivity, a perfect trait in cold environments as it helps to reduce heat loss. Furthermore, "The hair of the polar bear is exceedingly long, and yet it does not easily become wet. After he has been in the water the animal has only to shake himself, just as we trundle a mop, and he will dry in a few seconds. If this were not the case, when at home the poor polar bear, after a dip in the water, would soon be a mass of ice."[15] This is true, as wet fur is a poor insulator.

Early eyewitnesses noted that the bear's marine adaptation sprang from the need to find and surprise its main prey, ringed seals. Its apparent clumsiness on land belied its skill as a stalker. "Seals seem to be his most usual food," speculated Scoresby, "yet, from the extreme watchfulness of these creatures, he is often, it is believed, kept fasting for weeks together."[16] How an animal so awkward on land could catch alert seals, many could not imagine. But the Inuit, who had copied the bears' ambush-hunting techniques, provided answers. "The Esquimaux say, he prowls about examining the ice holes of the seals and, finding one close to high broken ice, there hides himself," wrote David Thompson, a Hudson's Bay Company surveyor and trader—the Natives called him "Stargazer" for his astronomical interests. "When the seals are basking in the sun and half asleep, he [the bear] springs upon them, seizes one, which he hugs to death, and, as fast as possible with his teeth, cuts the back sinews of the neck. The seal is then powerless and the bruin feasts on him at his leisure."[17] In fact, it is more common for a polar bear to kill a seal by crushing its skull with a bite or a swipe from its paw or by breaking its neck, but bears who crush their prey (including men) in a "hug" are a European conceit dating at least to medieval times.

These naturalists also noted that the natural boom-and-bust cycles of the Arctic cause bears to gorge whenever food is plentiful, to build reserves for lean times or periods of inactivity. "Before retiring into winter quarters," a Civil War–era book about animal habitations explained, "the Bear eats enormously, and, driven by an unfailing instinct, resorts to the most nutritious diet, so that it becomes prodigiously fat. In this condition it is in the best state of killing, as the fur partakes of the general fulness [sic] of the body, and becomes thick and sleek."[18] Here, as so often, observations of the animal included details of economical interest.

Writers frequently noticed that the bear becomes omnivorous in times of scarcity. It feeds, Scoresby wrote, on birds, foxes, caribou, or reindeer when it can surprise them, on eggs, and "indeed on any animal substance that comes within its power."[19] Even the diet of polar bears that are not starving is far more diverse than commonly acknowledged. As the physician Friderich Martens saw in Spitsbergen in 1674, they also feed on geese, lemmings, mink, beaver, and even starfish. They opportunistically kill belugas and narwhals near shore and feed on dead bowhead whales, where they wash up onshore, sometimes by the dozens. Twice, the Arctic explorer Adolf Erik Nordenskiöld found blood and hair of reindeer caught by polar bears on the Siberian mainland. Like the Dutch before him, Nordenskiöld traveled extensively on his quest for an open-water Siberian sea-lane and in fact was the first to complete it, in 1879, ice-locked, drifting through in his ship *Vega*. He was afterward made a baron, with the polar bear as part of his coat of arms. Somewhere en route, he watched three bears peacefully pasturing among the rocks. Though the principal food of the bear consists of seals, it does scrounge grass, mosses, seaweed, or lichen if necessary. Nordenskiöld concluded this from the fact that the number of seal-holes he discovered in the course of his journey was much smaller than the number of bears he encountered. The stomach of a bear he shot during his 1864 expedition contained nothing but earth mixed with plant remains.[20]

The polar bear's only foe besides people is the walrus, and a starving bear will take the risk of assaulting a herd in order to catch one. Already in 1385, at Greenland's Eastern Settlement, the widely traveled Icelander Björn Einarsson Joralafarer ("Jerusalem-Traveler") witnessed battling giants: a bloodletting between a polar bear and a walrus, which "always fight when they meet." Depriving us of the match's natural outcome, he killed them both, worried perhaps that one or the other of his prizes would get away.[21] Three hundred and fifty years later, the Norwegian Lutheran missionary Hans Egede settled the question of championship; long-held beliefs that the bear could, with a single stroke of his paw, cast a walrus up on the ice were no more than myth. A walrus often will kill a polar bear with its mighty tusks or, at least, "does not give over till they both expire."[22] The odds in such fights appear to be even. The drama, if one can secure front-row seats, must rank among Nature's most spectacular.

Long before the idea of "habitat" began to inform scientific discourse, the polar bear's range and that of its prey had been linked to environmental conditions. Synthesizing the work of the Comte de Buffon and other naturalists, the Anglo-Irish Romantic writer Oliver Goldsmith thought the "Greenland bear" exceptional, because it is "the only animal that, by being placed in the coldest climate, grows larger than those that live in the temperate zones. All other species of animated nature diminish as they approach the poles, and seem contracted in their size by the rigours of the ambient atmosphere. . . . In short, all the variations of its figure and its colour seem to proceed from the coldness

Hunter and hunted. Lithograph by Gustav Jakob Canton, ca. 1850. Some artists accurately portrayed the characteristics of Arctic species, including their behavior. As shown here, polar bears often kill prey by crushing its head. Courtesy of Staatsbibliothek zu Berlin, Stiftung Preußischer Kulturbesitz.

of the climate where it resides and the nature of the food it is supplied with."[23] Food availability does play a role in body mass, as does a region's mean annual temperature, and while polar bears are not the only compact animal thriving in the Arctic such biogeographic observations anticipated the theory of evolution and principles of ecology.

Nordenskiöld, who seems to have had a more prosaic nature than the poet Goldsmith, and with his feet firmly planted on Arctic ground, decades later noticed that "the Polar bear occurs principally on coasts and islands which are surrounded by drift-ice, often even upon ice-fields far out at sea, for his best hunting is among the ice-floes." His contemporary, Julius Payer, an officer on the Austro-Hungarian North Pole Expedition of 1872–74, correctly assumed that, despite the bears' ability to thrive and roam throughout the Arctic, distinct subpopulations exist.[24] Of the nineteen subpopulations now identified, several have never been surveyed, and estimates for others derive from unreliable aerial surveys. Even a trend for the whole species is difficult to assess, as subpopulations respond differently to climate change, hunting pressure, and food availability. The worldwide number of polar bears, estimated to be between twenty thousand and twenty-five thousand, is politically contentious and therefore often debated.

In their search for larger patterns, these naturalists found that questions of the animal's distribution quickly pressed to the fore. "Why does the white

Walrus killing a bear. Watercolor by James Kivetoruk Moses (1900–1982). Living on Kotzebue Sound, this Inupiaq artist may well have witnessed such a rarely observed incident. Biologists continue to tap Native knowledge about polar bears, as did their naturalist predecessors. Photo by Brian Sawnor, courtesy of Pacific Galleries.

OBJECT OF SCIENTIFIC CURIOSITY

Deyrolle in Paris, one of the world's oldest taxidermy studios, established in 1831. Originally, the mounted animals were used as zoological teaching material. Nowadays, some are sold to collectors or rented for movie sets, television shows, special events, and even store window displays. Courtesy of Mark Dantan.

bear enjoy the leaden sky of the pole and his native iceberg?" the American polymath John William Draper rhetorically asked. "Can it be doubted that, if the mean annual temperature should decline, the polar bear would come with his iceberg to corresponding southern latitudes?" No, it cannot be doubted. The oldest polar bear fossils found are from Svalbard and northern Norway and have been dated at 115,000–130,000 years old, before the beginning of the last Ice Age. But some biologists think that polar bears diverged from brown bears as early as 600,000 years ago. Fossils or bones from Denmark, England, and the Aleutians prove that during cold periods, polar bears *did* roam farther south than their current range, and the distribution of winter pack ice and shore-fast ice indeed marks the polar bear's southernmost limit. Professor Draper—who spoke at the heated 1860 Oxford evolution debate—was correct about polar bears then, though not in his application, during that speech, of environmental determinism to human races and history also.[25]

Polar bears were a milestone on our way to understanding biological change. On Svalbard expeditions in the summers of 1858 and 1859, the Scottish nobleman-explorer James Lamont watched them dive. Intuiting that the animal had become what it is by living on seals, he deduced that the seal and the walrus must have originated first. Lamont speculated that polar bears had evolved from brown bears, "who, finding their means of subsistence running short, and pressed by hunger, ventured on the ice and caught some seals . . . so there is no impossibility in supposing that the brown bears, who by my theory were the progenitors of the present white bears, were accidently driven over to Greenland and Spitzbergen by storms or currents." The palest brown bears with the greatest amount of external fat, Lamont thought, would have had the best chance to survive and therefore, reproduce. Upon his return, he wrote to Darwin, whose *On the Origin of Species* had been published in 1859. Encouraged by Darwin's response, Lamont elaborated upon walrus and polar bear evolution in his 1861 travelogue, *Seasons with the Sea-horses.* Darwin approved of Lamont's hypothesis and because Lamont's thinking on the subject predated the publication of *On the Origin of Species*, he later credited Lamont (as he did Alfred Russel Wallace) with independently conceiving the theory of natural selection.

As is evident in this chapter's opening quote, Darwin did consider bears in his masterpiece. But after he had been ridiculed for his thoughts on a future, insect-eating aquatic black bear, "monstrous as a whale," Darwin altered that passage in the second edition of *Origin* and removed it from subsequent ones. Lamont's observations and theorizing on natural selection vindicated the eminent naturalist—such a bear was entirely possible.[26]

A few words are in order here about an error that originated in that era and persists to the present, the "penguin–polar bear fallacy"—the portrayal of both species in the same environment. In my opinion, it is in part the result of polar confusion, a nineteenth-century conflation of the Arctic and Antarctic in the public's imagination. (Though this error predates Carl Hagenbeck's mixed antipodean-species zoo installations, I also hold the entertainer-entrepreneur responsible; see the "Zoo Bear and Circus Bear" chapter for more on Hagenbeck.) Our fascination with both animals, and perhaps even our confusion, is understandable: both arguably are the most charismatic species of their respective life zone; both are equally at home in the ocean and on polar ice; and both occasionally walk upright and are easily anthropomorphized. Even government-funded expeditions got it wrong. A postcard specially printed for the British National Antarctic Expedition of 1901–4, designed for crewmembers aboard *Discovery* to mail home, shows a Union Jack at the pole and a polar bear approaching it. Did the stalwart Brits perhaps think penguins were unsuitable symbols for the risks of polar exploration?[27] To those who cannot remember which animal occurs where, I suggest this mnemonic: in evolution-

Arctic fauna, by Gustav Mützel, 1898. A two-page spread from Alfred Edmund Brehm's *Thierleben* (*Animal Life*), a German multivolume encyclopedia that became known worldwide. The black-and-white bird on the far left is not a penguin but a thick-billed murre. Collection of Wolfgang Opel.

ary terms, polar bears split off from Eurasian brown bears and colonized the North via land bridges and sea ice. No such links existed between Eurasia and the South Pole—at least not within the shallow time frame of mammals.

But back to the question of polar bears' adaptive traits. Like Oliver Goldsmith, the well-educated eighteenth-century Greenland missionary David Crantz attributed the reduced size of vegetation and of many warm-blooded species—including humans—near the pole to "cold, inclement air and the foggy atmosphere."[28] The massive White Bear clearly was an exception; its survival under extreme conditions begged for an explanation. Denning—a pregnant female bear's most important behavioral adaptation to Arctic conditions—drew the attention of many naturalists, surrounded, as it was, by mystery. Unlike brown bears or black bears, most pregnant polar bears hibernate, preserving energy needed for nursing, and the young—born blind and sparsely furred—are sheltered from the elements. Bears do sometimes awaken and even leave the den. Early in the eighteenth century, the Lutheran missionary to Greenland Hans Egede reported that "in winter, instead of dens or caves under the earth, as in Norway and other places, here the bears make theirs under the snow," but then ruins his credibility, adding that "according to the information the natives have given me, [the dens] are made with pillars, like stately buildings."[29]

In truth, snow burrows, often discovered in a vacated state, are a marvel that can preserve bear and human alike and need no poetic adornment. A nineteenth-century popular natural history explains the amazing properties of a snow den: "The substance in which it is hollowed is a very imperfect conductor of heat, so that the traveler finds the caloric exhaled from his body is no longer swept off by the wind, but is conserved around him and restores warmth and sensation to his limbs. . . . There is no fear now of perishing by frost, for the snow-cell is rather too hot than too cold." A bear hidden thus "may be discovered by means of the little hole which is made by the warm breath, and is rendered more distinguishable by the hoarfrost which collects around it."[30]

A century and a half after Egede's observations, Nordenskiöld guessed correctly that pregnant female polar bears den well concealed, "perhaps in some ice-hole in the interior of the country." But he wondered about the males' whereabouts in the harsh season: "Whether the Polar bear hibernates during winter is not quite settled; various facts, however, point in this direction. For instance, he disappears almost completely from wintering stations during the dark time, and holes have sometimes been met with in which bears were concealed. Thus it once happened to Tobiesen that he went down with one foot into such a hole, to the no small dismay not only of the experienced walrus-hunter, but also of the bear."[31]

Polar bear head drawn by junior British naval officer Andrew Motz Skene, from John Ross, *A Voyage of Discovery*, 1819. One naturalist described the bear's head as an "elongated dog head," and Skene's drawing captures the animal's doglike alertness. Courtesy of University of Illinois, Rare Book and Manuscript Library.

In an era without radio-telemetry, such hunches were hard to verify. The male bears' absence from shore results from their prodigious treks, which resume when the sea ice expands again, early each winter. Even today, the males' wanderings are harder to trace than those of the females; radio collars do not fit them well—their head and neck are of similar girths, and they easily lose the device. Scientists now use glue-on satellite transmitters for that reason, and also because they hinder the animals less.

Between 1901 and 1907, Edward A. Preble of the U.S. Biological Survey spend several seasons in Canada's barrenlands, "Land of the Little Sticks." He finally set the record straight:

OBJECT OF SCIENTIFIC CURIOSITY

It is rather singular that the polar bears are seldom found on the land during the winter, on which account it is supposed they go out on the ice, and keep near the edge of the water during that season while the females that are pregnant seek shelter at the skirts of the woods and dig themselves dens in the deepest drifts of snow they can find where they remain in a state of inactivity and without food from the latter end of December or January till the latter end of March; at which time they leave their dens and bend their course towards the sea with their cubs; which in general are two in number.[32]

These seasonal disappearances and emergences of polar bears from the sea ice and their dens shaped Native ideas of the animals' regenerative and other magical powers, as a following chapter will show.

The frontiersman-poet Joaquin Miller, who at age sixty lost toes to frostbite in the Klondike after stumbling into Dawson starving, provided further reasons for variations in the bear's wintering. "As the Polar bear is able to obtain food all through the Arctic winter," he wrote, "there is not the same necessity, as in the case of the vegetable-eating bears, for hibernating. In fact, the males and young females roam about through the whole winter, and only the older females retire for the season." By the spring, Miller wrote, "the animal's heat has melted the snow [in the den] for a considerable distance, so that there is plenty of room for the young ones, who tumble about at their ease and get fat at the expense of their parent, who, after her long abstinence, becomes gradually very thin and weak. The whole family leave their abode of snow when the sun is strong enough to partially melt its roof."[33]

By his own admission, Preble, canoeing the barrenlands with fellow naturalist Ernest Thompson Seton, often saw and killed polar bears more than thirty miles from land; but he was also aware that females returned to firm ground every fall, "taught by instinct to seek the shore" and dig dens in the snowdrifts. An eighteenth-century fur trader had mentioned another trait that enabled polar bears, especially the males that stayed out year-round, to endure lunar cold. During the winters that trader could not get any bearskins from the Inuit, who, he thought, reserved them for their own use, for at that season the hair is "very long, with a thick bed of wool at the bottom."[34]

The Danish explorer Peter Freuchen, whose first wife was a Kalaallit and who spent many seasons on Greenland's ice, estimated that only half of all bears hibernate. "If they are not fat enough, they cannot remain idle for many months, but when they are well fed they can afford the luxury of sleeping all through the winter." Freuchen also noticed that bears used the same denning areas every year. "They knew their geography, the old bears," he recalled in 1953. "They picked a spot where the snow would cover them until the sun woke them up in spring."[35]

Cubs preoccupied curious natural historians and explorers as much as did hidden nurseries A nineteenth-century book about animal habitations portrays cubs as "of wonderfully small dimensions when compared with the parent," and not larger than rabbits when they leave their dens in March. They were easily captured because they seldom left their mother even when she was killed.[36]

The female in turn was envisioned as a model parent, affectionate and protective. Captain Scoresby observed that she defends her young "with such zeal, and watches over them with such anxiety, that she sometimes falls a sacrifice to her maternal attachment." He described a mother bear with two cubs pursued by armed sailors on the ice: "At first, she seemed to urge the young ones to an increase of speed, by running before them, turning round, and manifesting, by a peculiar action and voice, her anxiety for their progress; but finding her pursuers gaining upon them, she carried, or pushed, or pitched them alternately forward, until she effected their escape."[37]

The social skills of the largely solitary males got much shorter thrift but it was noted that they could be faithful mates. In his journals, the explorer Samuel Hearne wrote that "the males have a bone in their penis as a dog has and of course unite in copulation; but the time of their courtship is I believe not exactly known, probably it may be in July or August for at those times I have often been at the killing them when the males were so attached to their mistresses that after the female was killed, the male would put his two fore-paws over and suffer himself to be shot before he would quit her."[38]

Human biases toward the bear become most evident in summary statements about its "personality," a bundle of behavioral traits construed to reflect character. Most often, these observations assigned to the bear the role of adversary—hardly a scientific stance.

Some diarists turned the polar bear into a version of the Yeti, an abominable snowman "of a very large size, and of a hideous and frightful aspect, with white long hairs . . . greedy of human blood." Others, expressing mixed feelings, saw it as "savage and sagacious; apparently clumsy, yet not inactive," or, like Audubon, who never met one in the wild, as giving "the appearance

Polar bear cub in a specimen jar in the University of Edinburgh's Natural History Collections. The "wet" storage of zoological samples in alcohol allowed expedition naturalists to preserve larger animals in their entirety. Photo by Samantha Clark, courtesy of Edinburgh University, School of Biological Sciences.

OBJECT OF SCIENTIFIC CURIOSITY

of great strength without much agility."[39] Traits that appeared prominent to many observers were the bear's spirit of inquiry and its "clumsy cunning." It combined, they noted, aggressiveness with avoidance. Between the lines of Arctic journals, one perceives an animal hardwired to investigate oddities on the sea ice but also one fearing injury, which compromises its survival. Behavior labeled "aggressive"—approaching a camp or supplies—often was mere curiosity. Bears liked to inventory depots, abandoned vessels, or boats that had been left drawn up on the beach.[40] They sometimes ransacked the graves of sailors who had succumbed to the North's rigors, which gave them a sinister aspect. At other times, they invaded caches or huts, trying to steal from the nearly dead. "The night bears seem to be of a race of sneak-thieves," the leader of a doomed Belgian expedition wrote, condemning these opportunistic attempts. "The one that visited us last night pulled on our walrus twice, and we would infallibly have lost it if Strindberg hadn't been close enough to frighten the bear and make it let go of its prey."[41]

Explorers often remarked on the undiscerning appetite of polar bears. The medical officer Elisha Kane wrote that the plunderers devoured everything but some iron chests: meat, biscuits, coffee, sails, and his American flag. Others lost scientific instruments, candles, tobacco pouches, rubber bottles, and crampons to the voracious beasts. To protect their stores, the men sometimes covered them with sand on which they poured water, which then froze into a thick, solid mantle.[42]

According to Nordenskiöld, who often just walked up to a polar bear, the animal was not difficult to kill, because of its hesitant nature:

"Polar bears raid our stores," from Julius Payer, *Die Österreichisch-ungarische Nordpol-Expedition in den Jahren 1872–1874*. Quite a few images of the times show the animal as scavenger of expedition provisions, a result of its innate curiosity and explorers' dependence on their goods for survival. Courtesy of Alfred Wegener Institut.

When he observes a man he commonly approaches in hope of prey, with supple movements, and in a hundred zigzag bends, in order to conceal the direction he intends to take, and thus keep his prey from being frightened. During his approach he often climbs up on blocks of ice, or raises himself on his hind legs, in order to get a more extensive view, or else stands snuffing up the air with evident care in all directions, in order, by the aid of smell, which he seems to rely upon more than sight, to ascertain the true kind and nature of the surrounding objects.[43]

By emphasizing or exaggerating the strength and guile of polar bears, explorers implicitly commended their own bravery. But in the end, the polar bear, nightmare of early Arctic whalers, was not all that hard to kill, especially with modern firearms: "He is very rarely killed with a single ball, much less with an arrow that cannot break bone. . . . But a ball in the brain or heart is directly fatal," a Hudson's Bay Company man wrote.[44] Seen from the far-from-the action, non-scientific vantage of a newspaper editor of the time, the bear assumed a different shape—a character more in tune with middle-class urban

A rarity, even in captivity: Polar bear–brown bear hybrids at the Osnabrück Zoo, Germany. As grizzlies move farther north and polar bears spend more time on land due to climate change, interspecies liaisons could become more frequent. Photo by Molly Merrow.

OBJECT OF SCIENTIFIC CURIOSITY

Vrfus maritimus. Linn.

nach Maréchal gez. von Thle.   *gest. v. J.C.Bock*

Polar bear from Johann Christian Daniel von Schreber's *Die Säugthiere in Abbildungen nach der Natur, mit Beschreibungen* [*The Mammals in Images after Nature, with Descriptions*], 1774—the first print to employ the Linnaean binomial *Ursus maritimus* after Phipps coined that name the same year. The artist showed the hair fringe on a male's legs but erred about eye color. Courtesy of Biodiversity Heritage Library.

sentiments. It appeared to be "an engaging animal, with a distinct sense of humour and high domestic virtues." I will examine the bear's "domestication" and related image change in depth in the chapter about the circus and zoo.

•   •   •

In the light of recent events, Darwin's prediction that land-based black bears could begin to live like whales had it backwards. Instead, the most seaworthy of all bears could be reverting to landlubber looks and ways. In the spring of 2006, a trophy hunter accompanied by a guide killed an animal on Banks Island, Canada, that resembled a polar bear with soiled fur and sooty rings around the eyes. Closer inspection also revealed long brown claws, a dish-shaped snout, and humped back—all typical grizzly bear features. At seven and a half feet, this bear was much shorter than the average polar bear but had its small head, suited to hunting seals through holes in the ice. The guide knew immediately what his client had killed, and DNA tests confirmed it: the bear was the offspring of a female polar bear and a male grizzly. While the two species have mated and produced fertile cubs in zoos, crossbreeding in nature had never before been documented. Since then, other polar bear–grizzly liaisons in the wild have come to light. A bear killed in 2010 even proved to be a second-generation hybrid.[45]

Biologists now think, like Lamont, that polar bears evolved from brown bears that ventured onto the frozen ocean to stalk marine mammals, possibly after climate separated them from the main population descended from a common ancestor. This was not a single, clean-cut departure, and repeated pairings between both species have turned the family tree into a thicket. Shrinking sea ice could force polar bears to mingle with their southern cousins again, particularly as the latter now travel farther north. In coastal Arctic Alaska, grizzlies now feast on bowhead whale carcasses, sometimes in the company of polar bears.[46]

It remains to be seen if hybrids like these are evolutionary dead-ends or prototypes of a new species. (Genetic studies indicate that they are a rare and local phenomenon.) In the meantime taxonomists struggle with questions of classification. Polar bear nomenclature has always been somewhat diffuse: ice bear, sea bear, Greenland bear, or polar bear. Peoples with firsthand experience also use different names: *nanuq* (Inupiat), *nanook* (Inuit), *umka* (Chukchis), *ijsbeer* (Dutch), or *isbjørn* (Norwegians). To most Europeans from the thirteenth to eighteenth centuries it was simply the "white bear"—until 1774,

Weighing a bear on the ice of Alaska's Beaufort Sea in 2014. As part of Polar Bear International's Arctic Documentary Project, scientists are attempting to capture the rapid transformations that affect northern animals and ecosystems. Photo by Daniel J. Cox, NaturalExposures.com/adp.

when the English captain Constantine Phipps bestowed formal species status with a Linnean name: *Ursus maritimus.* Other scientific names suggested prior to the adoption of Phipps's designation included *thalassarctos, thalarctos,* and *thalatarctos.*[47]

With the occurrence of previously undocumented hybrids, new taxonomic conundrums arise. Buffon's ghost rattles its chains. What should we call the new creature, the White Bear that spends more and more time on shore? Grolar bear? Pizzly? Canadian wildlife officials suggest *nanulaq,* a graft of Inuit words for the polar bear and the grizzly *(aklak).* By a convention derived from big-cat hybrid taxonomy, the name of the sire comes first in such portmanteau combinations. The offspring of a male polar bear and a female grizzly thus would be *nanulak* or a "pizzly," while the offspring of a male grizzly and a female polar bear would be *aknuk,* a "grolar bear."[48] Our difficulty in choosing a name is reflective, perhaps, of our bafflement in the face of a quickly changing world. "Business as usual" no longer is.

Like a species' so-called personality—its mental and behavioral profile—taxonomy is a construct, an attempt to discern, to manage the rank profusion of life. Polar bears in particular live up to their reputation as shape-shifters. Science will continue to add to our knowledge of them, as long as they stick around. It is foremost in our imagination, however, that the animal continues to be made and remade.

From White Terror to Trophy of Modernity

A seminal moment in the life of a hunter arrives when he finds
himself the hunted: That dread second when he is frozen in his
tracks . . . he feels a primordial but familiar tenseness clamping
the back of his neck and he realizes that he is being stalked as prey
by a large beast.

—DOUG PEACOCK, *IN THE SHADOW OF THE SABERTOOTH* (2013)

DESPITE OUR GROWING KNOWLEDGE ABOUT POLAR BEARS, UN-scientific views of the bear as a man-eating monster persist. A poster on Longyearbyen, the administrative center of Svalbard, where three or four bears are killed in self-defense every year, asserts that the polar bear is the only mammal on Earth to actively hunt humans for food. The same poster advises that, after firing flares and warning shots, you throw down your hat, mitten, and scarf, which the polar bear will sniff, giving you more time—to do what, one might wonder.

Naturally, each time a polar bear kills a person, the media are abuzz with sensationalist headlines and gruesome images. The age-old fear of being consumed by a wild animal again raises its bristly head. In 2011, a starving polar bear attacked a Svalbard camp of the British Schools Exploring Society, killing one pupil, Horatio Chapple. It injured three other people before one of the expedition leaders—who himself suffered severe head and face injuries—shot it dead. "Eaton schoolboy savaged by polar bear," a *Daily Mail* headline shouted. Due to the ratings- and sales-driven nature of the media and the drama of such relatively rare incidents, they receive disproportionate attention. We thrill more to stories of humans *against* Nature than to those of humans *in* Nature, never mind Muir or Thoreau. Such coverage skews people's perception of risks. You are more likely to die in a car accident or from smoking than from being mauled by a bear. An investigating commission later found that the carnage in Svalbard resulted in part from an improperly handled shotgun and from neglecting to assign a night watch. The youth's death could have been prevented, but the image of the polar bear as "the half-ton killer that sees man as its prey" once again had been confirmed.[1]

Even when no recent deaths have occurred, our fear of the bear is kept alive. In 2013, a wildlife photographer inside a bear-proof Perspex box captured close-up images of a female Svalbard polar bear—again, a starving bear—trying to crack open this "cage." The photos of fangs in a slavering maw truly are terrifying. A microphone placed in the box picked up the photographer's racing heartbeat, giving those who viewed the subsequent television special the sense of being themselves menaced. "So THAT's what it's like to be eaten by a polar bear!" a related article in the *Daily Mail* concluded.[2] The often-mentioned fact that many of these bears are struggling to find food only adds spice to another newsworthy story: climate change.

Thus popular media cash in on one of our species' most anachronistic fears, the possibility of serving as food for wild beasts. The dread of it extends even beyond the grave. In 1899, a Norwegian member of an expedition to Russia's remote Franz Josef Land (an archipelago north of Novaya Zemlya) was dying of scurvy in an ice cave that held their supplies. His last request of his only comrade was that his remains not be eaten by a polar bear. He shuddered, like the poet Thomas Hood, at the possibility of a bear's "wet grinder" biting into his frozen spine, even postmortem.[3] The surviving sailor, Paul Bjørvig, honored his friend's request by keeping the corpse with him in the ice cave rather than burying it outside. Bjørvig endured two months alone in the polar darkness, reciting Ibsen to stay sane, until rescue arrived the following spring.

The phrase "serving as food" itself hints at subservience, at inferiority and a lack of control over nature. These feelings are hard to accept: we think of nature as largely subdued. But in the bear, we once again face the "staggering disproportion between man and no-man" that for so long has been part of our mental makeup as beings who, in the words of literary theorist Kenneth Burke, "build their cultures by huddling together, nervously loquacious, at the edge of an abyss."[4]

Of course, statistics from Svalbard and elsewhere show that we vanquish more bears every year than they do humans. Most polar bear attacks involve immature, hungry, and inexperienced animals. Older, savvier ones, so the thinking goes, have learned to hunt successfully and seldom regard humans a food—unless they become habituated through eating garbage or being fed.[5] But cultural preconceptions die hard, and even seasoned outdoorspeople fear polar bears more than they do grizzlies.

The outrage and the one-sided, morally charged discourse about man-eating bears are symptoms of an imagined human exceptionalism, a manifest destiny for the natural world that places us undisputedly at the top of the food chain and sees us as special, set apart. It starkly contrasts with the ideologies of hunter-gatherer societies, whose members experience the drama of eating or being eaten as a consequence of living among other large carnivores.

The earliest factual written accounts of the killing of polar bears come from the annals of the Nordic past. The sagas are vague about hunting techniques; unlike the Greenlandic Norse, who killed adult bears to sell the skins and to capture cubs for sale, Icelanders mostly seem to have acted in self-defense or in defense of their flocks. The sagas also mention that a prize was put on the heads of notorious sheep-killing bears. In the early fourteenth-century *Flóamanna Saga*, a boy, Þorfinnur, informs his father, Þorgils, that "a huge beautiful dog" is outside the homestead, bigger than any he has ever seen. Þorgils tells him not to go outside but the boy disobeys, wanting to play with the dog. The polar bear promptly sweeps Þorfinnur off his feet. Alerted by the boy's screams, Þorgils hurries outside and with his (named) sword, Jarðhúsnautur, "forcefully and in rage" strikes the bear between the ears, splitting its head, whereupon it falls dead to the ground. The boy is only slightly injured. Afterward, the bear's meat is prepared as food. Interestingly, the saga relates that the bear had only been playing with Þorfinnur.[6]

An entire book could be filled with details about polar bear hunting by Europeans and Americans who probed the Arctic between the sixteenth and early twentieth centuries. But I am more concerned with attitudes than with action and therefore will limit myself to a few typical narratives (including pictorial ones), which should suffice to outline the pursuit's tone and trends.

The Dutch sixteenth-century captain and cartographer Willem Barentsz (anglicized, William Barents) had one obsession in life: an ever-elusive ice-free Northeast Passage between Scandinavia and Alaska. It would kill him, eventually, in 1597, on the return from his third voyage. Before that, in its pursuit, he had many opportunities to learn about the White Bear. Overwintering near Novaya Zemlya, Barentsz and his company took potshots at each bear that crossed their path. In their struggle to survive, the crew had to keep bears away from their provisions or, better yet, turn them into provisions. During Barentsz's second attempt at finding the Northeast Passage to India,

Arctic nature dwarfs and instills fear in even its most formidable predator. From Frederick Whymper, *The Sea: Its Stirring Story of Adventure, Peril and Heroism*, vol. 3 (1877–80). Only toward the end of the nineteenth century can notes of compassion for a fellow creature be detected. Courtesy of National Institute of Water and Atmospheric Research.

in September 1593, some of his crew landed on the Siberian mainland south of Novaya Zemlya, to collect "a sort of diamonds occurring there," which turned out to be worthless rock crystals. Seemingly out of nowhere, a large White Bear charged and seized one of the landing party by the neck. "Who seizes me by the neck?" the man shouted and another, nearby, answered, "A beare," before running off. Then "the beare at the first faling upon the man, bit his head in sunder, and suckt out his blood." The rest of the men rushed to him, attacking the bear with lances and muskets. But the bear was not frightened, and, charging again, grabbed another man, "which she tare in peeces."[7] His comrades quickly fled. The experience may have made these men more likely to fire upon any polar bear they would see afterward. It is noteworthy that the skull-crushing related in this scene correctly describes the polar bear's method of killing seals. Many attacks on humans by grizzlies and polar bears follow this pattern.

Despite or perhaps because of its laconic voice, this account perfectly captures the terror men felt in an alien environment, and it became canonized, cited by other explorers. Barentsz's many run-ins with polar bears even yielded grist for the poet's mill. Ignoring the number of bears that the Dutch killed to feed themselves while overwintering, Hendrik Tollens's *The Hollanders in Nova Zembla* (1884) focuses on the bear stalking people. The darkness of polar winter only heightens their fear. Surprised by nightfall, the Dutch wander about on the sea ice near their hut, where

Detail from *Walvisvangst* (*The Whaling Grounds*) by Abraham Storck, between 1654 and 1708. Often starving or shipwrecked, explorers and whalers saw the bear as a threat as well as a means to fill their bellies. Many images show the bears outnumbered but still wreaking havoc. Courtesy of Rijksmuseum, Amsterdam.

They see the lamp set out for beacon-light.
Sometimes a bear with quick and fatal clutch,
Before the ready hand can wield the gun,
Assails the hindmost of the company.[8]

Building suspense and adding touches of psychological realism, Tollens envisions another encounter:

Ha! see they not yon polar bear advance?
He sniffs the tainted breeze; unwonted prey
He scents; with every pace he nearer draws,
Infuriate hunger fires his appetite;
The snowy mantle of his shaggy fur
Makes him an indistinguishable part
Of the surrounding whiteness; now he marks
His victim,—comes with stealthy step,—
Clutches the nearest of the luckless crew,
And drags him bleeding to his distant den,

A terror seizes all, they know not why;
They hear faint murmurings of a smothered groan
That ceases soon, expiring in a sigh.
Stunned and distracted with a nameless fear,
They darkling grope, to know what harm has come.[9]

Perhaps the late nineteenth century, no longer quite feeling the terror the bear once instilled, needed to imagine that of the sixteenth century, in a haunted-house sort of way. Gothic fiction as a fad, exemplified by the tales of Edgar Allan Poe, also in part is to blame. (Tellingly, Poe's novel *The Narrative of Arthur Gordon Pym of Nantucket*, which influenced Melville and Verne, is set in gruesome polar waters.) The Dutchmen's "nameless fear," the horror that "thrills their frames" in part spring from the bear's camouflage. Its near-invisibility in the Arctic landscape and half-light is also the subject of reflection in *Moby-Dick*, which strikes metaphysical chords in the reader:

Though in many natural objects, whiteness refiningly enhances beauty, as
if imparting some special virtue of its own . . . there yet lurks an elusive
something in the innermost idea of this hue, which strikes more of panic
to the soul than that redness which affrights in blood.

This elusive quality it is, which causes the thought of whiteness, when divorced from more kindly associations, and coupled with any object terrible in itself to heighten that terror to the furthest bounds. Witness the white bear of the poles, and the white shark of the tropics: what but their smooth, flaky whiteness makes them the transcendent horrors they are? . . .

Wonder ye then at the fiery hunt?[10]

A pale freak of nature, a cetacean aberration, inspired Melville's musings on whiteness, and the bear helps illuminate the horror of the white whale. Here was a whole tribe of bone-white creatures, fanged and clawed nemeses moving as stealthily on land as they did through the sea. Melville further elaborates on the enigma of the "white-shrouded" bear: "With reference to the Polar bear, it may possibly be urged by him who would fain go still deeper into this matter, that it is not the whiteness, separately regarded, which heightens the intolerable hideousness of that brute; for, analysed, that heightened hideousness, it might be said, only arises from the circumstance, that the irresponsible ferociousness of the creature stands invested in the fleece of celestial innocence and love; and hence, by bringing together two such opposite emotions in our minds, the Polar bear frightens us with so unnatural a contrast."[11]

Arctic travelers familiar with *Moby-Dick* or Jules Verne's work must have broken a cold sweat at the thought of famished ghost bears and the doom that would follow the loss of provisions from their raiding. The firepower of our weapons has grown, but the bear's near-invisibility, its non-color, still troubles us. A modern survival manual addresses the difficulty of detecting the bear in wintry landscapes and offers this safety tip: "The black nose and claws of a polar bear may be seen clearly before it is possible to see any outline of the animal, because the yellowish white of the fur blends with the snow-covered background."[12]

Perhaps Melville knew of or sensed etymological resonances. "Bleak," which describes the tone of his sea-tale as well as explorers' views of the Arctic, comes to us from the proto-Germanic *blaika-, "shining, white," by way of Old Norse *bleikr*, "pale, whitish, blond." This sense survived in medieval English, meaning "bare" as well as "pale"; in modern German it remains, as *bleich*. Facial pallor and deadliness connect snow, winter, and polar bear. At least one Dutchman blanched permanently, as the tale goes, under the claws of a White Bear. In 1668, Cornelis Gerritz Young Kees, the captain of a Spitsbergen whaler (whose name translated, appropriately, to *Hope for a Black*

Whale-fish), lived through a surprise attack by a polar bear he thought gravely wounded. He was so traumatized that upon his return to Zaandam, he had a gable stone carved and painted with the episode, and mounted it at the front of his house. The property became known as "the house of the man under the bear," the incident having become this sailor's badge. It is said that Young Kees aged overnight, that his hair turned gray, and that for the rest of his life he kept an ashen complexion. He commissioned a second painting of the incident, and had drinking glasses etched with the scene. His descendants still told the story in the early nineteenth century.[13]

In the context of anthrozoology, especially the widespread, well-documented esteem for white animals, Melville's take on whiteness appears ambiguous, prejudiced even—a break with tradition. Symbolically, it makes sense for his time and place: the whale as inscrutable, hostile godhead, the opponent of Puritan struggles. Like Ahab's obsession (whose object was modeled after a real-life, much-pursued white sperm whale named "Mocha Dick"), people's fascination with white bears probably also grew from attitudes toward the exceptional, often identified with the divine. Albino animals or those with leucism—a genetic mutation—have always sparked wonder and the imagination. Zoos treasure white deer, white moose, bison, gorillas, lobsters, and tigers, and the latter were hunted to such a degree that they became effectively extinct in the wild. Bounty hunters eagerly sought colorless specimens, for which they could net ten times the amount paid for more common creatures. Similarly, a white bear in British Columbia's rain forest, a black bear-mutant that the Tsimshian call *moksgm'ol* or "spirit bear," still commands awe.[14] In nineteenth-century and early twentieth-century Europe and North America, albino humans starred in "freak shows" at fairs, billed as "white moors," "ice-men," or "polar people." Polar bears or polar bear hides, seldom encountered in previous centuries, could likewise have been taken for singular oddities, and therefore deemed very valuable.

Karl I (1654–1730), landgrave of Hessen-Kassel, a principality in central Germany, commissioned Johann Melchior Roos to paint his menagerie, which included a "white bear," a gift from the King of Prussia.[15] The resulting eleven by twenty-two foot canvas, *Die Menagerie des Landgrafen Karl*, features more than eighty animals, mostly exotics, and quite a few white ones. This disparate group, from parrots to polar bear, rubs wings, humps, and haunches with each other in peaceful coexistence. It evokes an idealized, prerevolutionary social order, with the lion—symbol of the ruler—taking center stage. The painting afforded those who did not explore abroad a paradisiacal glimpse of nature, which in Europe had long been civilized. In its orderly, somewhat stilted composition, it also resembles an inventory or model of natural history collections, which at that time became more popular. It is said that the landgrave had a yen for white animals; during the filth-ridden Baroque, these embodied nobility, the immaculate, and luxury, but also vanity. (A contemporary painting in the same collection shows a white peacock.)[16]

While the polar bear ranked high in Inuit belief systems and cultural practices, in early modern Europe it remained subordinate to the "royal lion"—an outgrowth of medieval animal hierarchies. An eighteenth-century handbill for the Exeter 'Change menagerie gives "A GREAT WHITE POLAR" bottom billing, below various lions and even a "Flying OPOSSUM, from Botany Bay," and in a smaller font size. The ad claims that the animal is "Generally exhibited under the Title of the SEA LION, the most tremendous Animal of the Frozen Ocean." Perhaps the misclassification was an attempt to align the unknown bear closer with the show's top-ranking attractions.

Some cultures consider "ghost" animals such as albinos or "spirit bears" deities, omens, signs of good luck, otherworldly guides, or protectors. To Christians, the white stag symbolized Christ, as did the predominantly white unicorn. To hunt, capture, or otherwise harm white animals was taboo and brought bad luck. Ahab's demise could be read as a consequence of breaking such age-old prohibitions. In present-day online forums, hunters are still sometimes berated for killing albino deer or elk, though they do so legally. It would appear that anti-hunting sentiment with regard to polar bears at least in part stems from the animals' whiteness as well as the associated rareness.

The meaning of color, according to anthropologists and literary theorists, can magnify the meaning of an animal, and their combined meanings pack a double-punch. Compared with animals of a different hue, a beast the color of winter is almost always better, stronger, and supernatural.[17]

• • •

After Barentsz's voyages, contacts with polar bears proliferated. Whalers followed in the wake of explorers, though sometimes the two were identical. When whaling captains and European commercial interests arrived in the Arctic, the systematic pursuit of marine mammals—including the polar bear—began.

Non-Native settlers and visitors to the North quickly forged narratives of their own, situating the animal in the context of their own beliefs. Prone to quasi-magical thinking, British and Scandinavian sailors carried Old World memories of berserkers—crazed, bearskin-clad warriors built and shaped

Julius von Payer in a polar bear coat, on the 1872–74 Austro-Hungarian North Pole Expedition. Appreciating the warmth of bearskins, some Arctic explorers adopted Native clothing styles. With such outfits, the resemblance between the two species became even more pronounced. Courtesy of Österreichische National-bibliothek.

more like trolls than like human beings, men who bit the rims of their shields, who were immune to iron or fire. The unfamiliar creature fit that mold. It sometimes took ten or twelve musket balls to stop a furious polar bear, which did not seem to feel any pain. Perhaps the weapons lacked firepower or the sailors' hands shook. Though the Native people were poorly armed by comparison, they had long ago learned to combat the bears with spears and harpoons.

The polar bear of the sagas echoed in the superheated prose of Victorians. It recalled more heroic days, as in Charles Kingsley's *Hereward the Wake*, based on a historical Anglo-Saxon warrior: "Terrible was the brown bear: but more terrible the 'white sea-deer,' as the Saxons called him; the hound of Hrymir, the whale's bane, the seal's dread, the rider of the iceberg, the sailor of the floe, who ranged for his prey under the six months' night, lighted by Surtur's fires, even to the gates of Muspelheim. 'He has twelve men's strength, and eleven men's wit,' sang the Norseman, and prided himself accordingly, like a true Norseman, on outwitting and slaying the enchanted monster."[18]

In fact, medieval sources say nothing about the terror the Norsemen might have felt. We can only infer their attitudes toward the bear indirectly, as I have tried to do in an earlier chapter.

The superhuman, menacing polar bear similarly compelled the French science-fiction writer Jules Verne to craft a phantasmagorical scene, in a little-known story about a Hudson's Bay Trading company expedition to the "Cursed Land"—Canada's Northwest Territories, near Cape Bathurst. Out on the frozen ocean, the protagonists see "a huge object, of ill-defined dimensions, moving about in the uncertain light," scarcely a hundred paces from where they stand. "It was a white monster of immense size, more than a hundred feet high. It was pacing slowly along over the broken ice, bounding from one piece to another, and beating the air with its huge feet, between which it could have held ten large dogs at least."[19]

Eventually, the specter is revealed as an optical illusion, "only a bear, the size of which has been greatly magnified by refraction." But the similarities between this scripted scene and Inuit myths of a giant polar bear or a ten-legged bear are remarkable. One wonders if Verne did not simply cast into words an archetype of human fear, a memory embedded in the psyches of our cave-dwelling ancestors and shared by all who travel exposed on vast open plains. Without doubt, the Arctic's conditions—atmospherically, geographically, and psychologically unique—facilitate legend-building and mythologizing.

Verne's was well-researched fiction, but the snowy expanse could trick even old Arctic hands like Baron Nordenskiöld. Around the time Verne's story was published, Nordenskiöld noted, in his account of the Swedish expedition of 1878–80 to Siberia, "It happened that we were so deceived by an ivory gull, which had alighted in our neighbourhood, and in the mist resembled an immense Polar bear, as to make the common preparation for a bear-hunt, by ordering all the men to the tent or behind the sledges, so that the bear might not be frightened beforehand and so escape us."[20]

As Nordenskiöld's story reveals, the fears and beliefs of modern Europeans did not keep them from hunting polar bears. They routinely chased them in the water, especially when trying to catch live ones for zoos or menageries. A bear was much more defenseless afloat, and its natural instinct when wounded or clearly outnumbered on shore was to escape into the sea. A harpooned bear might rush a boat, especially when the bear was already tethered to it with a line or a noose. Such charges spawned any number of images and tales of waterborne attacks.

Analyzing the heroic quest narrative, the American mythologist Joseph Campbell pointed out that it is crucial for the protagonist to face unknown dangers and to gain some spiritually or physically valuable thing. As a placeholder for Arctic adversity, the polar bear perfectly embodied such a thing. Captured alive, pictured, described for science, or slain for its meat or skin, it signified the hero's trophy, his travails and rewards.

Two English nineteenth-century paintings that fall well within the Heroic Age epitomize the polar bear's role in visual mythmaking: Richard Westall's apotheosis *Nelson and the Bear* (1806) and Edwin Henry Landseer's memento mori *Man Proposes, God Disposes* (1864).

Landseer's monumental canvas alludes to the fate of Sir John Franklin (Nelson's subaltern at the battle of Trafalgar), "the man who ate his boots," who with his sailors disappeared sometime after 1845, while seeking to conquer that other chimera, the Northwest Passage. Using dark tones throughout this painting, Landseer, who'd studied live polar bears at the menagerie at the Exeter Exchange in London's Strand, cast long shadows upon "an English optimism and triumphalism, which was particularly apparent at mid-century."[21]

Franklin's had been the largest and best-equipped Arctic expedition to embark until then. His wife, Lady Jane Franklin, who never stopped hoping for his return, attended a soiree at the Royal Academy at which the "offensive" painting was shown. Her indignation was caused by the inclusion of two polar bears that, in Landseer's imagining of the aftermath, gnawed on a human rib-cage and shredded a red British ensign, symbol of national pride. Lady Franklin's shock at the sight of the disgraced flag could have been exacerbated by the fact that she had sewn it (or one very much like it) for her knight-errant before he embarked on his last journey. Allegedly, at home, she had thrown that silken flag over Franklin, who was stretched out on a divan, and he had startled, reminding her that the Navy covered corpses with the Union Jack before burial at sea. Superstition also surrounds the painting itself. *Man Proposes, God Disposes* now hangs in the study hall of the Royal Holloway (a college of the University of London) where administrators long felt it necessary to cover the work with a large Union Jack during exams. Rumor had it that a student who had looked directly at it went mad and committed suicide and that those who sat next to it would fail their exams or die.[22]

Every animal painting is also always a self-portrait, a story we tell about Nature and thereby reflective of our own nature. The red ensign in *Man Proposes,* which draws the viewer's gaze, recalls Tennyson's "Nature, red in tooth and claw"—but to pious Victorians, the horror of men having become bear prey was nothing compared to the evil whose name few dared to speak.

In 1854, word had reached London that Dr. John Rae of the Hudson's Bay Company had met some Inuit who had learned from others that about forty white men had been seen in 1850, dragging a boat south, and that later, the bodies of those men had been found. They most likely had died from cold and starvation, but John Rae's report included a disturbing detail mentioned by his informants. "From the mutilated state of many of the bodies, and the contents of the kettles," he wrote, "it is evident that our wretched countrymen had been driven to the last dread alternative as a means for sustaining life."[23]

That the men who had been commanded by the man who once ate his boots had allegedly resorted to this outraged the civilized British. To be known as men who were savaged by polar bears was tragic, if rather interesting—"to be known as men who ate each other, unthinkable."[24] In light of Dr. Rae's news, the ravenous bears in Landseer's work became interchangeable with men, identical to them—too close for emotional comfort, which Darwin's ideas had already disturbed.

Landseer's monumentalized animal stands firmly in the tradition of seventeenth-century *vanitas* still-life paintings. In this art form, bodily remains and sundry objects symbolize vanity and the fleetingness of wealth, power, and fame—indeed, of all human endeavors—in the face of death. It is unlikely that Landseer suggested that bears had killed any of Franklin's men; rather, he portrayed them in the scavenger mode that explorers often observed. To one re-

viewer, the painting's characters looked like "monster ferrets," which must have pained Landseer, who had gone so far as to borrow a polar bear skull from a Scottish museum in order to get the animal's face and dimensions right.

Westall's *Nelson and the Bear* reflects a younger, more confident empire. It poises the plucky, fifteen-year-old midshipman and future hero of Trafalgar at the edge of the pack ice, in a frockcoat, with buckled shoes and a bonnet resembling a chef's hat—not really dressed for such an outing. Nelson wields his musket like a club against an opponent that has flattened its ears against its head and looks more like a scared sheepdog than a polar bear.

In 1773, young Horatio's ship, HMS *Carcass*, like many before it on the search for the Northeast Passage, ground to a halt in the ice near Spitsbergen. *Carcass* and a second ship, *Racehorse*, were sailing under the command of Commodore Constantine Phipps, who on that same voyage named the polar bear *Ursus maritimus*.

Together with a shipmate, Nelson went after the bear, whose skin he wished to give to his father. That, at least, is the story the ship's captain, Commander Skeffington Lutwidge, started telling decades later. He added the companion and the loyal filial element only in 1809, four years after Nelson had bled to death on the deck of HMS *Victory*. In Lutwidge's story, Nelson's rusty, borrowed musket misfired and he was saved only because a rift in the ice had appeared, separating him from the bear. Westall's painting, however, shows only Nelson, a single, steadfast Briton facing the epitome of the hazardous North. Obviously, a companion on the ice would have diminished Nelson's glory. Westall also included, in the background, *Carcass* helping to scare off the bear by firing a cannon.[25] Besides adding to the hagiography of a national hero, the work celebrated Britannia and its mariners, tougher than walrus hide.

Westall had conceived the painting as one of a series of heroic episodes illustrating Robert Southey's *Life of Nelson*, begun in 1809 and published in 1813. Southey gave his hero a line ripe with braggadocio. "Do but let me get a blow at this devil with the butt-end of my musket, and we shall have him," Nelson supposedly shouted to his comrade after his shot had missed the bear. It gets stranger yet: Westall's painting was copied as an engraving for *The Life of Nelson* by John Landseer, the father of Edwin Henry Landseer.

• • •

Nelson and the Bear and to a degree even *Man Proposes* follow conventions of the exploration narrative, a genre seeking to terrify and to titillate. Such dramatizations of the quest—hand-to-paw combat, hull-crushing bergs, scurvy, and starvation—hallowed soldiers and explorers, especially in premature death. By the time Landseer finished *Man Proposes*, more ships and men had been lost in search of Franklin. The futility of Arctic exploration was starting to register, but hubris and vainglory persisted until 1912, when another

Richard Westall, *Nelson and the Bear*, 1806. An earlier, more confident nation worships its military hero, a paragon of British manhood. The incident depicted in the painting and the concurrent narratives likely are fictional. Courtesy of National Maritime Museum, Greenwich.

hero—Robert Falcon Scott—perished at a pole, and an iceberg ruined both an "unsinkable" ship and the confidence of a nation.

In the decades after Nelson's death at Trafalgar, the mercantile onslaught on Arctic wildlife only ramped up. In the second half of the nineteenth century, Norwegian walrus-hunters alone killed on average at least a hundred polar bears yearly. The Norwegian-Finnish harpooners regarded polar bear hunting as a "noble and dangerous" sport. Even decades before, Captain Scoresby had recounted how, on a single voyage to Greenland, his crew sighted one hundred bears, of which they killed more than twenty and caught four alive.[26]

Some researchers claim that explorers and Inuit hunters had a negligible effect on polar bear populations, because both groups killed bears primarily for clothing and food. Fur traders most likely had a greater impact, especially around their headquarters in Canada's western Hudson Bay. But whalers easily bested all others. When the return on investment in bowhead hunting diminished due to overkilling, they sought seals, belugas, and walrus for their oil and polar bears for their skins. In the Svalbard archipelago alone, 22,000 polar bears have been killed since the early eighteenth century—approximately the entire current population. Between the 1700s and 1969, an estimated 150,000 were taken from the Eurasian Arctic. Often, non-Native hunters used only the choice parts of an animal as food. The Austrian explorer Julius Payer described the scene near the doomed *Tegetthoff*, immobilized in the pack ice north of Novaya Zemlya: "A great number of bears' carcasses lay on the ice, for only the brain, the tongue, and the prime portions of the flesh found their way to the kitchen." When her crew abandoned *Tegetthoff*, it left behind sixty-seven cleaned bearskins, which proved too heavy a load.[27]

Northward expansion was powered by martial motives as well as mercantile goals. With the defeat of Napoleon in 1815, Britain had the world's largest navy sitting idle. Officers were let go or scraped by on half-pay until the second secretary to the admiralty, John Barrow, launched an ambitious exploration program that tasked his elite naval men ("Barrow's Boys") to fill in the blanks left on their maps. Like Civil War battlefields for young American mariners or seditious colonies for their European counterparts, the Arctic allowed men to prove their valor and earn promotions and reputations. In this analogy, the polar bear took on the role of insurgent to be defeated, captured, or killed. Journeys into the ice were prepared like military campaigns, polar bear skins or live specimens treated like spoils of war.

In accordance with the idea of the Arctic as colony, the nineteenth century conflated polar bears and Native peoples in racist ways. Observers commented on resemblances between indigenous northerners and bears and sometimes equated and denigrated both: "The dwelling of an aboriginal resembles a bear den," wrote the Russian priest Andrej Argentov, who traveled Chukotka's Kolyma River in 1880. "A bunch of people get together around weak unsteady light, and what is it they do? Gnaw on raw bones. This is polar man. In his habits, he is like a polar bear."[28] In Ilya Selvinsky's *Umka the White Bear* (1933), the polar bear Umka and his "tribe" are "uplifted" to the level of Soviet communism through careful indoctrination. The play reflects the government's anti-shaman stance and the collectivization of Chukchi hunting and reindeer herding. The protagonist's shedding of animal nature—as Maxim Gorki commented, "He quit walking on all fours and stood upright"— is a common theme in Siberian and Inuit myths, where it has, as I will show, a quite different meaning. Selvinsky's play so exaggerated its depiction of primitiveness that it was canceled in 1935 when some Chukchi complained that it was offensive.[29] Still, respect sometimes showed through cracks in the outsiders' chauvinist armor, when they acknowledged the skills that both bears and the Natives employed in their struggle for survival.

Compassion and even remorse also grew as the reckless and wasteful plundering of northern waters continued—feelings, which, in the late twentieth century, would lead to conservation efforts. Despite the fact that he ate bear meat like his ships' crews, the highly educated Nordenskiöld lamented the wholesale destruction of seals, walrus, reindeer, and polar bears out of sheer greed, the mentality of "if I don't kill it, another will."[30] In 1880, traveling as a young surgeon on a Greenland whaler, the creator of Sherlock Holmes, Arthur Conan Doyle, encountered polar bears near the island of Jan Mayen and pitied these "poor harmless creatures with the lurch and roll of a deep-sea mariner."[31] The "father of 'Eskimology,'" Knud Rasmussen, an inveterate hunter, empathized with a bear after falling, just as it had, into a sea ice opening. "It struck me that I no longer looked upon it as a piece of big game to be killed, but as a thinking and intelligent creature that was in the same distress as I was."[32] There is nothing like a dip with a polar bear to humble a man. As in warfare, hand-to-hand combat with the

The British lion gets licked, in *Harper's* 1876 take on yet another failed attempt to reach the North Pole. Especially during the second half of the nineteenth century, the sacrifices and futility of polar exploration became a frequent topic. Courtesy of Brooklyn Museum Library.

Polar bearskin bedding at a mining tent camp near Nome, 1900. Skins were prized as much as trophies as for their usefulness. Here they are used in the same way that the local Inupiat used them. From Alaska's oldest newspaper, *The Nome Nugget*, established in 1897. Courtesy of Peter C. Brown.

foe also more readily inspired fear, respect, and regret than anonymous long-range killing from aboard ships.

For practical and perhaps psychological reasons, it was easier to stay executions of cubs than those of adult bears. Members of a 1905 National Geographic Society expedition first orphaned a cub by shooting its mother, which had been circling their ship in search of food. They then lassoed the cub and brought it to the ship. But the little bear ("Buster") was inconsolable, and the captain was thinking about putting it down. The expedition leader, W. S. Champ, came to the rescue. "I was going down the gangway when the thought struck me. If I can get the skin of the mother to this cub, possibly it will quiet her." So the female's pelt was fetched and the cub comforted. Starving, it later fed on the fat from its mother's hide. Buster was caged for the rest of the journey—except at bath time—and sent to the National Zoo in Washington, D.C., where he lived until his death in 1936.[33]

•   •   •

In a few lines, Frank Buckland, an eccentric wildlife gourmet born to paleontologist parents, skewered the genre of polar bear hunting and exploration yarns as an outgrowth of male fantasies: "In most, I am afraid all, books of Arctic travel, we read accounts of polar bears being seen; then comes the old

Swedish sheet music for a polka, circa 1897. This cover anticipated the doomed Salomon Andrée balloon expedition's arrival at the North Pole. The merry bears and Inuit resemble each other, while the explorers, taller, distinct, engage in serious conversation. Photo by Frank Lateur, www .imagesmusicales.be.

story 'out with the rifles' and away somebody or other goes to kill the poor beast. 'Somebody or other' possibly misses the bear, who, of course, charges, and perhaps nips his enemy pretty smartly. The shooter comes home and writes, 'The ferocious brute then felled me to the ground, and made his teeth meet in my arm &c., &c.' 'Ferocious brute,' indeed! I think the boot is on the wrong leg."[34] Buckland felt pity for the bear in part because he identified with it. A forefather of the now-popular polar bear clubs, he sometimes could be found neck-deep in a river and often compared himself to the animal, as he too "languished in the heat and revived in the frost."

In 1899, five years before Buckland's barbed remarks, the eminent natural-ist John Muir, on the Harriman Expedition's *Corwin*, had witnessed a recent development: passengers—business magnates—chasing polar bears for mere sport, in this case, near Wrangel Island: "The first one overtaken was killed instantly at the second shot, which passed through the brain. The other two

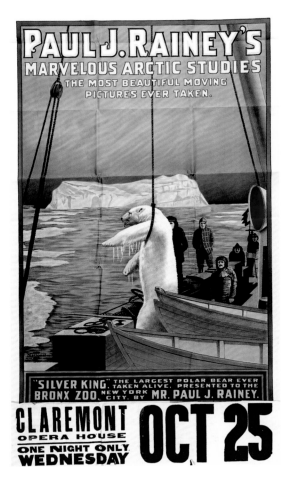

"'Silver King,' the largest polar bear ever taken alive." Poster for a nature documentary filmed in 1910 in North Greenland by the Pittsburgh big game hunter and millionaire Paul James Rainey. The bear Rainey "lassoed" ended up in the New York Zoological Park in the Bronx. Courtesy of Wellcome Library, London.

were fired at by five fun-, fur-, and fame-seekers, with heavy breech-loading rifles about forty times ere they were killed. From four to six bullets passed through their necks and shoulders before the last through the brain put an end to their agony."

This new type of hunting by the wealthy continues in the present. Ever the keen observer of nature and men, Muir described the bears' response to each type of wound, acidly judging the endeavor to be "as safe and easy a butchery as shooting cows in a barnyard from the roof of the barn." Agreeing with him, at least in this, the circus entrepreneur and animal trader Carl Hagenbeck in 1912 wrote that "the polar bear, once so formidable, now excites scarcely more fear than the musk-ox."[35]

Some of the new breed of tourist-hunters felt the same way. One late nineteenth-century yachtsman thought that "the 'polar' makes but a poor fight against the accurately sighted breech-loaders of to-day, and it is very rarely that one hears of the loss of a man in an actual encounter with a bear." Another handicap was the seascape's openness, which rendered the target easily visible and offered few places where a wounded bear could hide. Grudgingly, even this part-time sailor admired the bear's stamina. "One of my shots," he wrote, "had almost filled the abdominal cavity with torn entrails and debris, but, with this terrible wound and a broken hind leg, the bear had fought her way for more than a quarter of a mile through loose ice."[36]

The polar bear featured prominently on Theodore Roosevelt's wish list of big-game trophies. Although he never got a chance to hunt it, the well-read rancher, historian, and future president aptly summed up the White Bear's changed reputation:

> The grizzly's character during the last half century has been precisely
> paralleled by the change in the characters of his northern cousin, the
> polar bear, and of the South African lion. When the Dutch and Scandi-
> navian sailors first penetrated the Arctic seas, they were kept in constant
> dread of the White Bear, who regarded a man as simply an erect variety

of seal, quite as good eating as the common kind. The records of these early explorers are filled with examples of the ferocious and man-eating propensities of the polar bears; but in the accounts of most of the later Arctic expeditions they are portrayed as having learned wisdom, and being now most anxious to keep out of the way of the hunters. A number of my sporting friends have killed white bears, and none of them were ever even charged.[37]

Perhaps, more aggressive and curious bloodlines had really been culled from the polar bear gene pool.

The aeronaut and journalist Walter Wellman, head of an 1898 expedition to Franz Josef Land, typified a new casualness in which numbers compensated for lack of thrills. "All in all," he reported, "I think we had more fun out of bears than anything else during our day and night up near the Pole. Forty-seven, altogether, fell before our rifles, and the amount of sport involved in this slaughter would almost make a book of itself."[38] It would indeed but be dreary reading.

From the early twentieth century on, a different kind of encounter with and pursuit of polar bears evolved. Filming and photographing polar bears now sometimes took precedence over killing them. City slickers were "Bagging Arctic Monsters with Rope, Gun, and Camera."[39] This trend, too, has continued, though polar bear watchers today far outnumber those seeking the bear for blood sport or food. During the 1913–17 Crocker Land Expedition to northwest Greenland, the Bowdoin College alumnus Donald B. MacMillan chased a bear near the Native village of Etah with nothing in mind but a snapshot:

> One day I saw a polar bear swimming across the harbor. I ran down to the water's edge and called for two Eskimo boys to help me. They jumped into their kayaks. We headed him off toward a small berg, hoping that I might get a photograph. I had photographed a polar bear before, both in the water and on the ice, but never on a berg where they frequently take refuge. Before driving him toward the berg, I had stationed two of the boys on the other side to prevent him from plunging into the water.[40]

MacMillan got his photograph. "Upon seeing the boys he stopped long enough for me to take this picture," he wrote. But this bear was not spared a violent death either. Eventually, the boy who was with MacMillan in the boat shot the bear and, since it was his first, he thereby became a man, "a great hero

Winter Time, a German engraving from 1878. Removed from the stark realities of Arctic exploration, dead polar bears and polar bear representations adorned the middle-class domestic sphere from the second half of the nineteenth century to World War I. Author's collection.

from that time on." Native and non-Native uses of the bear, especially for its meat and fur, had long overlapped. With the advent of photography a live bear, outside a zoo, for the first time drew people who were not bent upon killing or capturing it, a trend I'll discuss more in this book's final chapters.

In summary, upwellings of compassion notwithstanding, a change in attitudes can be traced from the small, poorly armed, terrified parties of Barentsz's days—often starving, scorbutic, and stranded—to Victorian whalers' proto-industrial slaughter and eventually to the hunting cruises of Edwardian gentlemen. Familiarity with the bear, paired with technology and the belief in human superiority, bred, if not contempt, then arrogance, callous dismissal, or boredom.

Despite all that, the terror the White Bear had inspired in our species lingered like a substratum of the dark polar sea—particularly among artistic souls and those who never encountered it in the flesh. The Austrian expressionist Alfred Kubin, in his ink-on-paper drawing *Eisbär* (1902), slimmed down the creature; giant and ermine-like, it stretches on its belly across a high, icy cape, ready to gut a cabin tucked into a bay below. Warmth escapes from the smokestack, foreshadowing blood spilled on snow. The pending doom and bear's sheer size amplify the threat of animalistic hunger.

Though written under the influence of the winter blues and employing the bear as a metaphor only, the eponymous poem by William Carlos Williams makes a fitting textual bookend for Kubin's *Eisbär:*

> *his coat resembles the snow*
> *deep snow*
> *the male snow*
> *which attacks and kills*
>
> *silently as it falls muffling*
> *the world*
> *to sleep that*
> *the interrupted quiet return*[41]

Kubin's sinister artwork and Williams's poem both convey a kind of darkness, a note of dread. Ninety years later, the nature writer Charles Feazel imagines the bear hunting seals in their frozen-sea lairs, from the perspective of the prey. Here, too, the animal is the antithesis of safe domesticity, causing a sudden rupture of existence. After approaching soundlessly, it pounces, bringing "death from above in a blinding avalanche of ice and snow, accompanied by a

Julius von Payer's *Bai des Todes* (*Gulf of Death*) from 1897 envisions the end of Francis Crozier of HMS *Terror*, who assumed command after Franklin's death in 1847. The heavenly spotlight on the center is a marker of visual hagiography. Courtesy of Institute of Geophysics of the Academy of Sciences of the Czech Republic.

thundering crash, shattering the snug warmth of the seal's home. Then all that remains is the dark, and the cold, and the bear."[42] This specific fear is founded in reality. Numerous Inuit and some explorers' accounts describe polar bears breaking into igloos or tents, trying to kill the inhabitants. As the 2011 Svalbard incident showed, they sometimes succeed.

It seems that since the late nineteenth and early twentieth century, the image of the polar bear as a man-eater has been resurrected, and not just in the tabloids. I believe this to be a result of our decreased contact with the animal on its home ground. Besides, tourists who venture into polar bear territory today are generally not as well armed and knowledgeable as were their explorer and gentlemen hunter predecessors. We simply have lost the skills for combating large predators, which we now face almost exclusively on-screen or at zoos.

To Barentsz, Westall, Melville, Landseer, and any number of trophy hunters and entrepreneurs, the bear was a defining element in a "geography of fantasy," a metaphor of existential challenge and dread that was easily decontextualized and transported abroad.[43] But the demon they hoped to exorcise by means of superior firepower or art survived in the imagination. It keeps unsettling us, as an archetype of humanlike yet alien life—an abominable snowman, fanged kin to the Yeti or White Walkers. Despite the fact that deer kill more people than bears ever do (through car accidents), the White Bear personifies nature and a universe ultimately beyond our control. That is its true horror. In contrast with deadly disasters such as earthquakes or floods, death by bear is death by nature incarnate and individualized. It feels more personal, and so is our retaliation. We rationalize dispatching a man-eater in order to understand (via autopsy) what caused it to act and because carnivores that prey upon humans might do so again; but the killing of one also has elements of a vendetta, of Old Testament, eye-for-an-eye revenge.

Zoo Bear and Circus Bear

The practice of keeping animals regardless of their usefulness . . .
is a modern invention, and, on the social scale on which it
exists today, is unique. It is part of that universal but personal
withdrawal into the private small family unit, decorated or
furnished with mementoes from the outside world, which is such
a distinguishing feature of the consumer world.

—JOHN BERGER, *ABOUT LOOKING* (1977)

WITH NEW DEVELOPMENTS SHAPING SCIENCE AND PHILOSOphy at the turn of the eighteenth century, as well as a burgeoning middle class and expeditions to the Americas, Asia, and Africa, animal collections in Europe—until then largely a privilege of nobility— opened their gates to the public. As in the medieval menageries, polar bears drew a good deal of attention. Beginning in 1693, the first King of Prussia, Frederick I, kept a polar bear and other large mammals for public amusement in a baroque-style hunting enclosure inspired by Roman arenas. The animals were too valuable and difficult to obtain to be killed but, defanged and declawed, were pitted against each other in faux fights.[1]

Augustus II the Strong, king of Poland and elector of Saxony, felt that without a White Bear his menagerie was seriously lacking. On November 17, 1726, Augustus's minister therefore wrote to the Saxon envoy in St. Petersburg that "the king would very much like to have one or two polar bears, very large and handsome, as they can be." If any such beasts could be found, they were to be sent in cages on sledges to Mittau and then by sea to Danzig. Two came, from the Russian Empress Catherine I's menagerie in Moscow. She generously donated them, and they were promptly shipped. But the Tsarina died in May

95

1727, so the return gift—six crates of magnificent Meissen porcelain (including a silver-gilt tea service)—went to her daughter, Elizabeth.[2]

In 1800, Vienna's Tiergarten at Schönbrunn displayed its first polar bears, and until 1808, following the medieval tradition, one was still kept at the Tower of London. Two or three lived at the Ménagerie du Jardin des Plantes in Paris, an institution that, unlike the ducal or royal ones, was inspired by revolutionary ideals.[3]

In England, entertainers had been displaying all sorts of animals at carnivals and fairs since medieval times. The traveling menagerie, which derived from the processions of Europe's ambulatory monarchs and their entourages, first took to the roads at the turn of the eighteenth century. In a bid for respectability, the owner of one bragged he was doing "more to familiarise the minds of the masses of our people with the denizens of the forest than all the books of natural history ever printed."[4]

Private entrepreneurs quickly saw the lucrative side of displaying exotic animals. The fiercer a creature was, the more rare, and the farther away its original home, the larger the crowd it drew. A "ferocious Greenland bear" arrived in Boston in 1733, where its new owner showed it on his property among

Encounter of a Polar Bear with Two Leopards, attributed to the Augsburg engraver Johann Elias Ridinger, famous for his images of animals, before 1750. It is unknown if the painting is a scene from a menagerie or mere flight of fancy. The bear's size suggests that it is a cub, as the painting's other details are fairly realistic. Courtesy of Kunsthandel Rückeshäuser.

ZOO BEAR AND CIRCUS BEAR

Heeding the fin de siècle craze for things Arctic, almost all European porcelain manufacturers commissioned sculptors to design Art Nouveau polar bears. The material signified value and was particularly appropriate for white animals. Figurine group from Thuringia, 1900–1910. Courtesy of Marina Schuldt.

the hustle and bustle of wharves.[5] In 1747, another, "a remarkable White Bear," in chains, appeared at the Mulberry Garden near the Quaker workhouse at Clerkenwell, London. The bear, announced *The Gentleman's Magazine*, "is tame, and makes several postures at the word of command."[6] Between 1800 and 1821, the Exeter Exchange—housed in an arcade on London's Strand—exhibited a collection of live animals that included a polar bear. The building served as the winter quarters and eventual home of Gilbert Pidcock's traveling menagerie. In the course of the nineteenth century, more and more, such winter quarters turned into permanent exhibits.[7]

With the closeness of urban surroundings and the growth of a new intellectual climate, Western attitudes toward the hairy stranger among them once again shifted. In eighteenth-century England, "the encounter between humans and other animals took a singular turn with the discovery of the great apes and the rise of bourgeois pet keeping."[8] In cities, intimacy with non-domesticated species led to a sense of companionship. Nineteenth-century insights into animal intelligence and evolutionary relations further narrowed the animal-human gap. Animal toys replaced the actual wildlife that vanished from middle-class Victorian childhoods. The concurrent use of proper names for pets heralded profound changes in humanity's perception of the natural world. Teddies and Parisian lapdogs came to replace the Bear Garden's champion beasts. At the London Zoo, the practice of naming individual animals goes back to at least 1850. Throughout Europe, as cities expanded, wildness became sanitized, muted, enclosed; now, as trophies of empire, representatives of the animal world educated, edified, and entertained. In the case of the polar bear, what formerly had been a life-or-death meeting (for bears and for humans) became a static and aesthetic spectacle. "Looking at each animal," the art critic John Berger wrote, "the unaccompanied zoo visitor is alone. As for the crowds, they belong to a species which has at last been isolated."[9]

From the individuation of animals in bourgeois homes it was only a small step to the apotheosis of personhood—celebrity. This encompassed the animals as well as their procurers and handlers.

Nobody contributed more to the popularity of captive polar bears or the nature of modern zoos than Carl Hagenbeck. In 1848, Carl Hagenbeck Sr., a Hamburg fishmonger, exhibited six seals he'd received as bycatch from fishermen before selling them at a handsome profit. At age fifteen, Carl Hagenbeck Jr. took over what would become Europe's most famous animal-trade business. He soon supplied zoos, menageries, and wealthy individuals, including the Kaiser, and in his early twenties already ranked among Europe's top dealers in exotics. With a nose for opportunity, he branched out into the budding entertainment industry, mounting "ethnological" and large carnivore shows as well as a circus. His agents traveled the globe to catch or buy (or in the case of Natives, to hire) "wild" exhibits. Between 1866 and 1872 alone, Hagenbeck sold thirty-six polar bears.

A Hagenbeck pricelist from 1881 shows the commercial value of different animals, determined in part by their rareness and the effort required to capture and transport them. A pair of year-old polar bears brought two thousand Reichsmark, one-fifth of the price for an Indian elephant or African rhino; even a pair of king tigers was worth three times as much.[10] Still, it was a princely sum. By comparison, a German worker made at best six hundred Reichsmark a year. The polar bears in Hagenbeck's cages came from Svalbard and the Barents Sea, caught as cubs or full-grown adults, depending on whether they were to be sold to a circus or to a zoo.

In 1887, Hagenbeck crossed into the territory of circus entrepreneur, opening his "zoological circus" to tap another promising market. His encounters with wildlife had taught him to take advantage of the animals' natural proclivities—curiosity and playfulness. Condemning hot irons and beatings, he pioneered moderate training methods. Compared to the cruelly enforced dominance then customary, Hagenbeck's kindness as a trainer can serve as a barometer for shifting attitudes toward the natural world. By emphasizing the big cats' and bears' intelligence and tractability over their ferocity he recast the image many explorers had painted of them. This approach notwithstanding, an aura of unpredictability persisted—and *had* to, to entice paying audiences. Carl's brother Wilhelm, in charge of the Hagenbeck Circus and the first to introduce polar bear troupes into the ring, found the polar bear to be suspicious by nature and likely to turn on its trainer without the least warning. For the longest time, the animal had been considered untrainable. Wilhelm thought that, of seventy polar bears he had taught, only two really enjoyed performing their tricks. Nevertheless, at the 1893 Chicago World's Fair, Carl Hagenbeck appeared in the ring of his own carnivore show; substituting for a trainer who had fallen ill, he demonstrated his belief in his own methods.[11]

Starting in 1877, when his wild-animal business flagged, Hagenbeck recruited Greenlanders and Labrador Inuit for ethnographic shows in Germany, which in the colonial era became a fad. During this period, human beings regarded as "primitive" or as existing closer to a "natural state" often accompanied exotic animals in living tableaus. Hagenbeck's ethnic performers arrived in Hamburg by the same overseas routes as the wildlife and often—as in the case of the Sami or "Laplanders"—as the animals' caretakers. During Anthropology Days at the 1904 Louisiana Purchase Exposition (the St. Louis World's Fair), a group of "Esquimaux" in a "polar landscape" entertained fairgoers with traditional activities—snowshoeing, sledding, kayaking, seal hunting—and as the show's highpoint, "combated" a tame polar bear.[12]

Eisbärenkampf, engraving by Ludwig Beckmann, 1875. This fight between two polar bears at the Cologne Zoo led to the death of the female by drowning. The zoo kept polar bears from its opening in 1860 until 2000, when management felt the species could not be kept appropriately at its facility. Courtesy of Zoologischer Garten Köln.

On October 24, 1880, Berlin's *Charlottenburger Zeitung* ran a story about visiting Labrador Inuit performers and their meeting with the zoo's polar bear that is too delightful not to be quoted in full:

> The polar bear of the Zoological Garden, which usually is known for its contemplative calm, has been showing truly febrile excitement since the arrival of the Eskimos. As soon as an Eskimo approaches its cage, it runs with a loud grunt to the bars and seems to want to break through them to attack his natural-born enemy, whom it recognizes despite its long captivity. Also, the Eskimos cause a huge uproar in the building that houses beasts of prey, but it is hard to convince them to enter that building because of their insurmountable fear of lions and tigers. In general, the Eskimos have already settled in quite admirably.

The explanation for the hubbub could be very simple. Perhaps the restive bear smelled the sealskin clothes the Inuit must have worn, or the Native foods they were eating.

No treatment of live polar bears on display would be complete without addressing their role in films. Hagenbeck's man-versus-bear scene was reenacted on celluloid many times. In the 1974 film *The White Dawn*—a tale of three stranded nineteenth-century sailors—an Inuk spears a polar bear on an ice floe. According to the movie's commentary track, seals and walruses were killed in filming but only if they would have been killed anyway by the Inuit lay actors who fed on and utilized all of the slain animals' meat and skins. Animal rights activists nevertheless were upset about the polar bear scene, although the bear—flown in from the Seattle Zoo—was not injured in any way. We can compare this to the Danish Nordisk Films Kompagni's fictional safari film *Polar Bear Hunt* (*Isbjørnejagt*, 1907) or to pre-Code Hollywood's *Igloo* (1932), made when censorship codes were particularly lax. Framed as "an authentic story based upon incidents in the life of the Primitive Eskimo in the Arctic Circle," *Igloo*, a quasi-documentary with a love story, strove for authority and emotional impact by showing a real polar bear killing. In the death scene, filmed without a cutaway, dark blood pours from the speared animal's wound, staining its fur. Then as now, filmmaking was the art of make-believe: *Polar Bear Hunt* was shot not in the Arctic but in the channel between Denmark and Sweden during the winter of 1906, when it was frozen. For this "Arctic hunting" film, the director procured and personally killed a Hagenbeck polar bear, possibly the same one that had posed for a photo of the company's logo: a bear balancing on a globe. The authentic and explicit yet staged animal slaughter in this and similar "snuff flicks," according to film historians, constitutes a "sacrifice for the delectation of the spectator, a kind of 'morbid money shot' ensuring something real was being documented— death."[13] Attempts to frame existential realities for a viewer also are evident in modern-day polar bear trophy photos, which I will discuss elsewhere.

• • •

Cages and bear pits eventually made way for theatrical imitations of the animals' home habitats, stages striving for greater verisimilitude. Showing animals unhindered by fences or bars had long been a concern of Hagenbeck, who wanted zoo visitors to experience wildlife in more realistic settings. In 1896 he presented polar bears, seals, and various birds backed by an Arctic papier-mâché panorama. In 1907, the new Hagenbeck Animal Park in Hamburg-Stellingen's so-called Northland Panorama became a permanent fixture, changing zoo design worldwide.[14] The panorama had artificial ice floes and snow banks on several tiers separated by successive moats. Viewed from ground level, this created the impression of predators and prey

The showman and animal importer Carl Hagenbeck revolutionized wildlife displays by designing more natural-looking settings. Postcard of Hagenbeck's unfenced "Northland Panorama" at the Stellingen-Hamburg Tierpark, ca. 1910. Courtesy of Archiv Hagenbeck, Hamburg.

cohabiting in harmony in their faraway home. After centuries that had been marked by carnage, control, and collecting, wildlife now came to embody the yearning for Nature awakened by urbanization—a trend noticeable to this day. Not everyone approved. The director of the Bronx Zoo and of the New York Zoological Society, William T. Hornaday, strongly objected to this wide-angle form of display. For him, the educational value of a zoo animal stood in inverse proportion to its distance from the visitor, and Hagenbeck's bears just seemed too remote to have any impact.[15]

The interest that European and North American zoos in the late nineteenth to early twentieth century took in obtaining and displaying polar bears resulted at least in part from Nansen's, Peary's, and Amundsen's widely publicized polar exploits. Like their Viking forebears, Icelandic fishermen once again catered to the demand for White Bears. The newly fashionable animals also inspired one of the most outlandish expedition schemes of all times.

The origin of the idea is obscure. According to one version, when the Norwegian explorer Roald Amundsen first saw trained polar bears in Hagenbeck's Hamburg zoological gardens, he was so impressed that he asked Hagenbeck if they could learn to pull sleds. Hagenbeck said they could, and his right-hand man, Adrian Jacobsen (a former sea captain), took charge of turning bears into huskies on steroids. The first trial, with two polar bears and one sledge, took place the following winter, in 1908.

It's also possible that Amundsen got the idea from Julius von Payer, rather than from his zoo visit. In the 1870s, the Austrian discoverer of Franz Josef Land had captured two cubs, and his crew "in all earnest, prepared to break them in for the return sledge journey to Europe."[16] It was common for explorers and whalers to transport young bears to be traded to zoos or simply as mascots and souvenirs. One Russian steam-sailor, homeward bound from Franz Josef Land, carried four live polar bears on board, three of which already were two years old.

Cub on the quarterdeck of *Pandora*, 1875, in *The Illustrated London News*. Caught on a search mission for Franklin, the bear was intended as a gift for the Prince of Wales. Others like it went to zoos. Because the cub was noisy and irritable and scared away seals, the captain subdued it with an opium-chloroform cocktail. Courtesy of John Weedy.

The bears were so tame that they were chained only to keep them from getting into mischief—"stealing, tearing things to bits, breaking everything in sight." They played with the ship's dogs, and when quarrels broke out, one of the crewmembers cracked his whip to restore order.[17]

After consulting with Hagenbeck, Amundsen decided that six bears should haul three sledges on the final push to the pole. "These bears, when properly trained, are as tractable as oxen," he boasted in an interview. "They are at home in the cold of the Arctic and can easily be cared for and fed with seal meat."[18]

The Norwegian champion skier and zoologist Fridtjof Nansen, who had become somewhat of an oracle for other Arctic explorers, agreed that this was a splendid idea: "If it were really possible to train the polar bear for the purpose, he would naturally be an ideal draught animal for these regions: his strength and endurance are wonderful; like the dog, he can live on concentrated food; and, better than the dog, he has remarkable reserve powers, enabling him to live for a long time without any food. I am, however, afraid that the polar bear would be a somewhat risky and troublesome draught animal to use, as he might not always be easy to manage."[19]

From merry-go-rounds to Christmas cards, from circus acts to computer games, from fantasy novels to motorcycle club logos—the harnessed or ridden polar bear is a recurring theme. Every horse lover, Hell's Angel, and kid on a carousel critter enacts fantasies of power, domination, and control. The thrill is that of human strength multiplied, of limitations transcended.

Eventually, the sled scheme fizzled. Neither Hagenbeck nor his trainer wanted to embark on a lengthy expedition, and Amundsen doubted that he could handle the strange convoy on his own. Given the nature of the environment in which the trek was to take place, the training of bears as draft animals seems reasonable to a degree—at least as reasonable as Scott's use of ponies, which were supposed to conquer the South Pole but died one by one. The plan also served as a slick publicity stunt for both Amundsen and Hagenbeck. And in fact, the last chapter on this idée fixe had not yet been written.

Amundsen was still considering the experiment twelve years later. In 1918, near the beginning of his Maud Expedition to find the Northeast Passage, he had been mauled by a polar bear, while still nursing an arm he'd broken in a fall. Toward the end of that voyage, before he reached Nome in western Alaska, he adopted a polar bear cub after the crew shot its mother. He kept the cub aboard *Maud* and named her Marie, looking after her until, several weeks later, she became too combative, and he put her down with chloroform. Amundsen afterward confided to his diary that in the experienced hands of an animal trainer, the cub might have become well behaved.[20] He took the skin back to Norway to be stuffed, and Marie remains at his house in Svartskog near Oslo, which is now a museum.

In the 1920s, a representative of a large fur company made a renewed case for the use of draft polar bears, after watching one of the most interesting "experiments" ever attempted in the north country: an Inupiaq boy rode a small sledge pulled by two cubs. "Both bears had been in harness for some time, were fairly well broken, and showed no signs of viciousness or stubbornness," he reported. A trader's bear team, by his calculations, would be able to travel one hundred miles a day, compared to the huskies' twenty to forty miles. The bears would however consume much more food, which they'd have to haul. "Naturally swift, capable of running long distances without tiring, the bears would make the most powerful sledge teams in the Arctic," this visionary believed.[21]

• • •

Given the attention to and bonding with individual bears in captivity and especially in zoos, it is no wonder that they became stars in their own right, fussed

"Naturally swift, capable of running long distances without tiring, the bears would make the most powerful sledge teams in the Arctic."

over by the press, adored by those whom they amused. In the process, polar bears seemed more humanlike and were often treated accordingly.

The living conditions of captive polar bears have changed since Amundsen and Hagenbeck's days, influenced by new ideas about the animals' needs and by zoo visitors' expectations. The Polarium that opened in 1975 at Munich's Hellabrun zoo had a pool with concrete "ice floes" and a 1.5 inch–thick, bulletproof glass pane that separated visitors from the polar bears. A smaller adjoining outdoor enclosure was used for rearing cubs or to separate individual animals. The polar bear house itself had single quarters, birthing dens, work areas for food preparation, and a thirty-ton-capacity refrigerating room. The ultimate housing display is perhaps SeaWorld San Diego's "Base Station Wild Arctic," where "magnificent polar bears, beluga whales, and walruses have turned Mother Nature's most challenging conditions into a polar playground!" After a simulated helicopter flight, visitors arrive at a fake research station where they can observe the animals.[22] A perfect mash-up of circus and zoo, Base Station abrogates the authenticity of place, in this case a region ever more developed and diminished. Hagenbeck would have admired this act of showmanship.

Over the years, the urge to cross the gap between humans and the wildness (fettered as it may be) that cannot be bred out of zoo polar bears, or perhaps a desire to better get to know the ursine stars, has caused numerous incidents. In the Anchorage zoo, one of Binky's victims jumped over two safety rails to get a close-up photo of him. The other, a drunken teenager, entered Binky's enclosure hoping to swim in his pool. Such trespassing is not a recent phenomenon. In 1891, a female servant from Bavaria, Karoline Wolf, climbed down a rope into the Frankfurt Zoo's bear pit—after undressing and neatly folding her clothes—in order to be "eaten alive by a white bear."[23] Another woman, a mother and teacher depressed by her futile job search, in 2009, crossed the moat at the Berlin Zoo, swimming out to the bears—at feeding time. (She survived.)[24] People will forever seek operatic ways to end their lives, but *accidental* zoo maulings are telling, because they can reveal attitudes toward the animal. In 1987, two polar bears at the Brooklyn Zoo dragged into their den and then killed eleven-year-old Juan Perez, who had entered the enclosure after hours on a dare. The boy thought the bears were slow and afraid of people and water. After invading their space, he provoked the female, throwing bottles and sticks. Police, who suspected that more kids were in danger, riddled both bears with shotgun slugs and pistol bullets.[25]

The old animal magic, that attraction of people to bears, remains strong. Drawn like foxes to a bear kill, we take risks to breach barriers that once, long ago, did not exist. Perez's death and similar cases recall an Inuit boy's test of

Illustration from *Popular Mechanics*, 1923, of a fanciful scheme to use polar bears as draft animals in Alaska's fur trade. Impressed by their performance in the circus ring, the explorer Roald Amundsen planned to have some trained for pulling sleds to the pole. Author's collection.

courage and coming-of-age rite: his first polar bear kill. The crucial difference, of course, is the cultural context. Whereas Inuit children grew up listening to their elders, respecting the animal, observing its habits and how it was killed, young Juan had never been inducted into the White Bear's ways.

Heeding people's desire to connect, the Cochrane Polar Bear Habitat in Ontario has since 2004 been offering a truly immersive experience. In its wading pool, visitors can approach the bear in its very own element, separated only by two inches of shatterproof glass. For moments the division between humans and bears seems again to have vanished. Gazes lock, unhindered by bars. "Staring into the eyes of an immense polar bear while swimming only inches away," a representative of the center said, "is to be remembered."[26] The zoo's approach might well qualify as an experiment in providing a species with vital stimuli. We are that species. Up close and personal, *Homo sapiens* indulges the innate drive to interact with other life-forms, an inheritance that has shaped our kind for at least two hundred thousand years.

As shown in *Le Petit Journal*, in 1891, a woman climbed into the Frankfurt Zoo's bear pit—not the only case of suicide by polar bear. Author's collection.

Children and bears meet in the Cochrane Polar Bear Habitat's pool. The gaze that an animal returns holds great magic. Many zoos now try to provide visitors with close-up or even interactive experiences. Photo by Gerry Robichaud.

• • •

As forms of mass entertainment that grew from the games of Roman antiquity and medieval menageries, zoos and circuses share common roots. In both settings, captive animals live removed from their home habitats, habituated to varying degrees. As we've seen, modern zoos claim to educate visitors and to contribute to species conservation. Circuses emphasize training and performance while zoos claim to maintain at least a semblance of wildness, in part through landscaping that mimics an animal's original environment. For these reasons, polar bears have remained a fixture in zoos, and have even become newly popular there, but at the same time are being phased out in nearly all circuses. Animal rights activism and government regulations certainly played a role in that shift, though its primary cause may be that more appealing entertainment—such as concerts, television, and sports events—makes the circus appear a quaint throwback.

It is difficult to establish any continuity between classical Roman arenas and modern circuses. The medieval bear-leaders, acrobats, and jongleurs who attended feudal banquets or fairs were individual acts, and—Elizabethan theaters-cum-bearbaiting rings notwithstanding—no centers for such arts or organized larger performances existed until the eighteenth century. A 1768 equestrian act by the Englishman Philip Astley that also included trained monkeys and dogs is commonly regarded as the first true modern circus performance. Though by 1786, clowns entertained audiences between horseback stunts in New York and Boston, the exotic animals largely associated with the circus only joined it in the late nineteenth century.[27]

The wild animal shows of modernity, which began as stationary exhibits in cities, soon turned to caged wagons for transportation. They traveled to summer amusement resorts as touring units hired by carnival companies. During the winter they operated stationary "zoos" and generated additional income by booking their animal and human acts onto the winter dime museum and vaudeville circuits.

While at first they displayed native animals only, circus companies quickly upgraded to more expensive and rare exotics. In the United States, the first lion, in 1720, was followed by the first polar bear, in 1733. With names like "Opium Den," "Gypsy Village," or "Midget City," presentations suggested spectators were entering fantasy worlds. At Coney Island, in 1905, a "Moki [Hopi] Indian princess" danced in front of lions. "We carry a scientific lecturer which makes the exhibit very instructive for the better classes," one animal show claimed, in an attempt to shed the seedy carny image. Menageries also handed out souvenir booklets that referenced scientists or explorers.[28] There were aspects of natural history collections: an early nineteenth-century print of a traveling menagerie shows taxidermy exhibits on top of cages that contained living animals.

Such educational efforts barely disguised the main point of the circus, which gave it pull compared to museums and zoos: titillation. Like the Salem minister William Bentley, who visited Boston's Bowen's Museum in 1798, visitors might only find polar bears "sleeping and slumbering with an insolent contempt of every visitor." The circus, conversely, delivered polar bears that jumped through flaming hoops and rode velocipedes. Lights—action! Guaranteed.[29]

Circuses signaled the ambitions of modern expansionist states by including exotic beasts. Lions, tigers, rhinos, White Bears, and elephants fueled commerce and the Victorian imperial imagination while offering escape from the Industrial Revolution's dreary realities.

Built in 1900 as a combination of circus, menagerie, and variety theater, the London Hippodrome was an architectural reminder of the bastard lineage of this form of mass entertainment. It can be hard to separate the strands of the different institutions (especially as some entrepreneurs had an interest in both), but generally, menageries and zoos emphasized the exhibition of animals whereas circuses focused on animal and human performances. Circuses kept evolving, and in Britain, the decades between 1880 and 1900 mark the period when wild animal acts, rather than equestrianism, provided novelty and thereby, revenues.[30]

From the inception of the modern circus to its heydays, bears have been among the most popular circus performers because of their trainability, impressive size, effortless strength, and anthropomorphic looks. And among all bears, the White Bears from the north were the standout stars. The Bronx Zoo director William T. Hornaday called them the most showy and attractive as well as the most active and playful of all captive bear species.[31]

The earliest reference to performing polar bears in England is to a group at Bostock and Wombell's in 1904, but polar bears were already part of the German Circus Krone by 1888. Willy Hagenbeck (son of Carl's brother Wilhelm) began building an astonishing act with polar bears in Germany in 1904. At some point not just polar bears but also Himalayan black bears, Great Danes, monkeys, hyenas, and some ponies milled about his arena, chasing a rubber ball. When Berlin zoo director Ludwig Heck saw this presentation, he was left open-mouthed in astonishment as Willy strode calmly among his animals "like a shepherd with a flock of sheep." At a gala performance, Heck bestowed the title "Polar Bear Shepherd" on Willy. In 1908, Wilhelm Hagenbeck (who had premiered a twelve–polar bear act in 1898) presented a veritable herd of seventy-five trained polar bears. They slid, one after the other, down a sixty-foot chute into a water-filled tank half the size of an Olympic pool. It took Wilhelm fifteen

A polar bear and circus ball automaton by Roullet and Decamps, late nineteenth or early twentieth century. With wild animals disappearing from Victorian lives, such toys became common in bourgeois households. They emphasized mechanical functions over "cuddliness," as people were taken with machines. Courtesy of Bonhams.

years to teach these bears, which ranged in age from one to seventeen years. The show's odd "man" out was a black bear, acting the clown; its undisputed star, however, was Monk, a one-ton polar bear whom Hagenbeck often wrestled.[32]

The highlight of the Hagenbecks' circus ventures without doubt was the show they put on at the London Hippodrome. This venue was a temple to entertainment. It had both a proscenium stage and an arena that sank into a 230-foot, 100,000-gallon water tank (weighing 400 tons when full) for aquatic performances. Eight central fountains and a circle of peripheral ones ringed the tank. Side entrances to the auditorium could also be flooded, for the entry of boats. In prose as turgid as the setting, the *1909 London Hippo-*

drome Programme relates the climax of Hagenbeck's show, which even featured an artificial aurora borealis:

> Never before has so stupendous a gathering of the white coated denizens of the Arctic been seen together and the difficulty of obtaining so many of these, now rarely met with, animals has been incalculable. The Scene presented to the observer is almost beyond description. Below—the 70 Polar Bears disport themselves in the water and above—an apparently illimitable extent of icebergs, rearing their transparent summits high into the air, is exposed to view; weird indeed and wonderful is the effect obtained as these great masses of ice move slowly with the drifting floes, lit by the rays of the Midnight Sun—as it were—into their very depths. . . . All previous attempts at spectacular realism sink into insignificance beside this tremendous display.[33]

The Hippodrome act was loosely construed as a play about a search for the missing Franklin expedition. (Lest we are quick to sneer: IMAX and other wildlife documentaries sometimes follow similarly contrived dramatic plots.) In one rather amusing incident, the stage director Wilhelm Hagenbeck had a group photo of him and his bears taken afterward, and when the photographer's flash went off, all seventeen bears flopped belly-down into the ring's sawdust.[34] Their reaction should not be mistaken for cowardice. It was simply an instinctive response to a stimulus for which the bears had not been prepared.

After combining the idea of the circus and that of the zoological exhibit, Carl Hagenbeck toured with his brother Wilhelm and their trained animals, worldwide and successfully. In the United States, he quickly became a competitor to homegrown circuses such as Forepaugh's, Ringling Brothers, and Barnum and Bailey.

England had its own share of great polar bear trainers, chief among them Frank Bostock. Together with his wife, the daughter of circus man Frank Bailey, he launched the Bostock, Wombwell, and Bailey Circus in 1887. Six years later he sold out to his brother and, like many European artists to this day, went to America, where showbiz will always be bigger.[35] The barrel-chested, handlebar-mustachioed Bostock and his audiences loved living-history tableaus similar to Hagenbeck's, because they dignified entertainment with edification. In one, his polar bears reenacted the taking of a Russian fort. In an ensuing real brawl, five large "Russian [brown] bears" put Bob, a polar bear, into the show's animal hospital. Bob was not expected to live, and Bostock called this absolutely the worst fight he had ever witnessed.[36]

Acts with several species, or "mixed animal acts," became exceedingly popular before World War I, when Europe's colonial enterprise—the main source of imported live wildlife—was at its peak. Catering to cravings for exotics and faraway places, one mixed act at the New York Theatre comprised one lion-tiger hybrid, one Somali lion, one African lion, two Royal Bengal tigers, one Congo panther, one Indian leopard, two South American pumas, two polar bears, and four German boarhounds. The animals performed to "vociferous" applause and seemed to enjoy it, for "they bowed to the audience and gave a roar of apparent delight."[37]

The symmetrical arrangements and frozen poses typical of many carnivore and mixed animal acts emphasized the human dream of order, the desire to triumph over unruly nature. Dominance in the ring was derivative of "military arts." With their controlled routines and gaudy uniforms, the first true animal acts inside arenas reflected the regimented performances of equestrian drills and martial music. The true point of such acts was the display of human rather than animal skills. Conversely, mixed acts have been called the "happy family" genre of animal presentation, intimating biblical harmony—a prelapsarian Eden—with man in the supervisory role. And it *was* mostly men who cracked the whip in those days. Despite the presence of women like Mabel Stark, who joined the Al G. Barnes' Circus in 1914, where she tamed tigers, men long dominated in the world of big cats and in that of bears.[38]

Training, for bears born in the wild, began with their capture (which is, as we've seen, no longer legal), with the preliminary step of taming by animal keepers. Bears judged unfit for the ring were sold to zoological gardens and menageries. Most traders and circus men thought the polar bear, if taken young, was easily gentled. Bears can supposedly learn more tricks than any other animal, although some trainers consider polar bears less versatile than their brown brethren.[39] Trainers take advantage of the animals' natural skills. The bears' great sense of balance and their tendency to rear up predispose them to roller-skating, balancing on a ball, walking a tightrope, or even riding a motorcycle. They stand up on their hind legs naturally but have to learn to walk on them. Trainers and audiences favor such acts, because they make the animals look more human.

As transplants from the Arctic, polar bears can become irritable in warm weather, but in his memoir-manual, *The Training of Wild Animals,* Frank Bostock warned that

> even in cold, frosty weather, a polar bear, when being trained, will get
> completely played out long before any ordinary bear would consider he

had begun. In a very short time he will begin to pant and show signs of distress. In training her group of polar bears, Mlle. Aurora [a colleague of Bostock] took great pains to give the animals as little exertion as possible, and those who have seen this group perform will remember that the chief things they do are to take up positions on various stands and make pretty groupings. . . . There is the comforting feeling that the animals are not being made to do more than they are able.[40]

Mademoiselle Aurora herself was an original. W. Tudor, the manager of Bostock's Wild Animal Circus, one day caught the young woman driving his baby about in a dog cart pulled by two polar bears. When he chided her for endangering his child, Mlle. Aurora, whose real name was Lillian Miller, gave two weeks notice, unless Tudor agreed to sign the following statement: "I hereby agree with Mlle. Aurora as right when she said that polar bears are not treacherous and that they will not harm any one and they have never been known to hurt any one." Miller firmly believed in her charges' agreeability if they were handled right. Still, Tudor had the last word. Out of her earshot, one must presume, he nervously muttered that polar bears were "skittish steeds, just as likely to run away as horses" and that Baby Tudor would not ride behind them anymore.[41]

The spunky Miller is the earliest woman trainer to work with large carnivores whom I've been able to identify through an 1898 photo of her with five polar bears. Before she married John Miller, an animal trainer whose life she saved by screaming near the ring when an elephant almost trampled him, the young woman from Boston had been rather timid. Early in her marriage, she fell in love with polar bears the first time she saw them, asking her husband if she could train them. "They have less affection than cats and are fully as treacherous," she told reporters one year before defending her darlings to the wary W. Tudor. "5,000 pounds of husky polar bear answer the beck and call of 100 pounds of femininity," the papers gushed about Miller's show, "for even the frostbitten heart of a polar bear is susceptible to feminine influence."[42]

Trainers preferred bears that were about one year old. Initially, they might dab the bears' flanks with different colors to tell them apart. Trainer Doris Arndt, winner of a 1956 Circus-Oscar, reported that her polar bears initially looked to her like white blobs with three black facial spots. But she quickly learned to distinguish between them and like many before her, saw the bears not only as individuals but also as capable of complex social behavior. She recalls one male always protecting an old arthritic she-bear that the others picked on and even tried to drown.[43]

The symmetry of culture. Photograph of Tilly Bébé with twenty trained bears, ca. 1909. Originally a secretary at a law firm, this Austrian became the "Mae West of the Kaiserreich"—a silent-movie star and one of the first women to work large carnivore acts. Courtesy of Archiv Hagenbeck, Hamburg.

Trainers found that it was important to get to know the temperament and idiosyncrasies of each animal. Like other people familiar with the animal, such as Native hunters, biologists, and zookeepers, they speak of differences in the behavior of individual bears; to the casual observer, the animals seem largely interchangeable (apart from obvious differences in sex or age) and devoid of anything that could be considered "personality." Trainers however developed a repertoire of techniques for different bear characters, from the "unmotivated toddler" to the "obstinate" or even "volatile" "teen." For his famous seventy-five-bear act, Hagenbeck obtained bears that were seven or eight months old. A keeper spent the same amount of time "to educate them out of their savage state—by contact, kindness, sugar and fruit" before turning them over to Wilhelm for training.[44]

The circus was from its beginnings more honest than the zoo about its true nature as an artificial space set apart for the skillful manipulation of animals. Sometimes, finesse in this manipulation was visibly lacking. In a 1902 mixed-animal act, spectators saw the eye of a polar bear swollen shut "after fifteen minutes of constant chastisement in order to get him in a docile

"Dampfbad fetzt! .. Das fürchten die Eisbären mehr als Schläge!"

"A fail-safe training method," from the German magazine *Fliegende Blätter*, 1895. Methods that now strike us as brutal were congruent with pedagogic thinking of the nineteenth century, when corporal punishment of pupils and soldiers was still common. Courtesy of Bibliothek des Deutschen Literaturarchivs Marbach.

mood."[45] Victorian animal trainers used the same punishments headmasters and parents of that era used to command obedience from children. "You have to try and attach the animal to you," one of them wrote, "for by cruelty no wild animal yet was trained . . . . But unless their affection for their trainer is mingled with a certain dose of fear, you can do nothing with them."[46] To counter accusations by animal rights activists about "coercing animals," modern circuses stress that the animals "enjoy" performing and only will do so for a trainer they "respect," one who has won their trust.

Mademoiselle Aurora's trust notwithstanding, an element of unpredictability remains in even the best-trained bear. Polar bears are the most dangerous of captive animals, the circus historian John C. Clarke thought. "Unlike lions, tigers, wolves, hyenas, pumas, and leopards, all of which are trained to perform, the Polar bear gives no indication of its state of mind. It possesses what the card player calls a 'poker' face. Its expression never changes and, therefore, one never knows what it will do next."[47]

Even Wilhelm Hagenbeck, who had proved that the polar bear could be induced to perform in the ring, thought of it as suspicious by nature, awkward to train, and apt to turn on its trainer without the least warning. "A bear is like a tractor," said the trainer who doubled for Esther Williams in the film *The Big Show*. Circus polar bears could also be grouchy because they entered the ring hungry—"a fed bear is a lazy bear," a saying went. They were normally castrated, to take the spunk out of them.[48] Al G. Barnes, who specialized in wild-animal acts, thought that a lion or tiger would not stand a chance against a polar bear. Such fights could happen during mixed acts, when an animal felt its boundaries violated. Sometimes the big cat won and sometimes the bear did. A few interspecies conflicts played out to the bitter end. At Mundy's animal show in Jacksonville, Florida, Roosevelt ("a fierce Nubian lion") took on Peary ("a monster polar bear") in 1901. Peary (no relation to the polar explorer) had somehow angered the lion, "possibly by his color or his cold and reserved manner." The fight lasted "ten rounds," and the anthropomorphizing, blow-by-blow newspaper account detailed it to the gruesome finish. Toward the end, with the bear losing, the keepers were firing at the lion and jabbing it with red-hot irons to subdue it.[49] The question of the polar bear's superiority as "ultimate fighting champion" is still hotly debated in Internet forums where people speculate about the killing potential and strengths of different predators pitted against each other.

In a reflex known as "residual aggression," a suddenly startled animal will bite whatever is closest. In an arena that is usually the animal next to it, which might have done nothing at all. In the case of a bear on a leash, the closest thing is often the trainer's leg. Work with bears in cages resembles that with big cats, in that a greater distance is maintained between the trainer and animals, and not much physical interaction occurs. Nevertheless, several polar bear trainers have been harmed in this way.

In 1930, one of his polar bears killed the Czech-born Adolf "Cossmy" Kossmeyer, a Hagenbeck trainer. The elfin Cossmy often approached his bears "naked," that is, without a whip and "fork." His favorite animal was a large polar bear that sometimes modeled for artists. Cossmy always gave the bear a "kiss" when its work was completed. This was a reward, really, a piece of sugar or meat he kept in his mouth for the bear to take. (Since then, other bear trainers have imitated this "Kiss of Death.") One morning, as Cossmy was lathering and scrubbing the beloved animal, he stumbled over an empty can, and the startled bear charged and killed him. Ironically, just two days before, Cossmy had confided that he thought one of the lions would eventually be his death.[50]

Fatal accidents during the heyday of circuses were so common that they lent credence to an old, macabre circus adage: "bear trainers never retire." Captain Jack Bonavita—"a transitional figure in the life of animal acts as they moved from the big cage to the silver screen"—was a movie star, animal trainer, and former acrobat who worked for Frank Bostock. He already had lost an arm after a lion charged him at Coney Island. During a film shoot at a Los Angeles studio, a polar bear clawed him to death. He had been putting the bear through its routine when it became enraged and attacked. A fellow trainer ran two blocks for a policeman, who fired six shots at the bear, killing it. Bonavita's jaw had been fractured and his face and body badly lacerated. He died on the operating table at the hospital.[51]

Since Bostock's days, the make-believe circus world has been further refracted in the medium of film, which added touches of melodrama. In *The Big Show* (1961), a heartbroken and suicidal animal trainer enters the polar bear cage—not to perform her world-famous act but to get viciously mauled and killed by one of her bears. Later, her husband gets too close to the polar bear cage and the 1,500-pound Teddy, which killed his wife, grabs him by the head and ends his life also. Keeping production costs low and striving for authenticity, *The Big Show* was filmed at Circus Krone in Munich with real animal trainers doubling for movie stars.

In real circuses, rogue animals were permanently removed from a troupe, while those merely acting reflexively were kept and never punished for it—a year after Cossmy's death, his son was touring a brown bear and polar bear act that included the bear that had killed his father. The show had to go on, and it was too costly and difficult to replace a trained animal.[52] The mayhem and gore here described seem to confirm the bear's reputation as a man-killer. I therefore want to emphasize that most, if not all, of these incidents resulted from the conditions of captivity. The polar bear by nature is rather solitary, a predator that needs plenty of space, which enclosures do not provide.

With fewer deaths by circus polar bears in more recent times—due perhaps to their smaller numbers and to less-daring acts—their image changed similarly to the way it changed between the early explorers' and the gentleman hunters' days. The "white monsters from the Arctic" had been "reduced from a state of ferocity to intellectual perfection by superb training," as a 1977 Ringling Brothers and Barnum and Bailey Circus souvenir program declared. The brochure advertised "fancy-footed, solemn-faced, funny white bears." Al G. Barnes's "most vicious" bears had become "nature's own comedians. Her favorite jesters . . . each as big and as white as the biggest snowman you ever saw." The "snowy white pranksters" climbed ladders to the top of tall chutes and then tobogganed back to the ground (as they used to under Hagenbeck's reign), because in the frozen Arctic, "it is natural for polar bears to slide down the side of a snow-covered chasm. Thus the bears enjoy chuting the chutes," the program puns, just as, supposedly, they did at Coney Island's "Animal

Illustration from a circus program. Bears dressed up as humans or performing human activities are a popular motif, and not just in the circus. The bears seem to be having fun, judged by their cheerful faces, and have lost much of the ferocity that was formerly emphasized. Courtesy of Richard Ellis.

Avalanche" slide. In the accompanying illustration, nearly all the bears smile or look benign, contradicting trainers' comments about the animal's lack of facial expressions.[53]

The perceived humor of such polar bear acts stems in part from the cognitive dissonance of watching animals doing human things. The effect is enhanced by a fish-out-of-water element: the animals' "clumsiness," a result of plump physiques and the lack of opposable thumbs. At the same time, the bear as clown is unsettling because it combines playfulness with potential threat.[54]

In Western Europe and North America, television in the 1960s and 1970s brought circus acts to a wider audience. Simultaneously, televised nature documentaries made the role of animals in circuses and zoos questionable. Safari parks also made it possible to watch real wildlife in more natural settings. Still, in Eastern Bloc countries such as the USSR and the German Democratic Republic, circuses had been nationalized and, promoted as a "people's art form," remained successful much longer than in the West.

One of the greatest polar bear acts on the far side of the Iron Curtain was Ursula Böttcher's. Though she ranks among the most celebrated female animal trainers of the post-WWII era, she began her career as an usher and cleaning woman with the German Circus Busch. The diminutive Böttcher (whose first name, Ursula, means "little she-bear") ultimately choreographed ten adult polar bears of Siberian stock, which the Soviet Union had given to the East German government. Allegedly, she also worked with the offspring of Hagenbeck bears that had been chosen for Amundsen's expedition. Her biggest star, 1,400-pound, eleven-foot, six-inch Alaska, dwarfed his trainer, who weighed 130 pounds and stood just over five feet tall. The pair enacted the Kiss of Death in a steel cage in the center ring, while spectators held their breath.[55] In a 1977 interview, Böttcher admitted she had no delusions about her polar bears' nature—"If I gave them the chance, they would eat me." Alaska was the only one of her bears that she truly trusted. During a forty-five-year career, Böttcher got injured only once, when a bear knocked her down and bit her on the neck and shoulders. But in 1990, the Kodiak brown bears with which she also worked attacked and seriously hurt her partner, Manfred Horn, who a month later died from his injuries.

Böttcher's wards did not test boundaries often. In 1975's Florida winter quarters, she tried out a new arena to see how her bears would respond to a ring-curb wire-mesh cage, which gave spectators better views than did cages with steel bars. Mesh was common for big-cat acts but had never before been used with polar bears. During the rehearsal, two men with high-powered rifles sat as backup in the bleachers. The polar bears "looked at the cage, sniffed it, and one gingerly touched it with its paw, then, apparently satisfied, turned around and took a seat. After that, none of them seemed to give the cage much thought."[56]

Poster advertising the East German animal trainer Ursula Böttcher's act. Like the whip, the size difference between the trainer and her favorite bear, Alaska, emphasizes the theme of human control over "wild" animals—part of the attraction of such performances. Courtesy of Bernd Brunner.

When the East German state circuses were liquidated ten years after the two countries unified, their animals were dispersed. Two of Böttcher's polar bears, Olaf and Tromsø, went to the Zoo d'Amnéville in France, where they remain today. Tosca was donated to the Berlin Zoo, where she would give birth to the megastar Knut.

By the time Böttcher retired and her show dissolved, polar bear acts had been largely discontinued. The bears had been relegated to the accompanying menageries—sometimes pathetic, one-bear, one-wagon roadshows. There they were still making headlines.

In 2001, U.S. Fish and Wildlife officials seized seven polar bears of dubious origins from the Guadalajara-based Suarez Brothers Circus, which toured Central America and the southern United States. The animals had been poorly cared for, even physically abused, and their quarters lacked the air-conditioning and swimming pool the law mandates. One had already died from a preventable infection. The others suffered in the tropical heat. The circus was fined for violating the Animal Welfare Act and for falsifying import papers for one of the bears; it appeared that some had not been born in captivity but had been taken from the wild. According to the Marine Mammal Protection Act, any group offering "an education or conservation program based on professionally recognized standards of the public display community," can legally import, breed, and take from the wild marine mammals, including polar bears. But there is no oversight, and the spirit of the law is easily circumvented. Investigation of the Suarez circus revealed that three of its bears had probably come from Churchill, Manitoba, where polar bears spend significant time on shore. Seriously ill, one of the Suarez bears died on a FedEx flight, in transit to Memphis. North Carolina, Washington State, and Detroit zoos got the rest. One later had to be euthanized for lingering health problems. The case spurred new legislation, and it has since become illegal in the United States to provide polar bears for any traveling show or circus.[57]

The Suarez circus incident only exemplified conditions that PETA and similar organizations had long decried. Even in modern facilities, they claimed, polar bears do not have enough room to roam. Heat stress, lack of stimulation

Despite reforms in zoo design introduced by the German entrepreneur Carl Hagenbeck in the late nineteenth century, enclosures such as the Belgrade Zoo's can still be found. Photo by Alistair Bannerman.

or contact with con-specifics (in zoos), and inappropriate diets often worsen their plight, causing neurotic behavior. Zoo and circus representatives countered that most of their polar bears had been born in captivity and therefore were used to these conditions. In 2013, of the thirty-five polar bears then in German zoos, supposedly only Knut's dam, Tosca, came from the wild.[58] Zoo officials also say that we can learn useful things by observing animals even in artificial environments. Proof of that claim comes from a study testing the hunch that, to find mates in the Arctic's vast icescape, male polar bears smell other bears' paw prints. Scientists collected swabs from the feet of wild, tranquilized bears and tested their hypothesis at the San Diego Zoo. Male zoo bears indeed seemed to be able to identify the smell of females in estrus from the samples.[59]

While many polar bears still live in zoos, in what amount to huge aquariums, they no longer glamorize the circus. Their presence in the ring, though, is not entirely a thing of the past.

Forestalling protests from animal rights activists or visits from municipal inspectors, the small Galician circus troupe La Fiesta Escénica employs animatronic polar bears, which premiered at the Berlin Christmas show of Roncalli, Europe's most prestigious circus today. Its director credits Ursula Böttcher with inspiring the act. In the animation, remote-controlled servomotors change the bears' facial expressions—perhaps even "improve" them— and the mouth, nose, and ears "move as they would in life." Fur made in America by the same company that put hair on bears in *The Golden Compass*, on the ape in *King Kong*, and on *Star Wars'* Chewbacca, covers these six-foot, sixty-pound simulacra.[60]

In this futuristic glimpse of the circus, Hagenbeck's and Amundsen's trials come to closure. No more trainers or visitors will be mauled. The animal's fickleness has been reduced to one of electronic or mechanical malfunction. Enchantment here springs from the dreamlike performance, the flashy costumes, lights, props, and tricks that allow audiences briefly to forget the contrivance beneath the skin—or perhaps enchantment derives from the tension between the seen and the known. Like prior performances, this one tickles with cognitive dissonance, this time from watching machines doing animal things. Ultimately, enchantment might flow from an almost telepathic, remote form of control, from the sheer brilliance of our technology.

Honored Guest and
Ten-Legged Menace

> When the animal was nearly upon him, he had jumped away
> to his right. The furious bear took a wild swipe with his paw
> as it ran by, missing him by inches. Then, before it could turn
> to come at him again, Sakiak had unfalteringly shot it through
> one ear. The animal had collapsed in a lifeless heap, its skull
> shattered. And the man it had undertaken to hunt watched,
> unharmed, as it fell.
>
> —RICHARD NELSON, *SHADOW OF THE HUNTER* (1980)

I N HIS DOCUMENTATION OF YEAR-ROUND INUPIAQ SUBSISTENCE AC-
tivities, the anthropologist Richard Nelson goes on to explain how Sakiak
benefitted from the knowledge his people had accumulated over centuries of surviving on the ice, a knowledge sharpened gradually, like the fine
edge of a harpoon head. Had Sakiak not heeded two bits of traditional advice,
the outcome for him could have easily been the opposite: "First, bears are left
handed, so an attack is best avoided by dashing off to the animal's right. And
second, a wet bear must be shot where there is little fur to impede the bullet,
preferably in the ear or the anus."[1]

As Nelson's account shows, nothing could be further from the indigenous
mind-set than seeing the polar bear in the context of popular entertainment,
confined in a circus or zoo. To the region's Native inhabitants, it was but one
strand in a web of kinship, competition, and obligation, inseparable from the
landscape, a creature that signified home. Codes of managing its precarious
wildness—and of dividing the bear's flesh—were pervasive, a routine of daily
survival. Many of these Native customs and beliefs regarding the bear persist
today to varying degrees.

Beginning in childhood, a male Inuk was introduced to the ways of polar bear hunting through
stories, through exercises of strength and skill, and
through going on forays with adults—often, with
an uncle. The boy would learn by observation and
imitation, graduating from rabbit and ptarmigan
prey to caribous and seals. Inuit hunters sometimes reared polar bear cubs so that boys could
study their behavior and learn the ways of their
cubs' wild kin. Killing the North's most dangerous
animal was a youth's rite of passage. Harry Brower
Sr., an Inupiaq whaler in Barrow, killed his first
polar bear at age fifteen (in 1939) but as a boy also
raised a pair of cubs. When they became too old
and pesky, he gave them to the San Francisco Zoo.[2]

Inuit walrus-ivory carv-
ing representing a polar
bear, used in the game of
ajegaung. Thrown into the
air, the bear had to be caught
on the peg. This improved
aiming, catching, and
hand-and-eye coordination,
skills necessary for hunting.
Courtesy of University of
Aberdeen Special Collec-
tions.

An Inuk's first polar bear—traditionally often a
newly weaned bear or a female with cubs—is still a momentous event, be-
stowing great honor, because the boy's family subsists on the meat and providing for others is highly valued. A boy learns to butcher it under the tutelage of
an elder and may give the hide to a favorite person, or sell it for income of his
own. He will not brag about his success, though; that is considered immodest
and could offend the bear's spirit.

Cultures and subcultures emphasize what is important to them by linguistic differentiation. Middle-class Americans have numerous words for car types
and investment options, sailors have dozens for different knots. Canada's Netsilik Inuit know several polar bears: *anguraq*, the adult male; *tattaq*, the adult
female without cubs; *arnaluk*, the pregnant female; *hagliaqtuq*, the newborn;
and *namiaq*, the adolescent almost as large as its mother. Inuit even differenti-
ate between types of polar bear dens. Older male bears sometimes dig tempo-
rary winter shelters, called *tisi.* The exitless den of a bear that remains hidden
for several months is an *apitiq.* Denning bears are *apitiliit*, "those that have
snow to cover them."[3] Equally observant—and cautious—Siberian Chukchis
distinguish two dozen categories of bear, including the adult male with very
white fangs, the skinny, hungry, exhausted bear, the bear moving toward one
through water, and the bear moving toward one over land.[4] Scientists have
benefitted from Native observation skills refined through millennia and from
the resulting body of knowledge.

The earliest evidence of human predation on polar bears comes from Zhokhov Island in the East Siberian Sea. Armed with the simplest of bone and stone

A Greenlandic boy holds up a polar bear skin, token of manhood, in 1913. Killing a polar bear is still an important rite of passage in many northern indigenous groups, but clashes with tourists' and conservationists' world-views. Courtesy of Arktisk Institut, Norway.

weapons, Mesolithic hunters living in driftwood-roofed pit houses dispatched at least twenty-one polar bears there around 8,000 BP. An equal number of reindeer bones litter the site, which due to lower sea levels at that time was still linked to the mainland. With nearly four hundred polar bear bones, Zhokhov is not only the oldest but also the largest assembly of polar bear remains human hunters left anywhere in the world. Closer analysis of the bones showed that most came from adult females, which may have been killed in their dens—a practice widespread in the Canadian Arctic before it was banned. Many of the bear skulls had been cracked open, presumably to extract the highly nutritious brains.[5] Despite the fact that even a female bear yields as much meat as four small seals, large bone assemblies like the ones at Zhokhov are unusual. Before commercial whaling boosted the market for polar bear skins, the staples of Inuit and Inupiaq diets were seals, walrus, and whales.

A gallery of incised rock art designs on a bluff overlooking the Pegtymel' River valley thirty-five miles from the Chukchi Sea coast is further evidence of early polar bear hunting. Tentatively dated to between the fifth and eighth centuries CE, these petroglyph panels include at least four polar bear images. One scene shows a hunter on foot with a spear and three dogs cornering a bear, a technique used as late as the nineteenth century. Unfortunately, these images do not provide information about Native beliefs or attitudes toward polar bears. Here, the historical ethnographic record can be useful, though one should be careful in extrapolating ancient ideologies from the writings of cultural anthropologists; the group being studied might not be related to whatever group previously inhabited a region—like the dating of archaeological sites, its ethnic attribution can pose major challenges.[6]

To counter the spiritual danger that came with slaying polar bears, ceremonial procedures had to be strictly followed before, during, and after the hunt. Other acts were explicitly forbidden. As a large, relatively rare, but ceremonially important prey, the bear was the object of a great number of such taboos and observances.[7] Some hunters, or in some places, all women, could not even partake of its meat.

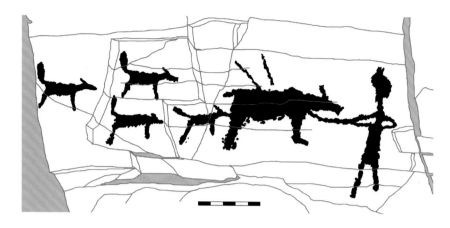

Polar bear hunt, a scene from the Pegtymel' petroglyph site in Chukotka, fifth to eighth century CE. This naturalistic rock art panel is the oldest graphic polar bear representation known. The hunt on foot with lance and dogs was still practiced more than a thousand years later. Courtesy of Ekaterina Devlet.

If the hunter or anybody in his community violated such taboos, retributions would follow: scarcity of game, bad luck, injury, disease, or even death of the hunter or family members. Codes of conduct demanded respect toward the hunted animal, with the bear's spirit or the master or mistress of game—a deity somewhat similar to Diana—acting as a dreaded enforcer. Many Arctic peoples believed that, if treated properly, killed animals would return reincarnated. Transgressions of the hunting rules required that a shaman intercede. During a trance-induced journey, he or she tried to appease the bear's spirit, often through offerings.

In preparation for the hunt, it was forbidden to speak boastfully about the animal, which was believed to hear and understand a hunter's every word. Terms that described but did not name and thereby anger ursine eavesdroppers were common, such as the Inuktitut *qakurturjuaq*, "great white one." At Igloolik (in Nunavut), in the special esoteric vocabulary reserved for shamans, the bear was *uqsuralik* or "Fat One." People used these names on the hunt as well as in songs and stories. "Old people say don't talk about killer whale, polar bear, brown bear, wolf, wolverine, the big-teeth ones," an Inupiaq elder remembers. "Don't talk smart or big."[8] Siberia's Yakut, who only know the polar bear through rumors or accounts from neighboring groups, respectfully call it "white old man" or "king of beasts" and use nicknames like "black" (for its skin color) or "master." Nenets and Siberian Yupiit tried not to step on the tracks of polar bears, which would otherwise sense that hunters were following them. The Nenets took extra care, moving the chunks of imprinted snow crust with a special wood spade, to allow passage of their sleds. Afterward, they returned the bear-tracks to their original places.[9]

Joseph Pootoogook, *Legend of the Blind Man and the Bear*, 1959. In this tale, a handicapped hunter kills a bear that is trying to enter his home, and its meat feeds his mother and sister. Sharing polar bear meat with kin and non-kin has long been an affirmation of group solidarity, a necessity of Arctic survival. Courtesy of Dorset Fine Arts.

After a successful hunt, Siberian Yupiit announced their kill to the spirit in charge of the animals, which otherwise might think that a hunter had stolen the bear from it. Even more important in an ever-watchful universe was the dignifying treatment of an animal's remains. The dead bear was a special guest. Dressed in new clothes, the hunter or his wife would offer the "tired" guest a drink of water. They would put a small willow twig under its body, as bedding. Chukchi hunters fed the head bits of dried reindeer meat, decorated it with bead necklaces, and kept it in the place of honor inside the *yaranga* (a yurt). They asked to be forgiven and sent off the bear with ritualized parting words: "Don't be offended; don't go far from our shore." The day after killing a polar bear, the Nenets would sacrifice a reindeer, the Chukchi a reindeer or dog. The celebration that followed typically lasted five days. After this thanksgiving, the polar bear's skull was either returned to the ocean or kept in the *yaranga* as a family talisman until the next hunting season. A new head then replaced it, and the old one was put back in its original environment with gifts that ensured the bear's goodwill and resurrection. "We don't kill a bear," Siberian Yupiit told the Soviet explorer Georgii Ushakov in the 1930s, "we only take meat from him and take off his fur coat."[10]

Similar rituals were observed in the New World, and many anthropologists see polar bear ceremonialism as part of a circumpolar bear cult that included Arctic and subarctic brown bears and the peoples that lived with them. Inuit and Inupiaq hunters, too, gave the dead bear a drink of water and kept its head in the house for four or five days. They smeared blubber inside the mouth to please the bear's spirit. They plugged its nose and covered its eyes with moss and lamp soot, sparing it the smell and sight of human beings. In some places, chunks of bear meat were thrown to the boys at camp, who tussled with each other for them. The scrapping, it was said, would turn these youngsters into good bear hunters. In parts of Greenland, the skull was turned to face the direction from which the bear had arrived on the drifting ice. Gifts were given to the bear, according to its sex: men's knives, harpoon heads, and rawhide rope to a male; women's knives, sewing needles, and, after contact with European traders, glass beads to a female. A gift of skin soles expressed the idea that though the bear had done so much walking, with new soles it would have no difficulty going home, from where it—or another bear that heard of such merciful treatment—would return to the hunter.[11]

Eastern Canada's Naskapi, Cree, Algonquin, and Ojibwa were the only North American Indians familiar with the polar bear, but it lived largely outside of their range. An eighteenth-century mestizo chief, Mes-ka-nee-powit wapask or John White Bear, lived near York Factory, Hudson Bay, and his children used the surname Bear. Around the same time, some Crees shot a *wâpask* or "white bear" on the mud flats of Hudson Bay near Churchill but were able only to sever and retrieve the head before the tide came in. They painted the bear's nose with ocher, oriented the head to the water, and, assuring the *manito* (spirit) of the bears that they had treated the head properly, asked it to float the skin ashore.[12]

Inupiaq men near Barrow scrape fat off a bearskin staked out on the tundra, between 1899 and 1908. With the arrival of whalers, miners, and tourists, bearskins became a valuable cash source for Native hunters. Taboos still guided the killing and processing. Courtesy of Alaska State Library, Rev. Samuel Spriggs Photo Collection.

Shooting a White Bear at Quebec's Rupert River, circa 1869, by Bernhard Rogan Ross, a naturalist and chief trader at the Hudson's Bay Company. One of the earliest polar bear photos and one of only a few that show non-Inuit Natives—in this case, Eastern James Bay Cree—with the bear. Courtesy of Library and Archives Canada.

There was another, less ritualized and non-lethal way of appropriating a bear. When the old beliefs were losing their hold and zoos and circuses clamored for polar bears, Inuit and Inupiat kept cubs of the bears they killed as pets in their homes. Such a cub they called *tiguaq*—"taken"—the same term they would use for a human adoptee. At least one family tried harnessing theirs with the sled dogs to pull a load when they were moving camp, which might have inspired explorers and traders to try the same. The cub, however, would not follow the dogs but veered off on its own course.[13]

Hunters proved themselves as worthy (and ingenious, in a meager environment) by not wasting parts of an animal. Beautifully fashioned tools and weapons also honored the one that had provided raw materials, or the one that would give its meat. Indigenous cultures seldom drew lines between the ceremonial, the aesthetic, and the everyday functional. More important than hunting techniques, ritual served as the most fundamental strategy to achieve ends, and expert craftsmanship showed awareness and care. Arctic Native peoples employed animal designs as much for decorative purposes as to propitiate prey or to acquire a predator's skills. Gestures of placation

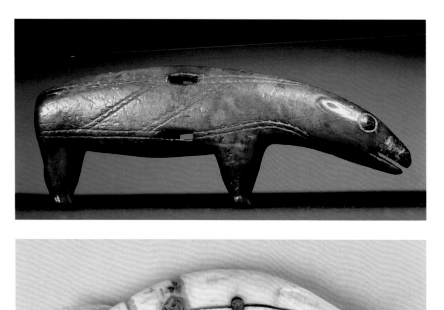

Polar bear ivory carving, probably a knife-handle of the Punuk culture, circa 1000 CE, excavated on Little Diomede Island in the Bering Strait. Everyday objects were fashioned with great care and often decorated, to express respect for the animals hunted. Courtesy of Werner Forman Archive/ Jeffrey R. Myers Collection, New York.

Fishing lure carved from a polar bear tooth, collected ca. 1930 in the central Canadian Arctic. Many everyday tools and items were crafted from polar bear parts. Courtesy of Prince of Wales Northern Heritage Centre.

marked life near the ever-threatening ice. The Smithsonian's collection of Arctic artifacts includes a wooden bucket of the sort that a Bering Sea Inupiaq whaling captain's wife would have used to offer the customary sip of fresh water to a newly caught whale. Carved-ivory ornaments on the bucket's rim represent polar bear heads and a whale. According to Inupiaq elders, these ornaments marked high status, symbolizing success in both hunting and political leadership.

Even polar bear bones came in handy. They were shaped into awls, arrowheads, combs, ladles, snow goggles, drag line toggles, meat forks, back scratchers, skin scrapers, drill bits, and bows for drills. Canine teeth became fishing lures, and other teeth, rattles. The *iputuruq*, a spear with a point formed from a long bone of a polar bear, was the traditional Inuit implement for polar bear hunting and remained popular even after rifles became common.[14] According to the Inupiaq elder and educator Ronald H. Brower Sr., in the old days men sometimes used polar bear ribs to make body armor. Seal hunters who stalked their prey and mimicked its movements fastened patches of polar bear fur to their left elbow and knee to help them slide across the ice while keeping them dry. Each time a seal napping at its breathing hole looked up, the hunter would raise his left arm, to shield his face, with the white fur as camouflage, and then freeze.[15] Perhaps this practice inspired stories about polar bears that cover their black noses with a paw while hunting seals.

In northwestern Alaska, ritual observances after the hunt included the Polar Bear Dance, a multiday feast and ceremony one anthropologist called "the most glorious of all Bering Strait occasions."[16] The dance was held in Little Diomede, Teller, King Island, Point Hope, and Wales after a successful polar bear hunt, to celebrate the hunter as well as the bear. On King Island, everybody gathered for the feast in a *qagri*, one of several communal men's houses built on the island's steep, rocky slopes. People believed that the bear's spirit visited during the ceremony, so they took great care to honor it and send it on its way again. The hunter put the bear skull on a bench in the *qagri*, where it "watched" the festivities. After the dance—on the fourth or fifth day—he

East Greenlanders imagined the moon—an elemental spirit—clothed in polar bear fur. This Yup'ik finger mask of wood and polar bear hair from western Alaska represents the moon spirit; women use finger masks in dances to accentuate eloquent arm movements. Courtesy of Werner Forman Archive.

would take it outside onto the sea ice, and "when the ice makes a noise as it moves, the spirit of the bear is regarded as having departed."

During the feast the hunter and his wife gave the participants sealskin strips for sewing, bearded seal or walrus rawhide line, and pieces of the bear's meat with the fur still attached. (After bear hides became an important commodity, only skinned shares of the meat were distributed.) Myths, often those that involved polar bears, were told. The hunter's wife or mother put out a spread of traditional foods. Then the dancing began, and could continue until the early morning hours. A participant of the last full dance held in 1960 recalled the bear's skull filled with water that hung from the *quagri*'s ceiling. As long as it was dripping, people kept celebrating. The dance songs detailed particular hunts. They described who the hunter was, which season the hunt took place, which weapons were used, if the hunter had approached the bear by foot or by boat, and how he killed the bear. Among the dances the hunter and his partners performed were pantomimic ones. "Stories are told by the movements and gestures that the dancer does," explained Marissa Oxereok, a former Wales resident, at a recent performance. "For the Polar Bear Dance, movements tell how big it [the bear] is, how great it is and how it walks." Though, regrettably, the ceremony today survives only in a pared-down form, the dance and memories of its former significance reaffirm bonds within the community and those between people and bears.[17]

The Polar Bear Dance honored the solitary hunter on foot, but especially before the advent of high-powered rifles, polar bears were often hunted collectively, with lances, bows and arrows, and dog teams. In the Bering Strait region and in Beaufort Sea, they were speared with harpoons from an *umiaq*, a sealskin- or canvas-covered whaling boat. Inupiat hunters attracted curious bears to within killing range: "If out hunting alone, the man would lie on the ice and 'play seal' by slowly raising and lowering his upper body off the ice. . . . Or, if the hunters were in a group, one man would be sent out on the ice alone to begin a crazed and furious dance. The motions of a man jumping and twirling can be seen for miles on the flat ice and any bear in the area would come closer to investigate."[18]

Sometimes a hunter butchering a walrus or seal attracted a bear unknowingly. A bear might also surprise him as he lay in wait at a breathing hole, mistaking his fur-clad shape for a seal.

Ironically, the more wary a good hunter was, the closer he would try to get to a bear before shooting, because a wounded, aggravated bear is even more dangerous than a hungry or curious one. Before rifles became widely available, Chukchis and Inuit faced polar bears at even closer quarters, armed with a

A polar bear attacks a Kalaallit kayaker who has lost his harpoon in this 1933 drawing by Kârale Andreassen. Arctic explorers commented on the scars many Inuit bore, testimony of their encounters with bears. Courtesy of Museon, Nikolaas Tinbergen Collection.

Short polar bear skin trousers from Smith Sound, Nunavut, 1899. Native hunters of the Arctic still use polar bear skins for clothes that modern products simply cannot match, such as fur pants and mittens, as well as *mukluks* or *kamik*, knee-high boots. Courtesy of the Trustees of the British Museum.

muskox spear, walrus pike (with a bayonet-style tip of walrus tusk or walrus penis bone), or a specially designed barbless head attached to a sealing harpoon.

According to Asen Balikci, an anthropologist with the central Canadian Netsilik, bear meat was shared with everybody who assisted, but the skin always belonged to the hunter who delivered the fatal thrust. A trophy and status symbol, the bearskin also was used for bedding and clothing. An average-size polar bear skin yields three pairs of pants and one pair of *kamik*, soft, knee-high boots. In northwestern Alaska, the hunter who first spotted a bear claimed choice parts such as the hindquarters and skin, because the bear had "shown itself" to him. Family members shared in the prestige from a successful hunt. Proud of a son's or a spouse's courage, the wives and mothers of Greenlandic polar bear hunters wore boots fringed with the "mane"—the long hair from the back of a male's forelegs.[19]

Like the men with whom Balikci lived, many of the Inuit encountered by explorers bore scars that spoke of their mettle. Captain John Ross, whose ship *Victory* got trapped in ice off the Boothia Peninsula (the northernmost tip of the North American mainland) in 1829, met Tulluahiu, a man about forty years old who was riding a sled pulled by his relatives. Tulluahiu had lost a leg in a hunting accident: a polar bear had ripped it from his body just below the knee, and he'd

King Islanders bring in a
polar bear. The "sled" in the
back is the bear's skin with
meat wrapped in it. After
distributing the meat, a
dance was held to honor the
animal and appease its spirit.
Photo by Father Bernard
Hubbard, 1938. Courtesy
of Santa Clara University
Library, Archives and Special
Collections Department.

almost died. *Victory*'s carpenter fashioned a wooden leg for him, which made Tulluahiu "serviceable once more to himself and his community."[20]

Even in modern times, killing a polar bear—one of the scariest creatures to approach on foot—affirms Inupiaq manhood. In the 1950s, Waldo Bodfish from Wainright recalled paddling with his crew toward thirty-some polar bears feeding on a whale carcass: "I was afraid, as all my companions were. Perhaps no man can come face to face with a polar bear without being a little frightened and the thought of going among a concentration of polar bears was enough to make even a brave man a little afraid."[21]

Few Inuit old-timers remember *apumiujuksiuqtut*—a test of grit and skills in which polar bears were hunted in their dens. After the dogs had sniffed out a den, hunters probed with a harpoon or spear to see if it was occupied. They then dug a hole at the top of the den just wide enough for the bear to poke its head through. When it did, eager to take on the intruder, a hunter would stab or shoot it. Afterward, the men pulled the bear out with the help of their dogs, which also hauled its meat back to the village. In late winter, with the snow crust thinning and the bears with cubs and crabby with hunger, this kind of hunting could be extremely dangerous: a man might fall through the den's ceiling or a bear burst out from below.[22] Present-day Inuit knowledge about den hunting is important not only for the cultural continuity it provides but also because it helps scientists in determining core denning areas and in finding dens where they can tag and examine bears.

Hunters heeded many of the old taboos as late as the 1980s, because old ways die hard, and because their observance protected them against bad luck and accidents. The Canadian anthropologist George Wenzel, who over the years witnessed more than forty polar bear hunts in the eastern Baffin area, noticed that generally, caribou, narwhal, and seal hunts took place in a rather relaxed atmosphere, while bears were approached "almost solemnly." The Inuit hunters he studied kept insisting that the bear was as intelligent as a human being and that "it understood when it was being ridiculed or belittled."[23]

Two stalwart anthropologists, Knud Rasmussen (between 1916 and 1918) and Jean Malaurie (in 1950), actively participated in northern Greenlandic Kalaallit bear hunts with sleds and dog teams. They left gripping accounts of hunting the bear with the world's northernmost people, accounts which deserve to be quoted at length here. Rasmussen joined up with Qolutanguaq, "a celebrated great hunter from Cape York," on Greenland's northwest coast. Both were on sleds pulled by trained bear dogs. Without need of the whip, they kept abreast of each other; "it was a race, and we knew that only a bear could excite them like this."[24]

Polar bear hide stretched out to dry in Qeqertarsuaq (Godhavn) on Disko Island, West Greenland. Bear skins outside a house signal a successful hunter to the community. Photo by Michael Haferkamp.

Rasmussen shared the excitement of Qolutanguaq, as "all hunters are children in the sight of big game, and every bear hunt is a challenge between drivers. The aim is to be the first on the trail and the first to shoot."[25] Malaurie also mentioned the pleasure the Kalaallit take in hunting bears, and their momentary regrets after the kill: "After all, he's the one closest to us," one of them said about the bear. For that reason and also to propitiate the bear, Native whalers still occasionally share a part of their catch with it.[26]

"When possible," Rasmussen wrote, "hunted bears always seek safety at the top of a steep iceberg, where the dogs cannot follow them. Even though the iceberg has vertical, slippery surfaces, bears can get a hold with their sharp claws." Rasmussen wrote that he had only once seen a bear lose its footing, near the top. "In falling it broke a hind thigh, and yet was able to smash a hole in the ice and seek refuge under the iceberg."[27] The hunt was never an exclusively physical pursuit. Some hunters knew spells that could stop or "surround" an escaping bear. In preparation for a hunt, an elder relative of the hunter might let down her trousers and shuffle about, so that the bear would feel as if it were losing its trousers and therefore move slowly.[28]

When the prey is close, a few dogs are loosed—by cutting their traces—to delay or surround the bear unencumbered by sleds. Many non-Native illustrations of this stage of the hunt from Rasmussen's time impress with their

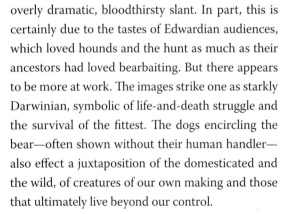

overly dramatic, bloodthirsty slant. In part, this is certainly due to the tastes of Edwardian audiences, which loved hounds and the hunt as much as their ancestors had loved bearbaiting. But there appears to be more at work. The images strike one as starkly Darwinian, symbolic of life-and-death struggle and the survival of the fittest. The dogs encircling the bear—often shown without their human handler—also effect a juxtaposition of the domesticated and the wild, of creatures of our own making and those that ultimately live beyond our control.

As soon as the hunter appears on the scene, Rasmussen continued, "the bear knows that he and not the dogs is its true foe. Unless it is killed with one shot it will fling the dogs aside and attack."[29] Often, the bear will also try to smash through the sea ice. Towering on its hind legs before pounding down with its massive shoulders and skillet-size paws, it hopes to cool its over-

An Inuit dog team devours hunks of polar bear meat on a scientific expedition to assess climate change in Resolute Bay, northern Canada. Dogs learn to associate the bear's smell with food and so become eager trackers and guards. Photo by Alastair Humphreys.

heating body in the water or to escape. The dogs attack the bear only from its right side, because "a very good dog knows that bears are left-handed."[30] It is unclear if the dogs "know" this or if it's the hunter who trained them who knows it. In Canada's Nunavut and Northwest Territories today, commercial polar bear hunts (trophy hunts) need to be conducted by "traditional methods," which means with a dog team. The dogs alert hunters to the presence of a bear, which is helpful when camping on or near sea ice. Some Kalaallit condition their young hunting dogs by wearing a polar bear skin, getting them used to a bear's smell and behavior.

After the butchering, the hunters prepare a quick meal of raw marrow and fat and of cooked bear tongue, while recounting past hunting exploits. These acts strengthen collective memory, and the hunters' ties with each other, the bear, and the land. The stories sometimes contain elements of the supernatural, like a bear that appears naked or as a sort of bear skeleton. In one such tale, three hunters, including a man who had recently become a shaman or *angakkoq*, chance upon an enormous bear. The bear promptly attacks the *angakkoq*, ripping his stomach open so wide that the hunter's intestines spill out and form a little heap on the snow. When the bear is about to renew his charge, the man "gathers up his intestines with one sweep of his arms, puts them back in his belly, and, walking bravely forward fells him with one blow."[31] The disembowelment and miraculous recovery echo the shamanic initiation treated more fully in the next chapter—it would be no surprise if the hunter himself had some bear power acquired by magical means.

Knud Rasmussen also collected a Greenland tale in which a hunter, caught by nightfall far from home, enters a hut. Its two owners offer him food and entertain him with games and wrestling displays. He marvels at their strength and size. As he bids them farewell in the morning, he turns to wave good-bye, realizing that his hosts were in fact a walrus and a polar bear. He hurries onward, afraid they might kill him in their animal forms. The veneer of civilization is thin. Featuring two of a shaman's most powerful helpers, the story speaks of their volatility. For any hunter who was not a shaman, it was a reminder that even people and animals that seemed familiar—indeed, the environment itself—could be dangerous.

The treacherous ice awash in mirages on sunny days, adrenalin flushing a hunter's veins, and above all, awe of the bear, inspired myths of man-eaters, monsters of the mind one might see as a metaphor of nature itself. An oversize polar bear with four, six, eight, or sometimes ten legs was variously known as Kokogiak (Inupiaq), K'ok'satkut (Siberian Yup'ik), or Kochatko (Chukchi). It lured people by lying on its back on the sea-ice, wailing as if in

Kokogiak—the ten-footed polar bear—in a walrus-ivory carving by Brian Kulik. A monstrous, devious creature, the Kokogiak lies on its back and wiggles its legs to attract hunters, which it devours. Courtesy of Long Ago and Far Away Gallery. Original composition by Wilbur Wallach.

distress or "crowing like a raven" and waving its legs in the air. If an unwary hunter approached, the Kochatko would tear him apart.[32] Although they are rare in southwestern Alaska, polar bears sometimes range as far south as Nunivak Island. Yup'ik hunters there thought that a wily polar bear would lie down with its legs in the air and, by bending them inward, imitate four hunters bent over and gutting a seal—a person should therefore be careful about approaching hunters on the ice.

In Chukotka, the idea of Kochatko became conflated with that of another bear, the "bald-headed polar bear," a giant, like the poet Ari Berk's, "built of ice and claws." This nightmare's fused ribs formed an impenetrable armor; sometimes it was thought to be solid ivory.[33]

A 1909 entry from Vilhjalmur Stefansson's Greenland expedition journals, described how a hunter could overcome the many-limbed menace, which in this case was stalking on all tens:

> Tarak told us Wednesday evening that the ten-footed bear lives mostly in
> the water like a seal. . . . When he walks on ice, the five feet of each side
> track after each other so the bear makes a double track like a sled. Walk-
> ing, the bear often gets his legs tangled up; there are so many, he can't

manage them all. Once a man was followed by a ten-footed bear. The man walked between two cakes of ice and the bear was caught in the crevice between them. If his feet had not become entangled he might have gotten off. As it was, the man speared him. When dying, the bear fell on his back, all his feet pawing the air.[34]

Ideas or archetypes are harder to kill than even an ice-armored polar bear. Kochatko still haunts the shrouded coast of Chukotka, affecting how Natives hunt real bears. "When killing a female bear with a litter," an elder from Uelen warns, "one shouldn't leave bear cubs alive, otherwise they will grow up into man-eating bears, 'koochatko.' An orphaned cub, in order not to die from hunger, starts scavenging, and after growing up attacks any animal—he is also not afraid of a man."[35] While cubs are too dependent on the mother to survive on their own, yearlings can do much better and indeed could get habituated to scavenging at remote settlements, which in turn might cause them to lose any fear of people. The bilateral agreement with the United States that set a quota for Native polar bear hunting still forbids killing females with cubs, cubs younger than one, and denning bears, including those preparing for hibernation. It is hard to decide if statements like the elder's justify what under the treaty would be called poaching or if orphaned polar bears *do* pose a threat to communities that warrants killing them.

Kochatko resonates with contemporary artists and storytellers also, and has been used to impart values such as the necessity of working together to avoid stumbling. Some non-Natives have taken this to extremes, turning the monster into a "particularly sensitive" creature that resents having to lead "such a violent existence." In one such case, the Kokogiak has changed beyond recognition: "One day a Qupqugiaq [Kokogiak, Kochatko] ate a caribou which had tundra grass in its stomach. This was a revelation for the Qupqugiaq: it is possible to live without violence, without selfishness."[36]

Many legends and myths offer lessons about cultural norms, survival, living skills, and relations among people, animals, spirits, and the land. Modern retellings often seek scientific or psychological explanations, reflective angles foreign to Native societies. Indigenous people rightfully criticize such cultural misappropriations and readings. In a world of spiritual longing, which idolizes "connection with nature" and "Native wisdom," the allure of such myths to non-Native audiences is self-evident. Romanticizing the culturally and biologically other can result from superficial knowledge about both, as much as from projecting desire onto them.

A Taste of
the Wild

I know that there are a lot of people who like polar bear meat
and a lot of people who don't like [it].

—MARY TAKKIRUQ, GJOA HAVEN (NUNAVUT, CANADA)

WE ARE WHAT WE EAT. THIS IS NOT NEW AGE MYSTICISM OR
even a matter of culture. Archeologists use bones and tooth
enamel to reconstruct the diets and migrations of Paleolithic humans through isotope analysis. While we are growing up, our bodies accu-
mulate chemical elements—carbon, nitrogen, strontium, oxygen—from the
foods that we eat and the water we drink, which in turn carry mineral traces
of the specific soils from which they sprang. These fingerprints of place stay
with us throughout life and even afterward, for a while at least, locked in our
skeletons. The plants and animals that sustain us are part of us, just like our
stories and memories.

Paraphrasing the French anthropologist Claude Lévi-Strauss, one could
claim that the North's Native peoples are taken with polar bears not only
because they are spiritually potent—"good to think"—but also because they
are physically potent—"good to eat." Throughout Arctic history the bear has
served as food, though in most indigenous societies, whales, walrus, seals,
caribou, or reindeer provided the bulk of the diet. Unfamiliar dishes or ingre-
dients like bear meat strike Western palates as surreal or exotic and might also
be seen as "politically incorrect"—but from our births onward, the culture
that surrounds us shapes our food preferences and what we consider "normal"
or acceptable. Food can be a marker of belonging, contributing to a group's
self-image and coherence. Food taken directly from one's surroundings is
symbolic of place, forming a link with a people's history. This is why even in

countries that banned polar bear hunting, such as the United States, Native groups with a tradition of hunting polar bears are permitted to keep hunting them (and other animals covered by the Marine Mammal Protection Act).

Together with the bear's humanlike appearance, the richness of bear meat and its rarity in modern diets seem to account for non-Native people's rejection of it. But our culinary preferences have changed. In nineteenth-century North America, bear meat (though not that of polar bears) was standard fare. Settlers also used bear fat to fry other foods and preferred it to butter—an English visitor complained that everything he ate tasted of bear.

As far as our relations with the bear family go, we are much more *Homo gustandibus* than *Homo deliciosus.* Despite the fact that in the Arctic, people have always eaten more polar bears than vice versa, the animal's reputation as an ogre persists, a psychological bias I have already examined in this book. That said, based purely on the percentage of meat in each species' diet, the polar bear (together with the orca) tops the Arctic food chain. Closer to herbi-

Livestock production is responsible for 51 percent of all greenhouse gas emissions. Reminding us of links between food and the environment, Vincent J. F. Huang takes a jab at the ecological consequences of our appetites, with *Polar Bear Hamburger, 2014.* Photo by Vincent J. F. Huang.

Skinning a bear on a U-boat in the Kara or Barents Sea. In 1943, skins became wartime souvenirs while the meat supplemented the crews' diet. U-711's sailors specifically wanted polar bear hides for the baby photos then in fashion—many had just married and were expecting offspring. Courtesy of Bundesarchiv/ Bildarchiv, Koblenz.

vore than to carnivore, *Homo sapiens* ranks somewhere between anchovies and pigs. Biologically, even shrews are more predacious than we.[1]

Unlike medieval royalty—or later, zoos—which pampered rare collectibles, explorers and whalers, always near starvation, treated the White Bears as survival rations. "Bear-beef" was often the only course on the menu for months. The meat is much greasier, however, than beef. A nineteenth-century treatise on food curiosities described polar bear fat as unpleasant—unlike the Inuit, some explorers preferred meat from a lean or even a starved bear. Chronically short of fuel, some Arctic travelers used a mixture of bear fat and seal blubber in their lamps, with results that gave off more smoke than light. Two ounces of bear fat fueled a lamp for one hour. Bearskins and bear meat could be seen hanging in the rigging of ships wintering in the ice, beyond the reach of foxes and dogs. In emergencies, fighting the cold, sailors sometimes burned the valuable hides, to save their own. Dutch whalers wintering on Svalbard in 1630 fed on one bear for twenty days, making two or three meals per day of it. During that winter, they killed seven more, which they skinned and roasted on wooden spits.[2]

Polar bear meat has received mixed reviews, from "exceeding coarse" to "strongly scented," to "passable, with a taste akin to lamp oil" (Arctic lamp oil, that is, rendered from whale or seal blubber), to "very good flesh and better than our Venison . . . as good savory meate as any beefe could be."[3] Fridtjof Nansen's captain, Otto Sverdrup, called it a "royal dish" and the explorer himself judged breast of polar bear cub to be delicious. Of course, hunger always has been the best sauce and could have swayed culinary opinions. "Heaven had sent us succor at a time of utter distress," one castaway recalled, of a polar bear windfall, "and our gratitude for this miraculous gift was apparent in our overflowing happiness."[4] The marbled cuts' flavor also varies with a bear's diet and age. A teacher in 1930s Alaska suffered fumes of seal pervading the schoolhouse as she was broiling polar bear chops on a bed of coals, which she attributed to the bear's diet. She liked the roasted heart much better. Despite his privileged background, Baron Nordenskiöld deemed the bear, "if he is not too old or has not recently eaten rotten seal-flesh . . . very eatable."[5] Captain Scoresby served bear ham to his ship's surgeon who, for a month afterward, thought he had supped on beefsteak.[6] Having run out of provisions on one of the numerous searches the British launched for Sir John Franklin, Dr. Elisha Kent Kane ate raw, frozen meat from a polar bear head that he had saved as a specimen and called it a godsend. He described the meat of lean bears as "the most palatable food" and "rather sweet and tender," but warned against well-fed bears, which were made nearly inedible by "the impregnation of fatty oil throughout the cellular tissue."[7] Frozen polar bear fat has the texture (and caloric load) of ice cream. A modern-day East Coast urbanite transplanted to Point Hope, Alaska praised polar bear meat as an absolute delicacy: "jet black, grainy like old gnarled wood, but . . . sweet and tender, ten times better than the best prime rib I have ever tasted."[8] Given the benefits of eating fatty meat in subzero environments, gustatory considerations seem trite. While one modern Alaskan compared polar bear meat to "last Thursday's pot roast basted with cod-liver oil," she swallowed three bites and came to appreciate

Julius von Payer's *Going Out to Dinner*, inspired by the Austrian Expedition to the North Pole (1872–74), on which Payer served as an officer. The lurking, barely visible carnivore reminds viewers that explorers sometimes became a polar bear meal instead of securing one. Courtesy of Tajan/Romain Monteaux-Sarmiento.

A TASTE OF THE WILD

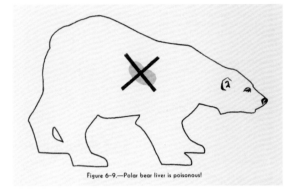

Figure 6-9.—Polar bear liver is poisonous!

Warning against eating polar bear liver, from a U.S. Navy survival manual, *The Naval Arctic Operations Handbook*, 1949. The organ has concentrations of vitamin A that are toxic for humans. Courtesy of Woods Hole Oceanographic Institution.

it. "Of course you belch all day no matter what you eat afterwards," she admitted but considered this a small price for keeping her engine stoked.[9]

Would-be connoisseurs should keep in mind the possibility of negative side effects from the consumption of polar bear meat. "I did not care to try how it tasted," wrote William Scoresby, "for I was afraid that my hair would turn grey before its time, for the seamen are of opinion, that if they eat of it, it makes their hair grey."[10] More serious is hypervitaminosis A, an excess of the vitamin that can be contracted from eating the liver of polar bears, seals, walrus, or huskies. Affecting the central nervous system, it can cause hair loss, extreme peeling of the skin, birth defects, liver problems, vomiting, blurred vision, loss of muscle coordination, and even death. One officer swore never again to eat bear liver, no matter how much it might tempt him, after his crew showed symptoms akin to carbon monoxide poisoning.[11] Native peoples have long been aware of this danger, as have explorers, though some felt no worse after eating of the liver. Research has shown that a healthy adult person can tolerate ten thousand units of vitamin A. Trouble, if it comes, comes between twenty-five thousand and thirty-three thousand units. One pound of polar bear liver—a fist-sized chunk and barely a meal—can contain nine million units of vitamin A. The occasional lack of liver toxicity that some explorers reported can be explained by differences in the age, hibernation, and feeding habits of the bear.[12]

Equally bad is trichinosis, a parasitic disease contracted by eating the raw or undercooked flesh of pigs or wild game. Its symptoms can include fever, muscle pain, and fatigue, as well as inflammation of the heart muscle, lungs, or brain, which have led to a few deaths. In 1897, the Swedish aeronaut and physicist Salomon August Andrée and his two companions perished on Kvitøya (White Island), Svalbard, after their balloon was forced down on the ice before they ever got close to the North Pole. They survived the forced landing, but the *Trichinella* parasite from a polar bear on which the trio later fed has been suspected in their deaths. Things started out well enough after their crash, with an unexpected bear meat bonanza. "The bear's roasted heart," Andrée wrote in his journal, "has a slightly bitter taste while the boiled meat with Stauffer soup is very nice." He had to make a fork from heavy wire for one of his crewmates because the polar bear meat was so tough that it bent the utensils they had brought. Then, for reasons unknown, Andrée ignored the rule against eating raw polar bear meat: "This evening, as I proposed, we tried to eat our meat raw. The raw kidneys sea-

soned with salt taste like oysters; the raw brain is also very good. . . . We took the best parts: two-thirds of the tongue, the kidneys and brain. Fr[aenkel] gathered the blood and, having added it to oat flour, made some kind of butter pancake. This new recipe was much appreciated."[13]

Research published in 1952 showed that some bags that the expedition's members had sewn from polar bear skin contained trichinosis larvae in cyst form.[14] Also, some of the symptoms they recorded in their journal hinted at the disease. Fraenkel got diarrhea the day after they ate of their first bear. A week later, all were weakened and had fever and swollen eyes. Another trichinosis casualty was the Dresden teacher and ornithologist Bernhard Adolph Hantzsch. He died less than a month after eating several meals of polar bear on his 1910–11 Baffin Island traverse. "I'm more dead than alive," Hantzsch scrawled in his journal two days before the end. Even dried bear meat can cause the disease, and people have become sick after eating jerked polar bear intended for their dogs—so cook those steaks well.[15]

One of the last photos of Swedish balloonist Salomon August Andrée. Andrée is shown here with the first polar bear he killed to feed himself and his two starving companions after crashing their balloon north of Svalbard in 1897. Trichinosis from polar bear meat may have contributed to their demise. Courtesy of Wikimedia Commons.

A TASTE OF THE WILD

• • •

In Alaska and Siberian Native societies, taboos concerning polar bear meat reflected not only the spiritual risks associated with the hunt but also the separation of male and female spheres. Further, as a creature of both land and sea, the bear occupied a position between both environments and their respective animals. Only the use of whales was regulated by equally strict rules. In addition to the hunt and preparations for the hunt, taboos guided the butchering, cooking, sharing, and disposal of remains as well as the actual consumption of polar bears. If a person broke wind while eating bear meat among eastern Greenland's Kalaallit, one had to say, "That sound seemed to come out from the ice!"[16] The proper observance of such taboos ensured that hunters were spared the wrath of the offended bear spirit and that bears would be reborn, released once again by the pleased master spirit of game. Some Inuit groups shunned bear meat altogether, because the animal too closely resembled a human. Individuals who had resorted to cannibalism during famines avoided it also—they believed that bear meat would make them crave human flesh.[17]

Varying across ethnic groups, unwritten rules regulated the possession of a dead bear. It could belong to the man who first saw it or its tracks, to the one who first wounded it, or to the one who first touched the dead body. Or it could belong to a female relative, someone not involved in the hunt. Often, different shares went to different people according to their contribution to the hunt or their relation to the bear's "owner." Polar bears were butchered at the kill site and the meat, wrapped in the hide, was hauled back to the village on a sled. Siberian Nenets hunters preferred to butcher a bear away from camp, as otherwise women might accidentally step on the bear's blood. Nenets women did not touch the meat with their hands, or prepare it, or even eat from the kettle the men used for cooking it. The Nenets thought that a woman who tasted polar bear meat would become combative or lose her mind—the bear's nature would contaminate her, in a manner of speaking. Melted bear fat, a delicacy, was taboo for a menstruating woman or one who had just given birth. (To circumvent this prohibition, she could disguise herself as a man by drawing a charcoal moustache on her face.)[18] Life and death, killing and procreating, male and female, wild and domestic were precariously balanced and complementary realms. They had to be marked continually, ceremoniously. As in the King Island Polar Bear Dance, Native Siberians treated the skull—seat of the animal's sentience—with special respect, often returning it to the sea ice after a period of honoring it inside their dwellings.

Frozen polar bear meat is cut with a hatchet during Iqaluit's spring festival in 2014. Foods taken from the sea and land serve as an important marker of Inuit ethnic identity and of values such as sharing and generosity. Photo by Anubha Momin.

To safeguard against revenge from a bear accidentally offended, some hunters disabled it by cutting off its paws, putting out its eyes, and severing its tendons and ligaments.[19]

Native peoples avoided polar bear liver for its vitamin A concentration, and, like explorers and whalers, fed it only to their dogs. The Chukchi dried, boiled, or grilled the meat. For a stew, they cut it into small pieces, which they cooked with the kidneys, intestines, and tongue. They also mixed polar bear bouillon with snow into a drink sipped from big wooden bowls with deer bone "straws."[20] Hudson Bay Cree from York Factory "long ago" ate polar bear and especially appreciated the paws. They dried the meat and rendered the fat into oil, which they stored in cleaned caribou stomachs.[21] Modern Inuit value the flavor nuances of different bears or parts of a bear. Some prefer den polar bears instead of bears caught in the open, because they taste better. Like their neighbors, the Cree, some consider the front and back paws (*tukiq*) the best eating.[22]

In the 1960s, the anthropologist James W. Van Stone witnessed a polar bear feast at Point Hope—a scene still common fifty years later in northern Alaska and Canada: "When a polar-bear skin and meat are brought back to the village it is the sign for a general gathering of friends and relatives at the home of the successful hunter. . . . A big pot of boiled polar-bear meat is usually supplied and everyone helps himself from time to time."[23]

Boy at Frobisher Bay, Northwest Territories (now Iqaluit, Nunavut), eating polar bear stew in 1960. Polar bear and other wild meats derived from fishing or hunting are healthier and cheaper than the store-bought foods in far-northern villages. Photo by Rosemary Gilliat, courtesy of Library and Archives Canada.

Until temperatures rose in the spring, people kept the bear carcass on the roof of their house, away from the dogs, and sawed off chunks as needed. Nowadays, they keep it in closet-sized electric freezers.

Wild meat such as the polar bear's is not only more nutritious but also much cheaper and fresher than store-bought food—a significant factor in places where cash and jobs are scarce and goods need to be imported from afar. A few years ago, the Nunavut town of Iqaluit organized an open-air market for local Inuit "country foods"—seal, caribou, and polar bear. While such meats are normally still shared informally, that initiative sought to raise cash that hunters could invest in ammunition, gas for snowmachines, and other necessities.

For many Inupiat, polar bear meat remains a favorite meal and a prestigious gift. When a polar bear has been killed, a call goes out on a village radio channel, asking people to get some. These days, the hunter normally keeps the skin, a trophy and commodity. The rest of a bear still is widely shared, a token of group identity and solidarity, a kind of Arctic communion. Unlike the whalers and explorers, who saw it as staple or last resort, indigenous peoples have always considered eating polar bear a reaffirmation of community and of their beliefs, as much as an act of physical nourishment.

• • •

Like the widespread idea that animal parts such as the blood, heart, or testicles give power to those who ingest them, the human craving for novelty and the desire to understand the unknown by tasting it have shaped human culinary exploration from the beginning. It is not surprising that, in a world of potentially lethal pufferfish entrées and coffee percolated through civet intestines, polar bear meat has found a place in fine dining. The Norwegian restaurateur André Grytbakk, manager of the upscale Huset in Longyearbyen, Svalbard, occasionally dishes out polar bear steaks with potatoes or a slice of roast in red wine sauce. He also offers a bear meat snack with lingonberry pickle. As it's "a rough kind of meat," the chef recommends a heavy wine with it, such as full-bodied Bordeaux from the Huset's 1,200-bottle cave.[24] The Radisson in

Bear shot in self-defense as it was trying to enter an occupied cabin in Hyttevika, southern Svalbard. In the archipelago, the meat of such bears sometimes is salvaged and given to restaurants or a daycare center. Photo by Arild Lyssand, courtesy of the Office of the Governor, Svalbard.

Longyearbyen, which bills itself as the northernmost hotel in the world, even issues certificates to diners who have "eaten a [!] polar bear entirely at their own risk." I was told these certificates also serve as liability releases for the hotel. According to one guest, the bear meat there is boiled for six hours and fried for another two, to kill parasites.[25] The Hvide Falk ("White Falcon") in Ilulissat, Greenland, also serves Arctic mammals protected by international conventions. Past spreads have included whale stew, narwhal sushi, thin slices of beluga, and cured polar bear meat. Some tourists feel tempted yet conflicted—curiosity battles convictions, sin conservationist scruples. "We must still protect the whales," one German woman insisted before sampling what to her were forbidden meats.

Luckily, polar bear is not often found on these menus. Though hunting the threatened species is illegal on Svalbard, occasionally one is shot in defense of human life. But foodies and hunters should both be forewarned: the environmental division of the Svalbard governor's office thoroughly investigates each polar bear death.[26] Only after that, and after a public health official has inspected the meat, does chef Grytbakk get his special of the day. A local daycare center also has received some of the meat. Because bears are killed infrequently on Svalbard, the dish is expensive: about $120 per pound.

Arctic gourmet cooking remains an exception, but holidays matter up north. In the far American Northwest, on Little Diomede Island, a stormy Bering Strait outcrop near the International Date Line, turkeys are hard to find. Undaunted, the islanders celebrate Thanksgiving by serving common local fare in the village school. These Ingalikmiut Inupiat still largely depend on the sea's bounty—blue crab and bowhead whale, seal, walrus, and polar bear, which they can legally hunt. Butchered properly, a polar bear yields up to five hundred pounds of meat, enough food for dozens of guests. Little Diomede resident and tribal coordinator Frances Ozenna has two favorite recipes:

Diced: Dice polar bear meat, leaving fat on some chunks of meat. Season pieces with bouillon, onion, Mrs. Dash Seasoning Blend, and salt. Boil.

(Chef's note: Polar bear fat is drier than walrus or seal blubber. It is neither fatty nor runny and is subtle in taste and very tender.)

Diced, variation: Cook polar bear meat with frozen, sliced fermented walrus flipper.

(Chef's note: When you eat the two together it sweetens the bear meat, and the bear takes away the greasy taste of the fermented flipper.)

Serve with mixed greens and [seal] oil.

Stew: For choice cuts, choose meat from the back of the polar bear shoulder blade. Dice meat. Marinate in refrigerator for one to two days with beef bouillon, Lea & Perrins Worcestershire Sauce, garlic, onion, and Mrs. Dash Seasoning Blend. After marinating, rinse well to remove some of the blood.

(Chef's note: A small amount of brown sugar can also be added to the seasoning.)

Boil a pot of water and add onion, Mrs. Dash, bouillon, salt, and Worcestershire sauce. Add meat and simmer for 1.5 to 2 hours. Add rice, potatoes, and carrots, if available. Thicken with flour, cornstarch, or elbow macaroni about ten minutes before the soup is done. Let stew rest before serving.

Serve with homemade corn bread or biscuits. Lacking polar bear meat, you can substitute brown bear or black bear. (Or pork.)[27]

RIGHT FRONT
POLAR BEAR LEG
DANEBORG, GREENLAND
3 JULY 2010 MCM

• • •

It is hard to anticipate how food preferences will change. In some future day, as a *Montreal Gazette* column from the 1950s surmised, southern Canadian cooks might be appraising polar bear cuts for steaks or bearburgers.

In that case, or if you ever find yourself at Grytbakk's Huset, don't hesitate. Bon appetit! *Niġiñaqsiruq!* Dig in!

The skinned right front leg of a polar bear killed in Greenland in self-defense, in 2010. Watercolor by expedition artist Maria Coryell-Martin, whose favorite dinner from this bear was tender back meat with a dark chocolate–whiskey sauce. Courtesy of Maria Coryell-Martin.

The Transformative Bear

As the carver holds the unworked ivory lightly in his hand, turning
it this way and that, he whispers, "Who are you? Who hides there?"

—EDMUND CARPENTER, *MAN AND ART IN THE ARCTIC* (1964)

ODERN INDUSTRIALIZED SOCIETIES, THEIR IDEAS SHAPED BY
mass media and the scientific worldview, find it easy to forget that
alternative explanations of the universe once were ubiquitous and
in some quarters persist. I hope in the remaining chapters of this book to
demonstrate that despite Western claims about value-free or "objective" perspectives, we sometimes still employ emotional, seemingly obsolete, often
quasi-magico-religious or symbolic modes of ascribing meaning to polar
bears, which significantly color our understanding of them.

Stories about people who change at will or are changed into animals have
been told for thousands of years and all over the world. Shape-shifters often
became whatever large predatory animal is typical of the environment in
which the story was told. Throughout northern regions, the wolf and bear
have been the most prominent guises. In the Norse sagas, we find cases in
which men undergo physical transformation and others in which their soul
departs from their body and takes possession of animals. The concepts of
multiple personality and biological mutability are not unique to modern psychology or genetics. According to Inuit belief, each person is made up from
four elements: blood, "inherited" by way of the mother's blood; bones, from
the father's sperm; name soul, from a deceased person (together with that
person's name); and flesh, from the game animals the person eats, which in a
metaphorical sense is true.[1]

For centuries before missionaries arrived in the Arctic, shamans were the
only full-time religious practitioners there—they were healers and seers,
wizards and weather-makers, voyagers to other planes of existence. In a

Luba Eynes's etching, *Legend of the Hunter and the Bear*, 2004. It is based on a Chukchi story in which a rich and evil polar bear–man steals the wife of a poor hunter. Using a walrus skull as a weapon, the hunter attacks and kills the bear-rival, who probably was a shaman. Courtesy of Native Arts Fan Club.

world fraught with danger, a world in which rocks and the moon could be animate and appearances deceptive, shamans drew on nonhuman forces for assistance. Dressed in skins, they acquired animal powers; donning masks, they assumed animal characteristics. Native seamstresses sewed hides into superimposed skins for people, but clothes made for shamans kept their animal identity. The wearer of such garments inherited qualities ascribed to the animal when it was still alive. Clothing made from the fur of a polar bear— boots, mittens, or pants—protected a person both physically and spiritually.[2] Shamans who had a polar bear spirit helper put carved walrus-ivory fangs in their mouths; growling and walking like bears, they *became* Bear. Their "adoption" by the bear spirit could happen lightning-fast or glacially, drawn out over days, years even.

David Crantz (1723–77), a Moravian missionary from Germany, had been asked by his superiors to compile a history of the Moravian Brethren in the Danish colony of West Greenland. Striving for balance, he interviewed both Native and non-Native informants. His *History of Greenland* (1765) remains a major ethnographic source about West Greenlandic Kalaallit. In the course of his research, Crantz got to know the church's competition, the shamans, and wrote at length about their initiations: "The candidate must lie in a dark house unbound, and after he has intimated his wishes by singing and drumming, if he is thought worthy by Torngarsuk, though few attain to this high

An Inuk of the world's northernmost human population in bearskin clothing, from Elisha Kent Kane's *Arctic Explorations in Search of Sir John Franklin*, 1856. Nessark ("Jumper-Hood") wears boots made from the animal's lower legs, with the soles and claws intact. Courtesy of University of Alaska, Fairbanks, Rasmuson Library.

honor, a White Bear comes and drags him away by the toe into the sea. There he is devoured by this bear and a walrus, who, however, soon vomit him up again into his own dark chamber, and his spirit re-ascends from the earth, to animate the body."[3] The Greenlandic shaman's soul seemed to leave his or her body during the catatonic "little death" of such séances. It journeyed to the bear lord of the afterlife and his domain, a quest from which only the truly steadfast and powerful could return.[4]

Torngarsuk, Crantz and his coreligionists presumed, was a kind of deity, but he (or it) seemed also to share traits with the Christian Devil. Among lesser spirits, Torngarsuk reigned supreme. He was believed to swim underground through the soil and rock, causing landslides. He ruled a netherworld at the sea bottom, where he made his home among the dead. He controlled the lives of sea animals and could take the form of a gigantic polar bear. In his *Myths and Tales from Greenland*, Knud Rasmussen fleshed out the cyclopean beast: "A huge polar bear lives far out in the sea and sometimes swims toward the shore, but the sea is too low in the fiords, and it then walks between the icebergs rather like it was walking through a puddle. When breathing, it raises such eddies that icebergs and women's boats are sucked up into its nostrils."[5]

Benjamin Gottlieb Kohlmeister, like Crantz a Moravian mission-teacher, reported similar lore from Labrador, where he was sent to serve. At the northern extremity of that coast, a range of high barren mountains with sharp peaks stretches inland from the sea. The local Inuit knew it as the abode of the master spirit of their mythology. Their name for the region, Torngait—"place of spirits"—derived from the presence of Torngarsoak, the Labrador variant of Torngarsuk. As the area was thought to be dangerous, hunters wore the claw of a raven and hung an inflated seal paunch on a tent pole fixed to the side of their boat when travelling there. The charms were meant to protect them against any malevolence from the master spirit.[6]

Hampered perhaps by the language barrier (he only stayed fourteen months) and by Christian notions, Crantz still acknowledged Torngarsuk as a largely benign spirit, "the oracle of the Angekoks [shamans] to whom they feign to have made many a pilgrimage, in his subterraneous happy mansions, in order to confer with him about diseases and their cure, about good weather, and such momentous matters." Crantz learned that Torngarsuk could assume any number of impersonations, though the most fearsome by far was that of the enormous White Bear.[7]

A shaman could find or be found by any number of helping spirits, but like their flesh-and-blood manifestations, the walrus and bear were the most formidable and therefore most prestigious ones. Both were adept divers that could transport a shaman to the residence of the ruler of all sea game. Cape Prince of Wales Inupiat believed that the physically manifested bear could dive to the ocean bottom and pick up a large rock, with which to crush a walrus's skull. While not observable behavior, this idea could reflect the bear's role as a vehicle on shamanic undersea journeys.[8]

Walrus and Bear battled each other as in life, proxies for antagonistic shamans. Or they might compete for a shaman apprentice: "Then a white bear comes through the entrance . . . and bites the witch-doctor on his big toe, drags him out to the ocean, and throws him into the water. A walrus instantly appears, which grabs his genitals, eats him and the bear. After that his bones, one after the other, will be thrown onto the floor where he has been sitting. When all of them are there, he will rise up through the ground and become alive again."[9] It is clear from this context that some supposed scenes of bear-human predation, as in drawings by the Greenlander Kârale Andreassen, sometimes really illustrate a shaman's coming into his powers. (The converted son of a shaman, Andreassen was privy to both the religious world of the Kalaallit and that of Christians, and his drawings are priceless sources.)

Occasionally, Walrus and Polar Bear would endow the same shaman, co-existing and manifesting at the command of that shaman. It seems that in those cases, walrus power was subordinate to polar bear power, or somehow included within it, reflecting predator-prey hierarchies. Rasmussen relates how Unaleq, an Iglulik Inuk, called upon these animal allies: "The mightiest and most influential of them all was Nanoq Tuliorialik ("the bear with the fangs"). This was a giant in the shape of a bear who came as often as he was called. . . . When that particular spirit deigned to occupy his body, he, Unaleq, could transform himself into a bear or a walrus at will, and was able to render great service to his fellow men by virtue of the powers thus acquired."[10]

An account from East Greenland from the early 1880s describes how, instead of waiting to be found by the bear, the neophyte ventures inland, to a lake: "I cast a stone out into the water, which was thereby thrown into great commotion, like a storm at sea . . . . a huge bear was disclosed. He had a very great, black snout, and swimming ashore, he rested his chin upon the land;

and, when he then laid one of his paws upon the beach, the land gave way under his weight. He went up inland and circled round me, bit me in the loins, and then ate me. At first it hurt, but afterwards feeling passed from me."[11] This loss of sensation during the trance was perceived as a form of death. Gustav Holm, who from 1883 to 1885 studied the Kalaallit around Angmagsalik, quotes Sanimuinak, whom the bear spirit had devoured. "At first it hurt," Sanimuinak told Holm, "but afterwards feeling passed from me; but as long as my heart had not been eaten, I retained consciousness. But, when it bit me in the heart, I lost consciousness, and was dead."[12]

When the novice comes to—wearied, stark naked, reborn—he realizes that the bear has become his spirit helper. Sometimes, the spirit bear is envisioned as so thin that—as in pre-contact ivory figurines—all its ribs are visible. In other versions, the fearsome lake-bear is bald, armored in ice, and impervious to spears, or "a lean monster, dog, or bear, with short legs and a tremendous head, much too large for its body, with a long snout."[13] Like skewed physical features, any unusual behavior of a bear that a person encountered betrayed its "spirit bear" nature.

The aspirant's ordeal is in essence a test of his worthiness: the bear challenges his dedication and strength, his ability to endure fear and pain, the hardship that comes with the shaman's office. Appropriately, the shaman's drum, whose trance-inducing voice summoned his spirit familiar, was sometimes made of a bentwood frame over which he had stretched a bear bladder.[14]

•   •   •

Artifacts recovered from the North's permafrost soils offer some clues to premissionary beliefs. Between 500 BP and 1,300 CE, before the arrival of Inuit in present-day Canada's Arctic and northern Greenland, the Dorset culture prospered in this barren region. We mostly know these accomplished hunters through finds from their house pits and hunting camps. The objects include bear skulls painted with dots, walrus-ivory figurines, and modified paw bones. The bear is the animal they most often portray. Some carvings have holes and could have been worn as amulets. The "X-ray style" of many Dorset polar bear figurines—in which lines were incised on the sides and backs of the figures—implies the skeleton beneath the skin. In shamanic thought, the skeleton symbolizes the soul, as it outlasts the decaying flesh.[15]

These markings also evoke the joints where hunters make butchering cuts, as well as the neophyte's dismemberment and bone-by-bone reassembly. The trailing limbs of some of the more abstract Dorset polar bear figurines do not mirror any of the living bear's postures. Such postures could indicate flight or dives to other realms, either by the shaman on his trance journey, or by his spirit helper alone. The same streamlined style characterizes the carved ivory harpoon heads of the Old Bering Sea culture, whose designs (carved on the foreshafts, or sockets of the harpoons, not the points) invoke the bear's bite and ally the Arctic's two most proficient hunters: humans and polar bears. It could even be said that the harpoon, or the hunter, becomes the bear. In some museum specimens, the harpoon heads have inlaid eyes, guiding the weapon by giving it sight. A rear counterweight on the shaft, shaped like a polar bear neck vertebra, often balanced the harpoon. Fittingly, polar bear shamans are sometimes shown armed with harpoons. One Dorset effigy combines the head of a bear with a falcon's body. The gyrfalcon is the North's signature aerial predator, and this amulet empowered its owner with both animals' strength and agility. A few ceremonial objects that juxtapose walrus and bear heads and others that merge human and bear features into a single figure might depict transformation.[16]

This two-thousand-year-old ivory pottery paddle from a female shaman's grave at Ekven, Chukotka would have been used for stamping designs onto crude earthenware. The handle's carved tip resembles a bear's head. The backside shows a "flying" shaman whose limbs have turned into the paws of a polar bear spirit helper. Courtesy of University of Oregon.

Anthropologists have proposed that, since these sculptures lack bases on which to stand, much Arctic statuary was designed to be held and explored by hand, as well as by sight, from various angles.[17] An Old Bering Sea ivory carving from Cape Dezhnev in Chukotka reveals aspects of a bear, seal, and bird as you rotate it. Such visual puns emphasize the multifaceted and fluid nature of life-forms, their basic mystery, as captured by the artist. At the same time, they bring into focus each beholder's subjectivity, the variant truths the blind men detect while exploring the elephant.

Accounts of shape-shifting are common in the Arctic. A Greenland tale that Knud Rasmussen collected during his expeditions tells of an old woman who avenged her son, whom a jealous hunter had killed. The old woman prepared to die. She sat down on the shore under a bearskin and let the tide cover and take her. Some time later, the killer was hunting a seal at a breathing hole when he heard the snow creaking. The sound came closer, and fog drifted in. The man's two companions heard "shouts as of one in a fury, and the screaming of one in fear." A monster had fallen upon and devoured the culprit. The remaining hunters fled to their settlement, seeing only the tips of the creature's ears

THE TRANSFORMATIVE BEAR

Jeremiah L. sells a carved polar bear figurine at an Ottawa street corner. Inuit sculpture invites tactile as well as visual exploration, revealing complementary, shifting aspects of reality, which are typical of the high Arctic's environment. Photo by Mike Gericke.

An animal-shaped rake with a fanged, gaping "mouth" also features seal and bear-human heads as a sort of visual pun. The object most likely belongs in a shamanic context. Ipiutak culture, from Point Spencer, Alaska, ca. 450–850 CE. Photo by Barry McWayne, courtesy of University of Alaska, Museum of the North.

above the hummocks as it crept along. None of their dogs had barked, as this was not a normal bear. The men eventually managed to harpoon whatever this was and when they came closer to the corpse, found the old woman's bearskin covering human bones.[18] An Inuit audience would have understood that the old woman's first death was only a transition; she returned from the ocean in the form of a vengeful spirit bear. She probably was a shaman and the bear her animal guide or "familiar."

As mentioned, a polar bear guardian spirit or *tornaq* can carry a shaman to the seafloor or moon, and a Chukchi statuette with a tiny human perched on its back that illustrates Nordenskiöld's travelogue hints at such journeys. Also from Chukotka comes the tale of a magical she-bear that picked up an orphan boy marooned on an ice floe and carried him on her back, safely to shore.[19] The bearskin itself sometimes functioned as a wizard's conveyance; one stretched-out Dorset polar bear figurine with a belly cavity and traces of red ochre inside might represent such a magic carpet or cloak.[20] By putting on bearskins, Chuk-chis in myths escaped persecution, punished offenders, or fought other bears. To announce their human nature, they simply peeled back the "hood," exposing a face hard to mistake, a face more expressive than that of *umka*, the White Bear. (The face is also a marker of individuality, not just of species identity, and it is generally harder to harm a person than a faceless opponent.)

It is not surprising that the bear's head is given special consideration in such stories. All sense organs except those for touch are located there, and it therefore could be regarded as the seat of sentience. As shown in the previous chapter, throughout the Arctic, the heads of this animal received special treatment. Evidence for this includes not only ritual prescriptions for disposing or displaying the skulls of butchered polar bears, but also miniature carved ivory skulls from Dorset sites and skulls placed at historic and prehistoric burials, to name but a few examples. On St. Lawrence Island, eighty-nine polar bear skulls were retrieved from a single grave, that of the hunter Kowarin, who died in 1910 and was buried near the village of Gambell.[21]

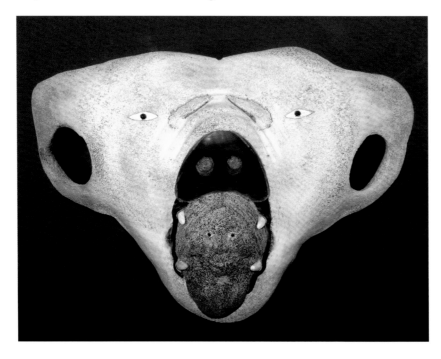

Sculpture in fossilized whalebone by the Inupiaq artist Harvey Pootoo-gooluk, from Shishmaref in northwestern Alaska. The face peering from the bear's mouth could represent the animal's spirit essence or *inua*, which is similar to the western concept of the soul. Photo by Corinne Caine, SavvyCollector.com.

Havets Moder in Nuuk, by the Greenlandic sculptor Christian Rosing, is fully visible only at ebb tide. It represents Sassuma Arnaa, the Mother of the Sea, with her creations. In times of scarcity, shamans placate her after journeying to the bottom of the ocean, often helped by a polar bear. Photo by Leiff Josefsen.

Tales of bear-cloaks that hide identities also come to us from Siberia. In one from Russia's easternmost settlement Uelen, a polar bear becomes the wife of a hunter after taking off her pelt and hiding it in a crevice in the ice. She later retrieves it and returns to her tribe.[22] The story personalizes the vulnerability felt by a new wife moving in with her husband and his family, especially in cultures in which polygamy was practiced. In this, as in other Native myths, the bear serves as a means for exploring social complexities and conflicts.

Before their exposure to scientific explanations, Arctic peoples made sense of any "disappearance" of wildlife (due to cyclical population changes, migration, or overhunting) within their own conceptual frameworks. A keeper of game spirit would withhold animals if taboos had been broken, until a shaman interceded for the community. People sometimes interpreted a shift in abundance from one season's seals and polar bears to the next season's walrus and whales as the transformation of the former into the latter.

The mythic origins of the bear species itself lay in transformation. In one version, a young Inuit woman, Nuliayuq, was too haughty to marry a successful hunter. Her starving parents, who could no longer feed her, loaded their boat and left her behind, hoping for better luck elsewhere. Nuliayuq swam after them. She grabbed the gunwales and tried to climb aboard. Her desperate father chopped off her fingers with an axe. Nuliayuq's fingers became the smaller marine life, such as seals and fish. The remaining pieces of her hands turned into polar bears and whales, and she, sinking, into Sea Mother, keeper or mistress of marine animals. Inuit elsewhere knew the Netsilik's Nuliayuq as Sedna, and in Greenland she was Sassuma Arnaa or Arnaqquassaaq, "the old woman." In times of scarcity, shamans traveled to her domain to ask her to send the people more game. If somebody broke a taboo, Sedna's hair got filthy, ensnaring the animals. A shaman then had to travel to the ocean bottom and appease the amputee by grooming her itchy, tangled hair, upon which she would release wildlife.[23]

As below, so above—the Arctic night sky holds similar evidence of transformative creation. Knud Rasmussen recounts this northern Greenland story told to him by one Aisivak. In it, a woman who has had a miscarriage runs away from her family. She comes to an igloo with bearskins lying in its entryway. The inhabitants turn out to be bears in human shape, but she stays with them regardless. She lives with one large bear who catches seals for both of them. He regularly pulls on his skin, goes out, and is absent for a while but always brings home some meat. One day the woman gets lonely—she wants to see her relatives again. "Do not talk about us when you get back to men," the bear says to her. He is afraid that men would kill his two young ones.

The woman goes home, where a desire to tell overcomes her. One day as she sits lousing her husband, she whispers in his ear: "I have seen bears."

Many hunters then leave on their sledges. When the bear sees them coming toward his house he bites his offspring to death. He does not want them to fall into the hands of men. Then he rushes out to look for the woman who has deceived him, breaks into the house where she is, and kills her. When he emerges again the dogs surround and charge him. He defends himself, and suddenly they all turn luminous and rise up into the sky. There they remain as Qilugtûssat—the Pleiades—resembling a pack of dogs that has cornered a bear.[24]

The myth *The Runners and the Great Polar Bear Hunt* charts the origin of another Inuit constellation. It tells the story of a group of four hunters who go after a polar bear with their dogs. During the chase, one of the men drops his mitten from the sledge. Afraid of freezing his hand, he returns home. As the other three, continuing on, pass by the house of a woman who has recently had a child and whose taboo period of isolation is not yet over, she comes outside and sees them. This is such a bad thing that the hunters, their dogs, and

Lower Yukon River (Yup'ik) mask of a bear-spirit, late nineteenth century. Though polar bears are rare in southwestern Alaska, they sometimes range as far south as Nunivak Island, where they are likely to make an impression. Courtesy of Dallas Museum of Art, gift of Elizabeth H. Penn.

THE TRANSFORMATIVE BEAR

the bear turn into stars in the sky, to warn people against breaking the rules. In the winter sky you can still see the hunters running in a row. Up in front of the hunters (the three belt stars of Orion), the dogs (Qimmiit—the Hyades, a star cluster around Aldebaran) have cornered the bear (Nanurjuk—Aldebaran, the eye of Taurus) from two sides, in a V-formation of small stars. Nanurjuk has been wounded, and if you look closely, you can see that this bright star is reddened by blood. Farther down to the right another bright star (Kingulliq or Rigel, the brighter "foot" of Orion) is the lone hunter left behind. (In some versions, Kingulliq is only the mitten the hunter dropped—because he did not break the taboo, he returned safely to Earth.)[25] In a universe where each thing told the story of its becoming, people were constantly reminded of the right way to live. One could not look at the night sky, let alone a bear, without considering the results of one's actions.

In times before people had fallen from grace, Alaska's Inupiat believe, animals that wanted to talk to them simply pushed aside their muzzles or beaks, as though they were masks. A face like a human's would appear—the *inua*, symbolic of the animal's sentient nature.[26] Miniature carved *inua* faces often peep at the observer from modern animal sculptures, like homunculi embedded in bone, wood, or stone.

In these Native cosmologies, animals lived in quasi-human societies, and shared human preoccupations. This was especially true of the polar bear, bipedal at times, nomadic, a den-dweller and skilled hunter of seals. In *The Woman Who Heard Bears Speak* we get a man-hunting bear's take on hu-

A contemporary Inuit example of the bear-back rider. Robert Kuptana's caribou antler carving, *Shaman Riding Bear*, 2009, captures the practitioner's journey to the spirit world astride a helper. The "flying" bear pose is also typical of Paleo-Eskimo figurines from 500 BP–1500 CE. Courtesy of Canadian Arctic Gallery, Switzerland.

manity: "Those shin-bone figures are terribly thin below," one adolescent bear says. "One almost feels inclined to knock them down." Some Inuit see the polar bear's "hostility" toward men as revenge for the mutilation of Nuliayuq-Sedna. This almost seems like a rationalization of guilt: if polar bears are Sedna's offspring, their clannish blood feud against the Inuit is justified, as is their preemptive killing by hunters. Conversely, if bears are too similar to the people who feed on them, the specter of cannibalism—a taboo in most cultures—arises.[27]

The concept of permeable boundaries between the human and other-than-human realms pervades and connects cultures throughout the North. One role of Nganasan shamans, from the Taymyr Peninsula in northern Siberia, was to perform the Clean Tent Rite, which could last for more than a week. During one such ceremony, observed in 1931, a pole draped with a polar bear skin was brought into a tent. Two men held it horizontally while the shaman leaned on it. He moved his arms as if swimming and chuffed like a bear, trying to drive away evil spirits. In the guise of the polar bear, he was swimming across the sea of the dead.[28]

The Russian ethnologist Galina Nikolaevna Gracheva described two bear pendants attached to the costume of a Nganasan shaman and symbolizing a he-bear and a she-bear. The shaman explained to her that he could hitch these bears to a sledge, and that they would take him wherever he wanted, so fast that the wind whistled in his ears and nothing could be seen.[29] His words perfectly captured the sensation of ecstatic transport. The Nganasan shaman Tubyaku Kosterkin also enlisted helping spirits besides the polar bear: an ermine, a mouse, a she-wolf with seven cubs, a seven-tailed dog, a brown bear, an eight-legged reindeer stag, and others.[30]

On the Bering Sea coast across from mainland Alaska, Chukchi youths who killed their first whale or polar bear had a simple mark tattooed near each joint of their limbs, an emphasis of skeletal junctures reminiscent of Dorset figurines. The same custom existed on St. Lawrence Island. Inuit, Yupiit, and other circumpolar peoples saw living bodies as inhabited by multiple souls, with each soul residing in a particular joint. Joint tattoos prevented instances of possession, as spirits could otherwise easily enter at these vulnerable places. Chukchi shamans also used amulets made from animal body parts that were likely to spring to life. In one case the dried skin of an ermine turned itself into a living ermine, which, in turn, morphed into a polar bear. The amulet's owner then sent it across the straits to harm an enemy.[31]

Sending out ghoulish assassins was also common in Greenland. A shaman could build such a *tupilaq* from bone, skin, hair, sinew, and even from

Greenlandic ivory carving, early twentieth century. This bear and skeletal anthropomorphic being locked in an embrace could depict a struggle between a bear-shaman and a *tupilaq*—an assassin created through sorcery. Photo by Michael Cichon, collection of John C. Miotke, Tampa, FL.

human corpses. One of Kârale Andreassen's drawings shows a *tupilaq* that is half polar bear and half woman, with long hair and pendulous breasts. Incantations breathed life into these Frankenstein puppets. But they could be just as dangerous to their creators—if a shaman sent a *tupilaq* after someone more powerful, it would return to destroy its maker. Since the late nineteenth century, and particularly during the twentieth century, bone or ivory carvings of these malevolent creations have supplied the souvenir market. This tourist trade can be traced to an incident that took place in 1884, when Captain Gustav Holm reached Ammassalik and asked what a *tupilaq* looks like. His informant found it difficult to sketch it for him and therefore carved one in wood.[32] *Tupilaq* production in various materials gradually spread across Greenland—collectors love these grotesques.

• • •

While some bear transformation motifs from Native North America and Siberia crop up in Norse culture, others are uniquely Germanic in nature. Thus, in Scandinavian folklore, a bear could be a changeling (secretly switched for an infant), or a human cursed to assume that form. But European traditions of shape-shifting that involve polar bears rather than brown bears are exceedingly rare.

I chose here to disregard the popular Norwegian tale "White Bear-King Valemon," in which a bewitched, transformed bear-king appears deep inside the forest, though polar bears did drift to shore and were killed in northernmost Norway. I believe Valemon's whiteness signifies its uniqueness or association with Christ, common markers of animals in European fairytales, rather than a polar bear identity. Similarly, in the late sixteenth-century Icelandic *Tíódel Saga*, a werewolf romance set in Syria, Tíódel can not only change into a wolf but also slip into the skins of a gray bear and a white bear (both perhaps brown-bear variants) as well as of other animals. In these forms, he dwells in the forest for three or four days each week, until his deceitful wife manages to trap him in his white bear-persona.[33] The conflating of wolf and bear is nevertheless interesting, as it plays to long-held perceptions of both as incorrigible man-eaters—even less justified in the wolf's case than in the polar bear's.

These stories aside, there remain enough Nordic cases of unambiguous polar bear-human transformation to support the cross-cultural pattern. In post-medieval Iceland, the bear's touch was a magic gesture; a mother bear's touch changed her cubs—which always looked like human children immedi-

ately after birth—so that they would remain bears ever after. In a folktale first recorded in the late nineteenth century, a man caught a polar bear cub that was "no other than a little girl," because its mother had not yet touched it. This supposedly happened on Grímsey, an island north of Iceland, where polar bears sometimes drifted ashore on Greenlandic ice floes. The man took this girl home, and she grew into a handsome and promising young woman. She showed no peculiarities other than an inordinate fondness for the sea. One day, she walked out onto the shore-fast ice, where her bear-mother reclaimed her by throwing a paw over her and changing her back into a polar bear.[34]

In *Hrólfs Saga*, Bödvarr Bjarki fights his opponents in the form of a polar bear while his human body sleeps. His shape-shifting ability seems to have been inherited: before Bödvarr was born, Queen Hvít hexed his father, Björn ("Bear"), making Bödvarr therefore the son of a man-bear, an enchanted being. Like the berserkers' rage, Bödvarr's ursine alter ego emerges only in battle.[35]

The *Hauksbók*, a chronicle of the settling of Iceland, mentions Odd, whose father and brother were killed by a polar bear. After finding the culprit, which was sucking their blood, Odd slew and then ate it, in revenge of his family. A sluggard before the event, he was later known as a harsh man. Odd was a shape-shifter too, and perhaps became one as a result of ingesting the bear.[36]

• • •

For his film *It's the Skin You're Living In*, the English performance artist David Harridine dressed in a polar bear suit and walked from Northern Europe to the south of England. As the journey progressed, the man under the polar bear skin gradually was revealed. Courtesy of David Harridine/Fevered Sleep.

Animal magic reverberates across space and time, and the question of how to relate to the Others has remained vital, universal. Some modern, non-Native artists borrow from Arctic animistic traditions, and in their work, too, the polar bear acts as agent of transformation.

In the poem *The Bear*, by Pulitzer Prize and National Book Award winner Galway Kinnell, a hunter tracks a polar bear he has mortally wounded, subsisting as he goes on the bear's blood, which he finds congealed in the late winter snow.[37] Arriving at the bear's carcass at last, he cuts it open and eats and drinks before crawling inside and falling asleep. He dreams of "lumbering flatfooted over the tundra" and feels the bear's dying. Having experienced the animal's pain in a dreamlike state, the speaker finds that the roles have been reversed: the hunter has become the hunted. He awakens in the spring in the shape of a bear and resumes the animal's wanderings. Lines about a she-bear licking her cubs nearby, "in her ravine under old snow," only reinforce the poem's theme of birth and emergence—the female polar bear arisen mysteriously from its hidden den has long been a symbol of immortality or resurrection. Notes of Whitman sound throughout, but here transcendence comes from destroying that which facilitates it. It can be read through the lens of Richard Slotkin's "regeneration through violence," which he sees as typical of the American frontier ethos, an interpretation that makes the bear syn-

Pudlo Pudlat, *Confrontation*, 1985. This stonecut print by a Nunavut artist shows a bear armed with a harpoon. A bear with a weapon, a drum, or wearing a parka is an artistic convention for depicting a shaman. Courtesy of Richard F. Brush Art Gallery, St. Lawrence University.

onymous with the land. On a more basic level, by taking a life, the hunter fully participates in Life, overcoming barriers we've built between ourselves and nature. The outcome, the unavoidable price to be paid, seems to contrast starkly with one of the central concerns that Kinnell articulates elsewhere, "a sense that so many things lovely and precious in our world seem to be dying out."[38]

By sheer geographic proximity to the polar bear range, Iceland has long been Europe's most fertile ground for imaginings of this animal, and this trend continues today. A music video for Björk's "Hunter" shows the singer shaking and convulsing and, with the assistance of computer-generated imagery, slowly and *unwillingly* turning into a polar bear. Such involuntary change or spirit possession is deeply rooted in shamanic traditions.

The Icelandic director Gisli Snær Erlingsson reprised the theme of travelers who move between worlds and identities. In his 2000 film *Ikíngut*, a nineteenth-century Inuit boy clad in polar bear fur has drifted across the Greenland Strait and faces a community of starving, xenophobic Icelandic fishermen and their families. They are convinced that the white dwarf speaking a foreign tongue is a demon or "flying polar bear" and they want him killed. Though they are nominally Christians and the story is fictional, the villagers' reaction betrays the durability of ideas that predate even the sagas. The director also toys with the fact that polar bears sometimes *do* strand as outcasts on Iceland's black beaches.

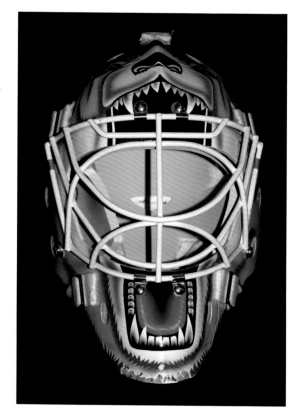

The martial persona of Quebec Nordiques goal-keeper Ron Hextall. Some ice-hockey players choose protective masks that project predator qualities, in an attempt to unsettle opponents. Photo by Nelson White.

Modern Inuit sculptors, visionaries in their own ways, sometimes render images of a shaman that has turned into a bear. The visual clue to the figure's shaman identity is often the bear's prizefighter neck, a vestige of humanity that contrasts with the neck of the polar bear, which is long and slender. Shaman-bears also sometimes wear coats that look like hooded parkas, or brandish telltale drums or harpoons.

Perhaps scientific ideas regarding animal nature and species transformation are unnecessarily limiting. Taxonomists either are "splitters" or "lumpers," but both kinds draw species boundaries. Heisenberg's uncertainty principle notwithstanding, many of us are still caught in a dualistic universe, believing that a thing exists clearly defined or not at all. But in the high-latitude twilight, with storms or mirages blurring the line between sea and sky, certainties crumble. In a whiteout, there is no direction, no depth, no middle distance or horizon. Shapes briefly appear and then vanish, as does life itself. In the long polar night, too, the tactile supersedes the visual. Northern hunters identify with both people, and the animals they respect yet kill, which poses a moral dilemma as well as one of mere classification. In order to transcend it, they have found ways to accept contradictions in a world of constant flux.

Anthropologists theorize that an Inuk behind an animal mask sees the world through the eyes of that animal but thereby also risks losing sight of his or her original, human nature. Like bearness, humanness must constantly be reasserted, redefined. Neither one is guaranteed or necessarily permanent.[39]

In Eskimo thought, wrote the visual media expert and anthropologist Edmund Carpenter, "the lines between species and classes, even between man and animal, are lines of fusion, not fission. Delight comes from the simultaneous perception of multiple meanings within one form." Metamorphosis, in other words, characterizes a world in which each form contains multiple manifestations that are revealed only in the becoming.[40]

It is no surprise that the bear, in its very resemblance to humans, helped to define human identity in many cultures. A reminder of kinship and permutation, it nevertheless marked an inviolable core by silhouetting a negative space: that which is not we.

Helper and
Protector

The witch doctor keeps his ceremonial gear and amulets or
charms up in a cache protected by the bones of the polar bear.

—CAPTION OF A PHOTO OF A NORTHERN ALASKA WHALING
BOAT WITH AMULETS AND EQUIPMENT (CA. 1905)

A NEWLY DESIGNED LOGO FOR MAINE'S BOWDOIN COLLEGE SPORTS
a polar bear in correct anatomical posture, rendered in a stylized
black line drawing. Gazing straight at the viewer, the bear stands on
three legs with its fourth raised and protectively resting on a capital letter
B. A ferocious, growling predator freezing prey with its stare was not the
image the college wanted to project, but a Bowdoin spokesman said that
there is "something appealing about having a mascot that is looking directly
at you."

The animal became Bowdoin's official mascot in 1913, at the school's annual banquet. Two years later, an alumnus of the class of 1898 who had been
a member of Peary's 1909 expedition to the pole gave the college a mounted
bear hide, which he presented with the words, "May his spirit be the guardian
spirit not only of Bowdoin Athletics but of every Bowdoin."[1] A Bowdoin coach
had requested a polar bear from the ex-pupil, as his trophy case was filling up
nicely but still lacked a fitting centerpiece.

The commander of a British infantry division known as the Polar Bears,
for their World War II service on Iceland, faced the opposite of the Bowdoin
designer's image problem. He rejected a uniform shoulder patch showing the
bear with its head down, as too submissive. "I want a defiant sign for my division," he said to a subaltern. "Lift its head up and make it roar."[2] Never mind
that polar bears in fact charge with their heads lowered.

The inflatable mascot of the Nanooks, the University of Alaska Fairbanks' hockey team. Players skate into the arena from underneath the bear as if emerging from the belly of the beast. Animal symbols, especially predator species, are popular with sports teams and convey regional identities. Photo by Michael Studinger, courtesy of NASA.

Schools, athletic teams, and military units thus have tried to partake of the polar bear's essence—its charisma and ascribed and actual physical powers—by choosing representations of it as their badges. One-upmanship is the name of this game: Nanooks beat Huskies, Cougars, Broncos, Eagles, or Wolverines, at least on a good day.

Such depictions of polar bears in military insignia or as the mascots or logos of companies, clubs, teams, and other regimented organizations should be seen in the context of medieval heraldry. Originally totemic communal symbols, these virile creatures of choice not only stood in for mythic ancestors but also had magical functions. The polar bear protected the warrior in battle and put fear into the heart of his enemy. Prowess and strength flowed from an animal familiar emblazoned on arms.[3]

Although rare, personal coats of arms did occur in Iceland. In the fourteenth and fifteenth centuries, some Icelanders were knighted and adopted noble emblems. Torfi Árason in 1450 obtained the right to a shield with a polar bear on a blue field and a half polar bear crest atop the helmet. Björn Torleifsson the Powerful had a similar design, but, powerful among his peers, boasted an entire White Bear on his headgear.[4] The coat of arms of the nineteenth-century Finnish explorer of Siberia, Adolf Erik Nordenskiöld, appropriately shows two polar bears rampant—"rearing up," with forepaws raised—in support of his shield.

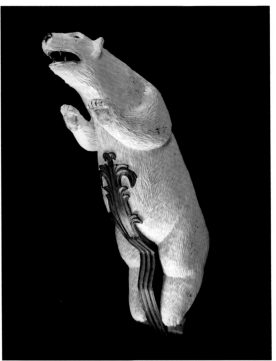

Imperial aspirations also could manifest by including polar bears in a royal coat of arms. After 1648, the animal adorned the seal of Frederick III of Denmark. Crowded by the tokens of other regions within His Majesty's realm, it proclaimed his right to rule Greenland—predating the actual presence of Danish officials on the island. Later, this Danish bear rose up on its hind legs, a more imposing, anthropomorphic pose. After home rule came to Greenland, the former Danish colony chose the polar bear as its own badge. Unlike the Danish version, which follows heraldic tradition by showing the bear with its right forepaw defensively raised (most knights wielded their swords with the right hand, and the left was "sinister," treasonous, unclean), the polar bear in Greenland's coat of arms raises its left, in acknowledgment of the Kalaallit belief that polar bears are left-handed. Biologists, however, have found no evidence of handedness in polar bears or other bear species.

With its clean, elegant lines, the polar bear's shape is instantly recognizable, lending itself to abstraction in logos and insignia. Protecting home, hearth, and honor, it struts on the coat of arms of the Norwegian town Hammerfest, the Siberian town Dikson, the district of Chukotka, and, by way of Byzantine bloodlines, has even sneaked into that of the royal house of Greece.

(*Left*) Coat of arms of Eduard von Orel, an officer on the Austro-Hungarian North Pole Expedition of 1872–74. In 1879, the Emperor Franz Joseph knighted Orel for his service on the expedition. The "majestic" or "noble" bear made a perfect heraldic symbol and reminder of men's Arctic exploits. Courtesy of Wolfgang Ladenbauer.

(*Right*) Replica of a wooden figurehead for USS *Bear* (later SS *Arctic Bear*). An embodiment of the ship's spirit, its purpose was to protect her and her crew. The U.S. Coast Guard's most famous vessel operated in Alaska, and later carried Admiral Byrd to the Antarctic. Photo by Wolfgang Opel.

· · ·

Bears mysteriously emerging from their dens in the spring have long been regarded as incarnations of immortality or, at least, of renewal. Hibernation in a subsurface world also resembles the shaman's trance and journey to the ocean floor. At home in two environments—terra firma and the sea ice and ocean—the polar bear was a perfect symbol of shamanic mediation.

In Native traditional medicine, polar bear parts helped people to maintain or regain health, a balancing act with physical as well as spiritual aspects. Cures were as manifold as the corresponding ailments, and often the curative power of an animal body part affected its human counterpart by analogy or by direct contact, a transmission based on the principle of "sympathetic magic." Native Chukotkans treated humans and their domestic animals with dried and ground bear gall. They also punctured polar bear eyes and dissolved ashes in the resulting liquid. Applied to the paddles of their *baidarkas* (skin-covered boats), this mixture conveyed speed and strength. Some Baffin Bay Inuit used polar bear oil against ear infections and congestion, and the fat to cure skin diseases and balding. Cumberland Sound Inuit made it into cosmetics and pomades. Seventeenth-century Icelanders smeared wounds with polar bear fat and drank bear bile to fight epilepsy. In yet another example of sympathetic magic found outside tribal cultures, in the kaiser's Germany, the hirsute bear's fat was believed to stimulate hair growth in men.[5]

Closely related to such uses of bear products were charms or amulets, a branch of preventive medicine, if you will. The polar bear's canine teeth were among the most widespread and powerful talismans of the North, and subject to lively trade. Some Nenets would offer as much as a reindeer for a single polar bear canine. Coastal hunters sold them to groups in Siberia's taiga to prevent brown bear attacks. It was thought that the polar bear's "nephew" would not dare touch a person who wore a tooth of its mighty "uncle." Throughout northeast Asia, people liked to take teeth from sacrificial places and only those teeth that had fallen naturally from old, weathered skulls—pulling them from the jaws was taboo. As in the hunt, the bear had to "offer" itself, or parts of itself. A Nenets child got its first bear tooth from its father, who tied it to the infant's crib after the mother had completed the birth ritual by cleansing the afterbirth with incense. The canine tooth tied on the crib or around a baby's neck protected the child from evil spirits, diseases, and nightmares. Bear teeth dangling from a grown man's belt spared the owner toothaches and lower back pains.[6]

Other amulets invoked and attracted prey, often the same species that had yielded parts for the amulet. They could also bestow an animal's keen senses upon the wearer. According to the Russian ethnographer Vladimir Bogoraz, the soul of the bear resided in its nose, claws, paws, and canines, and successful Chukchi hunters carried bundles with dried bear noses and pairs of leather-wrapped pupils that helped them to spot and scent game.[7]

In his account of the "Samojeds" (a catchall term for western Siberian peoples), the circumnavigator of Eurasia, Nordenskiöld, describes a source of polar bear teeth in the northwest of the Yamal Peninsula: "On the rising ground close to the beach, there was a sacrificial altar, built up of about fifty Polar bears' skulls, walrus's bones & c., placed in a heap. In the center of the heap, two idols were erected, cut out of drift timber, their eyes and mouths having apparently been recently smeared with blood. There were likewise two sticks, from which hung bones of reindeer and bears."[8] More than two thousand miles to the east, near some old house pits in Chukotka, he came upon "great collections both of large numbers of lichen-covered bears' skulls (at one place up to fifty)." These were "laid in rings with the nose inwards; and of reindeer, bear, and walrus skulls mixed together in a less regular circle, at the center of which reindeer horns were piled up."[9]

Polar bear skulls also lay scattered along the beach. This and the many ivory bear figurines he purchased from the "Chukches" led Nordenskiöld to believe that the animal played a great part in the locals' imagination. Craving bodily comfort as much as peace of mind, "the natives often have a small strip of bear's skin on the seat of their sledges" (to keep their backsides from freezing, the seafarer noted as an aside).[10] On a journey to the Yamal Peninsula in 1913, the Russian scholar B. M. Zitkov also found a sacrificial mound of polar bear skulls and learned that the Nenets had been piling up skulls there for more

Necklace of polar bear molars from Labrador, collected in 1893. Only teeth that had fallen naturally from old, weathered skulls could be used, not those from a freshly hunted bear. They warded off evil spirits and disease. Courtesy of the Trustees of the British Museum.

Baron Nordenskiöld at a "sacrificial altar" with bear skulls, on the Yamal Peninsula during the Swedish Arctic Expedition of 1876, in *Harper's Weekly*. Seen as the seat of the animal's sentience, bear skulls in particular were objects of taboos and veneration. Courtesy of Brooklyn Museum.

than one hundred years. The custom clearly transcended tribal boundaries, owing to the skull's importance as the seat of sentience and the soul.

Busily gathering not only artifacts but also the myths and legends that linked far-flung Siberians like ocean currents, ethnographers learned more about polar bears as benevolent creatures. The Yamal Peninsula Nenets believed in a leader of all polar bears that lived at sea and never came ashore. In one tale, lost hunters encounter this master spirit (Tai-Nyaluy Vark), which shows them the way home. A culture hero like Prometheus, Tai-Nyaluy Vark also introduced fire to the Nenets and taught them how to use it. A Chukchi equivalent, the "master of place" Kyt Olgyn, similarly laid the foundation for reindeer herding when he gave a wild female white deer (a caribou) to a starving, childless couple. The Evens of the Laptev Sea coast recall how a woman escaped her abusive husband by putting on a polar bear hide given to her by a kind she-bear—an act of interspecies female solidarity expressed through a protective garment.[11]

· · ·

Parallel practices and beliefs shaped the lives of people on the opposite side of the hemisphere. In northern Greenland, Knud Rasmussen reported, Kalaallit wore amulets next to the skin or on special belts, placed inside the kayak or under the bed, or sewn into clothes. For such an amulet, or *arnuaq*, a body part of the bear or a carved bear representation was preferred. Parents sewed skin from the bear's palate into a child's cap for strength and protection. But as in Siberia, teeth could never be taken from a freshly killed bear, only from one that had died from natural causes, or from an old skull. Here too, fear of the bear spirit's revenge guided behavior.[12] One expedition scientist described a canine tooth nursing mothers "used as a kind of clasp to a seal-skin string, which passes round the body and keeps the breasts up. Her milk supply cannot fail while she wears this."[13] The claws and nose skin of a polar bear likewise were potent amulets.

Warriors in northern Alaska wore amulets of the "land bear" (the grizzly) on their right arm and those of the polar bear on their left, to borrow the strength of both animals. The Inupiaq myth *The First Bears* explains the two species' common ancestry and differing habitats. It tells of a woman who birthed twins; one was covered with brown fur, the other with white fur. Because of their strangeness, she abandoned them. While the White Bear-child ran off across the frozen sea, the brown one scrambled across the tundra and into the mountains.[14]

A different sort of bear amulet—knapped from microcrystalline quartz or "flint"—was obtained near Barrow, Alaska, between the 1880s and 1919. Some of the thirty-seven chipped-stone amulets from that region, now at the University of Pennsylvania Museum, came from archaeological sites and others from ethnographic collecting. Most are whales, with bears—polar and grizzly—the second most common representation. Traces of lamp soot and grease remain on a few, hinting at ceremonial purposes.[15] We can guess this from the practices of Inupiaq whaling captains of the historical period, who marked

Gray-chert bear amulet, possibly of the Birnirk culture, 500 to 900 CE, collected in 1883 by Thomas Kennedy at Point Barrow, Alaska. It was knapped as arrowheads were, by flaking off slivers with pressure from a bone tip or antler tine. Photo by Joel Castanza.

Miniature ivory polar bear skull, seen from above. This intricately carved, rare Late Dorset artifact from Greenland's Qaanaaq (Thule) District may have served as an amulet. It would have been worn or kept with a hunter's or a shaman's possessions or included in a grave. Photo by Paddy Colligan, courtesy of Greenland National Museum.

amulet boxes in a similar manner. The captains and their harpooners also wore soot and grease smudges on their faces, tallying the whales they had taken before.

Polar bear bones were the objects of special observances. At Cape Prince of Wales in western Alaska, where he taught at the mission, Harrison Robertson Thornton found assemblages like those in Siberia, in this case, on food and boat storage platforms. Despite Thornton's dismissal of Native beliefs as "superstitious" and his misuse of the term *bruin*—a proper name only for a brown bear—his description is worth quoting at length: "The tops of the posts, which support the platforms, are frequently ornamented with the rump-bones of the polar bear— either as trophies of the hunter's prowess or as talismans against evil spirits and other forms of superstitiously dreaded harm; for, as we have intimated in our account of the 'bear dance,' this part of Bruin's anatomy is obviously thought to be peculiarly significant and important. In like manner, the skulls of the bears that the hunter has killed are preserved and kept in a circle near his igloo."[16]

Where the mythical overlaps with the mundane and the past with the present, respect must be paid to the powers that guide human lives. Elders still alive remember many of the beliefs here described, as well as the rituals to ensure good luck performed in their youth. According to one such tradition, a rock in the northernmost part of Greenland's Thule District is the human foster mother, now turned to stone, of a polar bear. It is told that a widow adopted this bear and that some hunters killed it because it was raiding their caches, after which she turned to stone from grief. When people passed her on their way to the winter hunt on Ellesmere Island, they smeared blubber around the mouth of the stone-woman or offered cigarettes and other tidbits, perhaps to make amends.

Just as often, in stories, a bear might prove to be anything but benign, a reminder of its fickle nature. Martha MacDonald, a folklorist at Newfoundland's Memorial University, collected stories about a similar rock in Labrador. There, a bear threatened some Inuit women and children who were fishing for salmon, and a drum-beating shaman turned it into a rock. It is said that on a day when you can see that single white boulder across the bay from Nain, visitors will be arriving—a reasonable assumption, as people prefer to travel when the weather is nice and the sea calm.[17]

Webs of kinship and obligation routinely included the bear, as is evident in a Central Inuit tale that Franz Boas recorded. In this one, a widowed woman nurses and raises a bear as a pet. (Hunters or natural causes orphaned it, we must assume.) Growing up, the bear begins to hunt seals and salmon, bringing

Illustration for Derek Wilson and Cynthia Colosimo's *The Polar Bear in the Rock* (2010), a bilingual children's book based on a legend about a Labrador Inuit shaman who, by drumming, transformed a polar bear. A similar rock exists in northern Greenland's Thule District. Courtesy of Cynthia Colosimo.

them to his "mother" before eating any himself, providing for her as a male relative would and receiving his own share from her hands.[18]

As we saw in the chapter on transformation, the guardian spirit that Bowdoin's designer tried to evoke could be an edgy associate. In the Arctic's extreme environment nothing ever was simple or without risk. Life's greatest danger, in the words of an old Iglulik shaman, was that "man's food consists entirely of souls"—the very animal spirits that were so easily offended.[19] Unlike Bowdoin's bear and the Disneyfied, caring bear-mother, the spirit bear is ambiguous; like the shaman, it can heal or kill. Both shaman and bear are liminal creatures, moving freely between realms: earth, water, ice, underground, the heavens, the natural and the supernatural, the sacred and the profane.

One person's protector can be another's attacker. In an Inupiaq tale from northwest Alaska's Noatak River, two in-laws war in the form of shaman-bears. It all begins rather harmlessly, with a man whose wife keeps fattening him and who discourages him from hunting. The man's mother warns him that the wife is going to eat him. One day while he is out walking, the wife, who has turned into a polar bear, stalks him. He starts to run—a big mistake, according to bear biologists—but a grizzly appears, fighting and killing the polar bear. Then the victorious bear turns into the man's mother.[20] Once again, a polar bear fable addresses divided loyalties of two kinds of kin: kin by blood and by marriage. Similar though ultimately at odds, they differ like bear species.

For each legend about hostile polar bears there seems to be one empha-sizing the animal's kindness toward humans. A common motif throughout northern latitudes is the rags-to-riches story, or rather, the famine-to-plenty-of-meat story. These stories often feature orphans and other outsiders on the land, stressing the importance of family or community, without which a per-son was doomed.

In one version, told by Arctic Bay elder Sakiasi Qaunaq, hunters abandon an orphan, who is then adopted by a village of polar bears. The bears teach him to hunt and to survive and when he is grown up, return him to his peo-ple.[21] Another Noatak River tale features Katak ("Waterbucket"), a young boy with a small pet polar bear. When the two are cast adrift on an ice floe, the bear catches food for Katak and warms him by letting him sleep on its stom-ach. Eventually it helps Katak back onto stable shore-fast ice.[22] It is no surprise that Native stories about polar bears and young boys, such as Qaunaq's, be-come popular illustrated children's books.

Quite a few stories turn on reciprocity, the tit-for-tat of good deeds without which humans could not live in the Arctic. *The Hunter and the Polar Bear* tells

Inupiaq toggle showing a man turning into a bear, ca. 1850. Toggles for pulling dead game were charms as much as tools. This one could depict a spirit helper and was perhaps attached to a kayak or sled, especially during a polar bear hunt. Photo by John Bigelow Tay-lor, courtesy of Thaw Collec-tion, Fenimore Art Museum, Cooperstown, NY.

of a luckless, poor man who, bidden by a bear he meets on the ice, travels "down into the sea a long way" on its back. They arrive at an igloo where the hunter is asked to pull a spear from the hip of a wounded bear. He obliges, the wound heals, and the first bear takes off its "parka," becoming a man. Later, changed into a bear again, it carries the hunter back to the pack ice. The man, after finding that he has been gone for a whole month, turns into a good (read: "lucky") hunter for the rest of his life.[23] It is easy to see in this a reflection of the shaman's journey to an otherworld to correct wrongs, guided by a spirit helper. In this telling, the themes of transformation and assistance mesh, as they did in actual ritualistic practice. One can assume that after the event described, the polar bear kept acting as the hunter-shaman's associate. The story's reach is wide enough to have inspired a modern artist's illustration. It could also have been the source for a nineteenth-century walrus ivory amulet in a London collection.

• • •

Inspired by the Grimm brothers' fairytales, the librarian and museum director Jón Árnason in the 1850s recorded Icelandic traditions that predated the age of print. Until the thirteenth century, Norse colonists rubbed shoulders with *skrælingjar*—Greenland's Thule Eskimo population—and with polar bears, though seldom in a friendly manner. Still, Árnason found that Icelandic lore, like that of the Inuit and Siberians, featured helpful and nurturing polar bears.

Norse mythology teems with *fylgjur*, spirit companions that sway a person's fortune and fate from his birth to his death—embodied signs of the zodiac, if you will. In the hyperborean witching hours of winter days and summer nights, one might mistake them for shadows or mirages. Icelandic *fylgjur* or "followers" could appear as a bear, but they could also reveal themselves as a swan, boar, eagle, wolf, ox, or pig. In pre-Christian times, they only became visible on rare occasions. "They are," wrote Jón Árnason in *Icelandic Legends*, "to the man they follow as guardian spirits and either regulate or personify his luck or success in all things."[24]

The *fylgjur*'s influence on individual lives lingered, detectable still in the nineteenth century. The bear's benign magic partly emanated from its fleece, Árnason recorded: "It is an excellent thing to spread the skin of a bear under a child as it is born, for all infants received on that fur obtain thus the 'bear's-warmth,' or, in other words, become so warm-blooded that they never feel cold."[25] This kind of sympathetic magic—of powers gained through contact or association—could help explain the late nineteenth to mid twentieth-century fashion for photos of babies on polar bear rugs. Some of the animal's strength might rub off, and parents perhaps hoped that a male child so posed would grow into a "slayer of beasts" or his urban equivalent, the shrewd businessman (much like Auðun, the polar bear–trader from Westfjord). Naturally, polar bear skins in this context also were status symbols, pricey and often replaced by cheaper, more common sheepskins.[26]

In *The Grímsey Man and the Bear*, one of the dozens of stories Árnason compiled, a farmer gets trapped on rotten ice between his island and the mainland. A she-bear beckons him to follow her into her den, which he does, though hesitatingly. Then, "the animal laid herself down upon him, spreading herself out over him and her young ones, covering them all as well as she could, and, by her signs, managed to make him take her teat into his mouth, and suck, together with her cubs." Thus he passes the night and the next day and three more. On the fourth the bear leaves the floe and, on her back, carries the man home to the island. There he repays her with two wethers from his sheep pen. In a variant of the story, he spends five weeks with the bear, living off her milk and the seals she hunts.[27]

The theme of polar bears nourishing the bereft—as in the case of the Inuit widow—also is central in an Icelandic tale recorded in 1403, and one wonders if some cross-fertilization between Thule Eskimo and Norse stories occurred or if archetypal ideas are at work. In this version, a bear benefactor gives birth to cubs under a widow's bed. It regularly goes to the seashore for fish and other edibles, giving to the widow what the cubs do not eat. The bear leaves when the cubs are old enough to travel, but the woman remembers it long afterward, for its help.[28]

Accounts such as these highlight attitudes of respect for wildlife and acknowledge dependency on it, both hallmarks of hunter-gatherer societies that are largely dismissed in farming societies. Besides stressing reciprocity as a mechanism for Arctic survival, they echo Kalaallit beliefs about people living or denning with polar bears. They raise the question if ideas and perhaps gift exchanges linked the Norse and their Native American neighbors, despite their general enmity.

Many sympathetic bears enliven Árnason's pages: one spares a pregnant woman, another digs a well for the people of Grímsey. But with them walk the man-eating, tabloid bears, and humans bent on killing: a young man single-handedly slays twelve polar bears; another Grímsey man uses his child to lure a bear from its den; a third stabs a bear with sheep-shearing scissors.[29]

A red thread of blood-feuding runs through the Norse sagas, and revenge drives many a tale. Árnason duly passes on some ancient warnings. He cautions against teasing or baiting bears "for they are sure to take vengeance." A mortally wounded bear should be respected in its agony, not abused: "When he has received his death-blow, he lies down quietly and licks his gaping wounds; and if, after this, the hunter takes the dastardly advantage of giving him a further blow, the man's life is from that moment doomed. If a bear, after receiving his death-wound, roar once or more than once, it is to call upon his relatives to take vengeance upon his slayer; and the next year there will come as many bears to the place as roars were uttered."[30] Spiritual retribution and human restraint—these are concepts any Kalaallit would have recognized.

The *fylgjur* too, went astray during the twilight years of Norse culture. They were now instruments of witchcraft, "answering to followers of an evil kind, ghosts that have been roused from the marble sleep, whom none can lay, and spirits who only appear when mischief is in the wind."[31]

From eighteenth-century Iceland comes a report of *bjarndýrakóngur*—a polar bear king—that seems strangely diluted, a tamer version of the spirit bear of the pagan sagas. The *bjarndýrakóngur* is an extraordinary beast of gigantic size, sprung from the union of a walrus and a polar bear, with a horn sprouting from its forehead. The horn is aglow, lighting the area around it so that the bear can find its way in even the darkest midwinter night. The master of all polar bears, the *bjarndýrakóngur* understands speech and in its infinite wisdom uses its horn only in self-defense or when angered. One story tells how, during a Whitsun service at Grímsey's Miðgarðar church, the ursine monarch approached from the island's outskirts with an entourage of twelve (or thirteen) polar bears. Surprised at this sight, the minister and his congregation stood outside and watched the procession. The clergyman bowed to the bear-king, who in passing returned the courtly gesture. Near Borgamór

Bjarndýrakóngur, the "polar bear king" of Icelandic folklore, with "ruddy cheeks" and "a glowing horn on his forehead," imagined by Icelandic artist Jón Baldur Hlídberg for *Meeting with Monsters*, 2008. The Christ-like figure combines elements of pagan bear worship with those of the more recent religion. Courtesy of Jón Baldur Hlídberg, www.fauna.is.

the bears came upon some sheep, and the last in line killed one. When their leader saw this, he immediately ran his horn through the offender, mortally wounding it. After that, the party marched south, toward Grenivík, where they all disappeared into the sea.[32]

Through the distorting lens of this late feudal society, one can still see the mythical bear of old, though this account could also mark a year in which an unusual number of polar bears landed on Iceland's shores. It is interesting to note that the *bjarndýrakóngur* is a bear that has been "neutered." He does not kill for sustenance like a normal bear, but only from a sense of justice. He dispatches the offending bear with the unicorn's romanticized weapon, much like a knight with a sword. This is another sign of his noble breeding, his domestication.

In the Christian liturgical year, Whitsunday—the day the polar bear king first appeared—commemorates the descent of the Holy Spirit upon the *twelve* apostles and other followers of Jesus Christ. The etymology of the feast day's name preserves color symbolism: "White Sunday" was named after the white clerical vestments worn on that day instead of the usual red ones, or perhaps after the white robes of the faithful who expected to be baptized on that Sunday.[33] The file of polar bears suggests these catechumens, clad in white, and the associated purity of the spirit.

"Regal ruler," "northern monarch," undisputed "king" or "lord" of the Arctic, "majestic" . . . the polar bear has been and still is called all that. The names acknowledge the bear's position at the top of the food chain but also allude to its "nobility"—the strength and "dignity" it displays on its home ground, its apartness, its status, and the lethal power it wields. These are all qualities traditionally associated with human royalty. The animal's aristocratic titles also pay homage to masculine power, a link I'll examine in the context of the bear's gendered sexuality in the next chapter.

With its Christian-monarchic overtones—the twelve followers, the Whitsunday setting, the light figure leading the way, and the scepter-like horn—the legend of the *bjarndýrakóngur* presages Heinrich Heine's *Atta Troll*, published in 1843 in the German *Zeitung für die elegante Welt*. This satirical verse epic's mouthpiece is Atta, an escaped dance bear—a brown bear. Atta symbolizes many of the attitudes Heine despised, including the view that God exists in the believer's form. Atta imagines the deity as an enormous, elevated polar bear:

> High upon his golden throne
> In yon splendid tent of stars,
> Clad in cosmic majesty,
> Sits a titan polar bear.
>
> Spotless, gleaming white as snow
> Is his fur; his head is decked
> With a crown of diamonds
> Blazing through the central vault.
>
> In his face bide harmony
> And the silent deeds of thought,

And obedient to his sceptre
All the planets chime and sing.

At his feet sit holy bears,
Saints who suffered on the Earth,
Meekly. In their paws they hold
Splendid palms of martyrdom.[34]

In one of Canto VIII's stanzas, Atta warns his cub of becoming an atheist, a "monster void of reverence," a stance that should be read as satire. While Heine caricatures pious Biedermeier domesticity, Atta also dreams of revolution, of waging war against the human species. Just because people walk upright, wear clothes, and practice arts and sciences, the bear asserts, they should not consider themselves superior to other creatures. If all animals united in solidarity, Atta thinks, they could end the rule of humans and replace it with an animal republic. Here, Heine mocks populism and simplistic egalitarianism. But as in all good fables, his quixotic protagonist meets a fitting, and from the perspective of political elites, well-deserved end: a Basque bear hunter eventually kills Atta, who reaches Paris—center of radical action and thinking—as a rug.

A popular writer of the current era has resurrected spirit helpers and polar bear–like colossi in his fantasy fiction and, like *Atta Troll*'s creator, has also been charged with godlessness. The English writer Phillip Pullman's *Northern Lights* (released in the United States as *The Golden Compass*) is the first book of a trilogy about a world populated by angels and gypsies, by witches, shamans, and an apostate nun. Inspired by Milton's *Paradise Lost*, the plot centers on the overthrow of "the Authority," a thinly veiled metaphor for God.

Pullman's *panserbjørne*—a race of huge white "armored bears"—live on Svalbard. One of their kings, Iofur Raknison, emulates humans by drinking liquor and wearing opulent clothes. Another, Iorek Byrnison (a mongrel form of the Norwegian name Bjørnson, "bear-son") aids in the rescue of kidnapped children. In this potpourri of the imagination, Nordic folklore blends with real bear biology. The *panserbjørne* are solitary but form a loose society; their duels follow ritualized procedures and seldom end in death; their liver is toxic. Pullman also borrows freely from northern ethnography. There are clans and taboos in Pullman's universe as well as allusions to shamanism. All human characters in the story have a "dæmon," a spirit or soul that takes the form of an animal and that frequently changes shape during childhood but after puberty stays fixed. These dæmons, like the animal-spirits associated with shamans, are known as "familiars," an ethnographic term; they die when a person

Polar Bear, a seventy-pound sculpture by Andrew Chase, 2011. Like the armored bears of Pullman's popular fantasy book series, it stresses the bear's natural strength. The polar bear's sheer force and determination is sometimes perceived as machinelike. Courtesy of Andrew Chase.

dies and vice versa. A human without a dæmon is "like someone without a face, or with their ribs laid open and their heart torn out: something unnatural and uncanny."[35]

The Golden Compass was briefly banned from some school library shelves in a Canadian Catholic school district for its anti-Christian tone. But it was also adapted for the screen, where it reached even larger audiences. The book cover of one edition shows a child on the back of a polar bear, like the already mentioned *The Orphan and the Polar Bear* by Sakiasi Qaunaq. The bear on the cover of this particular edition of *The Golden Compass* is wearing no armor, which softens its image. It is an iconic reprisal of the mythological theme of riding bears. Such images, like white teddy bear toys, irrevocably pair childhood "innocence" with the polar bear's "purity."[36]

Eventually, the production company for the film adaptation of *The Golden Compass* partnered with the World Wildlife Fund (WWF) to promote the "plight" of the polar bear and by inclusion, the film and the book. The film studio's website contained a quiz that allowed readers to discover their own animal spirit—and linked that spirit to WWF's symbolic animal adoption pro-

A nursing assistant robot developed in Japan, ROBEAR resembles a polar bear. Its friendly face and humanoid stance put patients at ease. It was designed to create the impression of "strength, geniality, and cleanliness," all of which are reinforced by the white color, also typical of hospital equipment and furnishings. Courtesy of RIKEN.

gram (really just a financial sponsoring of animals). Another partner in the venture, the Coca-Cola Company, launched a massive multipronged marketing campaign that used the White Bears.

•   •   •

In light of the color symbolism already addressed, it is no coincidence that Heine's brown bear visualizes the Supreme Being as white—purer and more virtuous than himself. With this conception, Heine supports the thesis of his contemporary, the radical materialist philosopher Ludwig Feuerbach: the human idea of God is the projection of idealized human qualities upon an imaginary being.

The same could be said about many people's ideas of the polar bear.

Sifting the evidence, it appears that humans everywhere and at all times have tried to appropriate animal powers and appease animal spirits. Through hunting charms or young adult genre fiction characters, we construe a form of externalized moral consciousness, a big protective brother, nurturing mother, strong partner, or stern, easily angered father. In an uncaring world, we long for comfort, reassurance, for help from forces mightier than we—for Nordenskiöld's "peace of mind." And what force of nature could better alleviate this existential vulnerability than the powerful, humanlike polar bear?

Lover,
Super-Male,
Mate

To most of us in the Arctic, all polar bears seem compellingly male . . . *anything* that outweighs me by more than five to one seems like it ought to be male.

—CHARLES T. FEAZEL, *WHITE BEAR* (1990)

IN A MID-1950S MAIDENFORM AD MEANT TO TITILLATE WITH EXOTI-cism but which nowadays feels offensive, the "Eskimo maiden" wears a white fur hood, fur mittens, and a brassiere engineered like twin Cold War missile heads. Behind her, putting paws over her eyes—a husband home early from work, surprising his wife with a *Guess who?* move—towers a polar bear. The woman seems ready for some bawdy game.

The sexualized depiction of human-animal situations in advertising and art seems largely a modern phenomenon, though it still veers dangerously close to taboo. The strict prohibition of zoophilia, a hallmark of the Abrahamic religions, threatened transgressors with death. The Enlightenment considered such acts crimes against nature, a sentiment bolstered by the animal rights movement, which thinks the practice abusive. Perhaps the greatest danger of bestiality, at least from an ontological perspective, is that it blurs categorical boundaries.

Since before Leda and the swan, there nevertheless circulated a body of stories about interspecies liaisons, sometimes involving one nonconsenting party. In medieval Europe, male bears were believed to have a penchant for kidnapping and raping women. Religious minds took animals as metaphors for the cardinal sins. As raiders of beehives, bears combined lust and laziness;

187

The scandalous *Bacchanal* by Leo Putz, first displayed in 1905. It is one of several paintings by the artist that show bears mingling with young women in sexually charged situations. Photo by Siegfried Unterberger, courtesy of the Athenaeum.

we still call a group of them a "sloth." Despite the Church's efforts, traces of the magic that pagans had once ascribed to bears lingered in Christian times. Offspring from such "unholy" unions—half-human and half-bear—were celebrated as founders of royal lineages.[1] Siward or Sigurd, an eleventh-century Northumbrian earl and vanquisher of Macbeth, was the son of a bear-eared Scandinavian named Bjorn. Bjorn owed his furry appendages to "a certain nobleman whom the Lord, contrary to what normally happens in human procreation, allowed to be created from a white bear as a father and a noblewoman as a mother."[2]

Perceptions of the male bear's heightened sexuality survive even into the present. To a degree, such association may simply have been transferred from the familiar brown bear to the unfamiliar polar bear.

As late as 1905, a rather tame work of art by today's standards—Leo Putz's painting *Bacchanal*—could cause public outcries. Putz had submitted it for the Ninth International Art Exhibit at Munich's Royal Glass Palace. The jury first accepted then removed the piece, citing a controversial law passed five

A Mermaid and Polar Bears, by Arthur Wardle, a study for his 1912 painting *Lure of the North.* In the imagination of Edwardian gentlemen, the North and its bears stood for mystery and elusiveness, qualities they also idealized in women. Courtesy of Christie's Images Limited.

years earlier that censored displays of the "immoral" in artworks, theater, and literature (and incidentally, outlawed pimping). Interestingly, the painting's lewdness, its potential to incite lust *in public,* not its hints of bestiality, got Munich's burghers excited.

The controversial canvas is not that exceptional; scenes of nude or barely dressed women acting amorously with animals were common expressions of male Art Nouveau artists' whimsy and back-to-nature stance. Putz's work foregrounds four naked maidens in a glade who cavort with fearsome large predators: a leopard, a black panther, a brown bear, and a polar bear. Perhaps not by coincidence, the bruin has paired off with the dark-skinned woman while his pale arctic cousin hugs the platinum blonde. Joy radiates from the women's faces, but were their expressions changed, the postures and scenario would suggest a mauling rather than foreplay. In another one of Putz's nude studies, an upright polar bear can be seen among revelers in the background. Similar in content and style is Arthur Wardle's *Lure of the North* (1912), in which three polar bears, jolly as seals, surround a bare-chested mermaid holding a lyre. She personifies the high latitudes as a locus of Edwardian desire, while unintentionally referencing Sedna, the Inuit guardian goddess and mistress of sea creatures.

In the German magazine *Jugend*, Putz would later give shape to a less cheerful, though no less masculine, nationalistic vision: the conquest of Russia. In his World War I painting *Russland!*, a slain polar bear giant—the body of Russia, the uncivilized beast—bleeds among the dead, in a city engulfed in flames. As in the shamanic séance, in these artworks only a knife's edge divides rapture from annihilation.

A straight line seems to run from such erotic scenes to the maneater, in full makeup, on the bear rug.

Some early manifestations seem rather innocuous. In *Prinzessin Josephine* (1898), Adolf Münzer's study for *Jugend*, we see the "princess" (colloquial German for a spoiled, narcissistic woman) rather unceremoniously plunked down on her polar bear rug—a colonial souvenir—regarding herself in a mirror. Clothes lie scattered about, and a feathered hat tilts rakishly on the bear's skull. Perhaps Josephine is a symbol for the belle époque's vanity, or perhaps she is simply deciding which hat to wear on a rendezvous. In most pre–World War I photos and paintings where it is shown, the bear rug is part of opulent interiors and sometimes of exotic fantasies, like those materialized in the A. Goldwhite painting of an "odalisque," reproduced in these pages. From this perspective, the feminine and the faraway are both veiled in mystery—and the bear serves as a stand-in for the inaccessible, unknowable Arctic. At the same time, the fur rug implies the male's absence; he is "out there," in the world, pursuing its trophies while, cloistered, the beloved awaits his return.

With the camera disseminating images more widely and publicly, pictures that juxtaposed women and bearskins became less risqué in the United States, where the (censored) film industry flourished. More flesh was bared on polar bear skins in European boudoir art of the 1880s to 1920s than in the American starlet photographs of the 1920s to 1950s. Starting with silent movie icon Pola Negri, a list of divas shot languorously posing on polar bear skins reads like a roster of the silver screen's glory days: Jean Harlow, Ann Miller, Ann

Adolf Münzer, *Princess Josephine*, 1898. This illustration from the German magazine *Jugend* is unusual for its satirical tone. It mocks the paintings of women on polar bear rugs that were popular at the time. Courtesy of Deutsches Literaturarchiv Marbach.

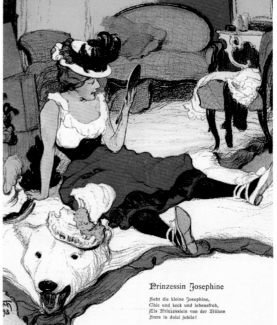

Prinzessin Josephine

Seht die kleine Josephine,
Chic und keck und lebensfroh,
Als Prinzesslein von der Bühne
Stets in dulci jubilo!

LOVER, SUPER-MALE, MATE

Sheridan, Joan Collins, Ann Crawford, Carroll Baker, Edwina Booth, Lisbeth Scott, Olga Baclanova, Dolores Del Rio, Rita Hayworth, Veronica Lake, Marlene Dietrich, and Marilyn Monroe, the last on at least two different occasions. Perhaps the most famous of these photographs is that of Jean Harlow, taken in 1934, as a *Vanity Fair* assignment. In 2010, the original print and negatives of that photo were auctioned off for 57,500 dollars. The image is so iconic that its shooting was reenacted in the 1965 biopic *Harlow*, starring Caroll Baker. Conversely, the "beauty basking on a polar bear rug" has become such a cliché that postmodern visual artists ridicule it. There now are images with ridiculously faux rugs, gender-benders featuring a male sex symbol, rock musician, or pudgy comedian, and even Hitler on the pelt of his favorite German shepherd, Blondi.

In "respectable," bourgeois art prior to World War I, the models stand demurely, often ramrod straight, on the rugs or else lounge on chaises, their feet planted on the fur; the rug more often than not is part of lavish furnishings. In the Roaring Twenties, the women are more likely to lie on the hides, which now are central to the composition. Scantily clad and seeking full-body contact, they have gone horizontal—a more seductive pose. Such still lifes of white-on-white—almost all subjects were Caucasian and many were blondes—helped launch the culture of celebrity and longing, as well as beauty ideals that the film industry fosters to this day. Murky undercurrents run through these set pieces: conquest and trophy, smooth beauty and hairy beast, fair and fair-skinned "game"; amusement, sport, trickery, a contest determined by skill, strength, or chance; a taste of wild flesh—all frozen in the gaze of the alpha male, the director or photographer, and the viewer. The photo "shoot" reenacts the original hunt that yielded the skin. The lone hunter stalks again, and to some degree, the image-maker and bear merge. It would be no surprise if the rugs in such images came mostly from male polar bears. They are much larger than those of female bears, and make a more desirable trophy—size *does* matter. Symbolically, it is the *male* competitor that is outclassed or killed in archaic warfare and sport, as he is in the trophy hunt. At the same time, these seemingly unblemished women on virgin-white fur look pure, innocent even.

An Embarrassing Confession, by Charles Joseph Frédéric Soulacroix, ca. 1860. The women's seated pose is typical of "proper" nineteenth-century polar bear rug images. The bearskin here is a token of wealth not of sexuality. Courtesy of Gail Zawacki.

The living bear has more rarely been cast as a recipient of sexual attention. One of the few female polar bear paramours in Western literature comes from an obscure mid-nineteenth-century novella, James Hogg's *The Surpassing Adventures of Allan Gordon.* Pretending to be a factual account, this Crusoe-like fantasy tells of a castaway sailor in the Arctic who lives on a wreck off Greenland with a polar bear as his provider and partner. The bear, a cub he names Nancy, catches fish for Allan, thus keeping him alive. There is clearly a romantic dimension to the relationship, though it is couched in the terms of Victorian propriety. Allan recalls how Nancy "lay in my bosom and though certainly a most uncourtly mate she being the only one I had I loved her sincerely I might almost say intensely."[3]

Eventually, the wreck drifts to a settlement of the last survivors of the Norse colony in Greenland, where Allan takes several wives. Unhappy at her displacement, the now-grown bear disturbs the community with her nightly moaning, and the gleam of jealousy in her eyes frightens Allan. "I could not

A. Goldwhite's *A Nude on a Bearskin Rug*, an oil painting of an odalisque, ca. 1900. Depictions of the "odalisque"—a nominally eastern woman lying on her side, displayed for the spectator—typify the sex, lassitude, and exoticism that ran through much Orientalist painting of that period. Courtesy of Bonhams.

leave my wife and my other supposed beautiful inamorata to sleep with a huge white she bear," he decides, "yet I had resolved to do it rather than drive her to desperation."[4] Afterward, Nancy leaves but faithfully returns to rescue Allan when other polar bears attack the colonists.

Hogg constantly reminds his readers how powerful and large Nancy is, and how easily she could hurt Allan, even if only by accident. It is easy, from a Victorian male's perspective, to see this bear—a femme fatale—and the ones that massacre the Norse, as ciphers for the Arctic in all its volatile yet attractive otherness.

From the early days of European exploration comes the contrasting tale of a maiden bear-slayer, a female Robinson Crusoe, refracted by multiple chroniclers. This is the gist: The heroine, Marguerite de la Rocque, was a relative of the nobleman-privateer Jean-François de la Rocque, *sieur* de Roberval, whom King Francis I appointed lieutenant general of New France (now Canada) in 1541. This lord de Roberval marooned the young woman on an island off the Labrador Peninsula, the "Île des Démons," after he found that she was having an affair. A seventeenth-century Dutch Calvinist version specifically presents Marguerite's ordeal as a deserved consequence of sexual transgression, in this case, of premarital intercourse. During her two and a half years on the island, Marguerite buried her lover, her maidservant, and a newborn child. She supposedly lived in a cave and killed bears and other animals to survive, and when Breton fishermen rescued her, took the furs with her back to France. A sixteenth-century scribe claimed that one of these bears was "as white as an egg"; but it is impossible to determine whether this was indeed a polar bear, or even if the episode really happened as described.

In its early forms, the account paints Labrador as a dystopia, a godless place that contradicts the era's propaganda about the New World as an Eden of unlimited possibilities. It's an upside-down world where even women of noble birth have to fend for themselves to stay alive, where "daily the rampant beasts did not fail to give her alarms." Even bears are different there, the "wrong" color and quasi-demonic.

An alternative reading of this episode as proto-feminist fable is possible—in later retellings, it becomes a pioneer-era story for young adults and a prize-winning novel, Douglas Glover's *Elle* (2007). These emphasize how Marguerite survives her male mate (and everybody else) in enforced isolation and how she lives self-sufficiently, and entirely by her wits. In the Rabelaisian, postmodern *Elle* (titled, appropriately, "She," "Her," or "Herself"), Marguerite has no need for her lover's "rusty and useless" harquebus. She never kills any bears, but in female solidarity identifies with a she-bear that involuntarily saves her from starvation,

an emaciated, old mother polar bear. When the bear dies from malnutrition, Marguerite dresses in its skin and dreams of a bear lover. Her "uncle," the *sieur* de Roberval, meanwhile develops a fear of bears, of supernatural retribution.[5] In another story variant, he casts Marguerite out to cheat her of her inheritance—an indictment of feudal patriarchal patterns.[6]

One hundred years after Hogg's romance of Allan and Nancy, a scene from the precursor of Hollywood screwball comedies, *Laughter* (1930), provided ironic comment on modern male-female relationships while poking fun at the filmic convention of the bear rug. Perhaps unwittingly, the movie's director also acknowledged the actual biological proximity of brown bears and White Bears in evolutionary terms. Through the self-deprecating filter of humor, we see Nancy Carroll and Frederic March's characters in *Laughter* as different yet closely related species, able to connect and have offspring—a theme also found in northern Native myths. As performers (and shamans) are wont to do, Carroll and March slip into transformative robes and roles—he into a polar bear's, and she into a grizzly's. In their postures—she crouching submissively, he kneeling above her—the pair seem to parody the gender relations typical of the day, and to exaggerate the size difference between the sexes in humans and bears.

This bodily disparity also was striking in Ursula Böttcher's 1960s circus acts and contributed to their success. The 5'1"-tall East German animal trainer approached her polar bears in a skimpy dress or tight bell-bottom pants and had her favorite, Alaska, bend down for the "Kiss of Death," in which Alaska gently removed a sugar cube that Ursula hid in her mouth. The nuzzling pair was so remarkable that in 1978, the GDR honored it with a postage stamp. Their size difference made the act even more impressive, as the "midget" dominated the "monster," a visual representation of human presumed superiority, with potential for male-to-female violence.

For the audience, there was an element of voyeurism. The Austrian silent movie actress and lion- and polar bear–trainer Tilly Bébé typically wore schoolgirlish costumes in the ring, showing more leg than was common at the time and displaying an infantile coquettishness that spurs predator instincts in some men. According to film critic Thomas Elsaesser, Tilly's "combination of animal trainer and brothel madam had something of both the repressed and the forbidden about it."[7] Many other woman animal trainers wore tight or revealing outfits in the ring, and it's likely that spectators watched them as intently as they did the animals.

Regarding women, polar bears, and maleness, the line between titillation and violence remains treacherous, as the following example shows. In 1891,

Marooned for having premarital sex, Marguerite de la Rocque (Roberval) shoots polar bears on the "Isle of Demons" near Labrador. The sixteenth-century tale has been retold repeatedly, with changing details and emphasis. From *A Child's History of the United States*, 1872. Courtesy of New York Public Library.

a Frankfurt servant in some unspecified trouble wanted to commit suicide by polar bear. The supplement of a Parisian daily described how the woman, Karoline Wolf, undressed and, singing quietly, climbed into the polar bear pit. After its initial surprise, "the beast" attacked her, first clawing off her breasts. The "singularly chosen, terrible comforter" then shredded the rest of her body, ending her sorrow (and pain). Undeniably graphic, the original news item and illustration don't allude to any sexual violation or even to the sex of the bear. (The image discussed here is reproduced in this book's zoo chapter.) Surprisingly, Michel Pastoureau's caption for the illustration in his 2011 history *The Bear* specified that the bear raped the young woman before devouring her. In this version, the bear, figured as "he," also had escaped from the zoo and thereby become the transgressor, a sexual predator par excellence.[8]

Exaggerated to the point of caricature, as many male fantasies eventually will be, the temptress on the rug before long became grist for the feminist mill. In Mary McCarthy's novel *The Group* (1963), Norine, one of the female protagonists, finds that her spouse simply "wilts at the approach of intercourse," because Norine is a decent woman—when he's with her, her husband feels he is "fornicating" with his mother.[9] After counseling from a friend, a behaviorist, Norine deploys some raunchy accouterments: black chiffon underwear, dark silk stockings, cheap perfume, and a polar bear rug—think Sacher-Masoch's *Venus in Furs*— things her spouse would associate with a "fallen woman."

Polar bear costumes were popular props of German professional photographers from the 1930s to mid-1960s. Impersonators would solicit business at holiday destinations. They often acted in traditional male roles and posed mostly with women (or children), sometimes flirtatiously. Courtesy of Michael Schimek.

The polar bear's skin itself is sometimes a quasi-animated agent in erotic episodes. In the contemporary British writer Ian McEwan's eco-satire *Solar*, a has-been, aging scientist now draped in "human blubber" returns home to find his wife's lover, his young, up-and-coming assistant, at their apartment. In the ensuing confrontation, the rival slips on a polar bear rug and hits his head on a glass table. Instead of calling emergency services, the scientist— epitome of rationality, not of impulsiveness—arranges the scene to make the accident appear like a murder committed by another of his wife's vigorous lovers. Tellingly, in this, the novel's key passage, the bear rug seems alive: "As

LOVER, SUPER-MALE, MATE

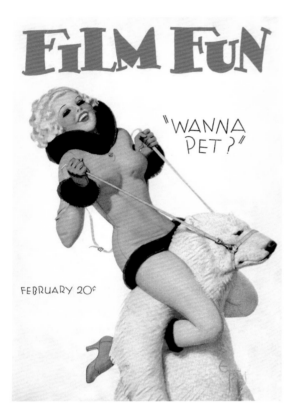

FILM FUN

"WANNA PET?"

FEBRUARY 20¢

Bareback or bear-back riding on a *Film Fun* magazine cover by Enoch Bolles, 1936. Depictions of humans atop polar bears are widespread, suggesting control and dominance, occasionally with sexual overtones. This one has also served as the logo of a motorcycle group. Courtesy of John Raglin.

his [the rival's] right foot landed on the bear's back, it leaped forward, with its open mouth and yellow teeth bucking into the air." Later, the bear's (not "the bear rug's") hard glassy eyes are described as "murderous."[10] It is as if the protagonist's latent aggression toward the lover has been transferred onto an animal proxy. Also, in a sarcastic stab from McEwan, the scientist, "a weakling," did not kill the bear himself, which would have been the traditional token act confirming manhood. Instead, his father-in-law gave him the rug as a wedding gift—a clear reference to impotence, disempowerment, and the tension between in-laws already discussed. The wife, much younger and better-looking than her husband (she resembles Marilyn Monroe, of the famous rug shots), is the proverbial "trophy wife." Their marriage has remained childless. The physicist never liked the rug, its "leering, wide-open mouth and bared teeth," and once, slipping on it himself, almost broke his ankle.

The Arctic, in this novel, functions as it did in the minds of British explorers, as a testing ground, an escape valve for society's pressures, a place of freedom and purity. It promises a rawness that elsewhere exists only in a compromised form. The physicist frequently travels there, released from his "box of miseries," an early Victorian home of gray London brick. On one trip, he barely dodges a polar bear, and this existential wake-up call becomes the highlight of his vacation and, he believes, a life-long memory. This idealization of the North—for which the polar bear often stands—makes the physicist's conflicted "relationship" with the bear rug all the more intriguing.

The German-Italian writer Claudio Michele Mancini takes the topic to extremes, in a poem that ridicules vulgar décor and sexual longing.[11] It is told from the point of view of a living-room polar bear rug, and laced with innuendos. The husband ignores the rug, but the wife regularly pets it, and each time the husband leaves on business, undresses and stretches out on it. She and the bearskin then lie "as newlywed," and the rug, openmouthed, witnesses the wife's "breathtaking methods." When she rises, after "heavenly minutes," the narrator's heart breaks and he asks God why he is only a polar bear rug.

Let no one mistake erotic encounters on bear shag for mere lowbrow frivolity; such trysts take place in works of "serious" literature. Richard Dehmel, Joseph Roth, Thomas Mann, and others used the device to signal bourgeois tastes and mores—in the context of which they explore acts of illicit or risky sexual behavior, from incest to homosexuality—as well as expression of repressed feelings; one scene involves a gay nobleman who bites his prone lover. In the Freudian climate of their time, these writers equated sexuality with animal nature, and that stance still prevails. It even makes sense from the perspective of evolutionary psychology. For the more common, heterosexual, "trophy-wife-on-a-bearskin" situations, a biological reading could be this: the human alpha male, in part defined by and selected for his economic resources, impresses his mate—and his competition—by wrapping her in or bedding her on (literally and figuratively) costly animal furs. While there are literary and visual representations of women seductively stretched out on the skins of brown bears, leopards, or tigers—large predators all—polar bear rugs are by far the most common motif. Given the species' comparable size and degree of ferocity, we must assume that color or the bear's "northern-ness" account for this preference.

A psycho-physiological component remains. Seeing such images or reading such scenes, we imagine the tickle of coarse hair brushing bare skin. Sparks fly when skin touches charged fiber or hair. Conversely, ecstatic or highly pleasurable activities can induce piloerection: "hair-raising" or goose bumps. In *Brave New World*, Aldous Huxley used a promiscuous sex scene on a bearskin rug for the ultimate effect in tactile voyeurism: at the sensory-enhanced "feelies," moviegoers "separately and distinctly" experience each of the rug's hairs, among other sensations.

Frisson produced by the friction between smoothness and coarseness plays a role in bear eroticism, especially considering male hairiness, a secondary sex characteristic. Some famous fetishists of Freud's time rubbed against faux-bears. The writer and journalist Leopold von Sacher-Masoch, is still remembered for lending his name to what in those days was labeled a perversion. Aroused by punishment and humiliation, he reportedly en-

Polar bear envy or pride of possession? The male voyeuristic gaze is normally external to the images of women on polar bear rugs, directed at them. Here, a man is shown looking. Postcard from the 1920s by the Austrian illustrator Robert Sedlacek. Author's collection.

Professional wedding photo taken at the Los Angeles County Natural History Museum. The identities the couples chose reflect real predator-prey relationships. Interspecies liaisons in many Native myths express tensions between human in-laws and blood relatives. Photo by Mark Brooke, courtesy of Jed and Jillian Carter.

joyed impersonating a bear and getting tied up and being administered to by "an opulent fur-clad woman with a whip"—an off-color animal trainer or bestial dominatrix.[12]

Even some modern, feminist writers cannot resist sexualizing the bear. In Audrey Schulman's novel *The Cage* (1994)—about a woman wildlife photographer on an expedition near Churchill—the main character hears a bear breathing "as heavy and methodical as the breath of a person making love." The novel's central, eponymous motif originated with the 1982 National Geographic documentary *Polar Bear Alert*. For that documentary, filmed near the polar bear mecca of Churchill, a cameraman entered a rebar cage to get close-up footage of menacing bears. In another scene from *The Cage*, the photographer imagines evisceration as a form of erotic death, during which the marauding bears reach into the protective cage, "rip the biceps from her flailing arms, the bowels

Walrus penis bone capped with carved ivory polar bear front and back finials. Such *oosiks* are made exclusively for the tourist trade and have become coveted souvenirs and collector items. Photo by Grant Turner, courtesy of Long Ago and Far Away Native Arts.

from her belly, the tendons from her neck." Her life ends, she imagines, when her head rolls back for the bears' touch, "as though for a kiss."[13] Again Eros and Thanatos fiercely cohabit, and the shaman's inception as well as Böttcher's act and Gordon's adventure fit in with Schulman's writing.[14]

Unsurprisingly, the bear penis bone or baculum (Latin: "stick" or "staff") is highly prized by some males of our species. Whole or ground up, it is sold illegally as an aphrodisiac in some Asian countries. A polar bear's baculum averages 7.5 inches in length compared to the human male's 6-inch, boneless penis. At twenty-two inches or more, the walrus *oosik* (from an Inupiaq word for penis) is a much more impressive implement. Traditionally, Siberian Yupiit and Inupiaq hunters used fossilized walrus bacula to club seals, and perhaps the occasional rival. They now sell as tourist curios, often mounted on dainty stands and capped with a carved-ivory polar bear head.

As their bacula reveal, polar bears are not significantly better endowed than men, especially in proportion to their body size. In fact, in some respects the white giant seems actually undersexed. It does not produce prolific offspring, like the rabbit. Its mating season is limited to roughly five months (February till late June), compared to the year-round readiness of *Homo sapiens*. Reasons for the polar bear's reputation as super-male must lie elsewhere. Possibly, the baculum makes the bear appear, at least in the imagination of human observers, always ready to mate. More likely, the polar bear's overall vigor and its aggressiveness in combating rivals combine with its humanlike attributes to account for the imagined virility. The idea that the bear's anthropoid traits and stamina promote its sex symbol image finds further support when we consider the gorilla, an animal sexualized in a similar manner, from Victorian explorers' abduction and rape stories to jealous King Kong.[15]

Consequently, anybody who overcomes the bear gains super-male status from the bear's elevated maleness. In the days before firearms, a successful Native polar bear hunter was indeed highly esteemed in his community. For sports hunters today, the bear ranks among the most desired trophies. Guided hunters, who normally don't butcher the bear they shoot, sometimes ask their guide for its baculum, as a swizzle stick for stirring cocktails. One can imagine the "hunting stories" told over drinks in exclusively male company.

The Canadian wildlife biologist Andrew Derocher considers polar bear testes unremarkable. The public thinks otherwise. When Derocher discovered two female Svalbard yearlings with ambiguous genitalia (possibly caused by hormone-disrupting pollutants) and published a scientific paper about it, a journalist wanted to cover the "story." It also seems that polar bears with high levels of toxic chemicals in their bodies develop a smaller than average baculum and testes and that these pollutants reduce the bone's density, compromising the bears' ability to reproduce. Though the link between toxins and brittle bacula remains tenuous, tabloids jumped on it with headlines like "Polar bear dicks are BREAKING" and "Polar bear penis bones are snapping in half due to pollution." *Oosik* envy gave way to *oosik* pity. "Congratulations," the environmental magazine *Grist* sniped, "we're all collective cockblockers now."

Kettle drummer of the Royal Scots Dragoon Guards with polar bear skin cap. The unit's first caps were a present from Tsar Nicholas II, who became the regiment's colonel-in-chief in 1894. Accouterments of male potency, the "bearskins" add sixteen inches in height to already impressive troopers. Courtesy of the Royal Scots Dragoon Guards Museum.

Sex sells. According to Derocher, weird sex sells even better, and "weird sex linked with polar bears merits the front page."[16]

Meanwhile, the theme of purity resurfaced five decades after the heyday of leading ladies on fleece—this time in a nonsexual guise, in the bear's appeal for the conservation movement. Now, its noncolor stood for "virginal" wilderness and the bears' assumed perfect fit with their "pristine" environment. Commerce, however, co-opts ideals, and in the new millennium white fur is not only en vogue but also again eroticized, as in this adventure tourist's satirical trip account: "Though all we saw were three brownish semi-animate specks rooting about a rocky foreland, a photographic orgy instantly broke out. A hundred little erections sprouted from compact zoom cameras, ejaculated in a flash and detumesced with a satisfied hum. They had ticked an important box. It was odd to think that, just twenty years ago, the only tourists here were on kill-a-bear-or-your-money-back Arctic safaris."[17]

A marker of the marvelous and exotic, the live bear in its true habitat has become a luxury good, as the bear rug in the ostentatious parlor used to be. The above snapshot from aboard a cruise ship near Svalbard sums up other attitude changes from the days of big game hunts to those of eco-sightseeing tours, a shift I will examine more in a following chapter.

Despite its close association with sex, sensuality, and wealth, polar bear fur never made inroads in the world of high fashion, even before the era of wildlife conservation. Unlike the pelage of mink, otter, ermine, lynx, and other fur-bearers, polar bears' guard hairs just are too coarse and numerous in relation to the soft, highly insulating undercoat for the pelt to be considered luxurious. They also make garments very bulky. A person wearing polar bear fur is more Hulk than Mata Hari. The sartorial use for the skins has been mostly limited to Natives and polar explorers, to pants, mittens, and *mukluks* or *kamiks*.

· · ·

In northern indigenous cultures from Greenland to Siberia, tales of intercourse with polar bears reference a mythical time when the boundaries between humans and other-than-humans were thought to be permeable. Shape-shifting occurred commonly. While possible, "marriages" between people and bears always were dangerous. Made easier by the two species' close resemblance, such "promiscuity" resulted in the shared ancestry of humans and bears of which many myths speak. Of twin brothers born to a woman, one could be a cub and the other a child. The sole offspring of a human couple could be a bear. In one Inupiaq tale, a woman gives birth to a brown bear and a polar bear, in

LOVER, SUPER-MALE, MATE

a story that functioned as a "mythological explanation" of the three species' similarities.[18] Among the wealth of Native tales about polar bear–human cohabitation, those in which a man and a she-bear have sex far outnumber those of a male bear engaging with a woman, perhaps because men roamed farther and more often outside the domestic vicinity. Bears and hunters were rivals, "cousin adversaries," most obviously in their contest for seals, but also in defense of their life and families.

The association between polar bears and Inuit or Inupiaq males began at a young age. In some groups, the first dog whip a boy owned had to have a handle made from a polar bear's *oosik*. In the central Canadian Arctic and elsewhere, dogs were part of a triumvirate of hunting. Aligned with the nondomestic sphere, they were crucial in cornering, tiring, and distracting bears so that hunters could move close for the kill. Dogs sometimes were analogous to a man's penis, and in some Siberian myths, the bear's mother was a woman and his father a dog. In some places a boy's first bear kill signaled his coming of age—he officially became a man, entitled to marry and set up his own household.

Sometimes a freshly killed she-bear's warm body tempted a hunter to reenact carnal communions of the mythical past. In one such transgression, the bear infected one of the hunter's eyes, eventually killing him despite the efforts of five shamans to save him. In this instance, the hunter's disrespect of the bear's spirit and resulting disruption of the cosmic equilibrium, rather than moral notions about bestiality, seem the reason for punishment.[19]

The Moon-Man, Aningat, an Inuit source of shamanic power, protector of young boys and hunters, is affiliated with the bear. Polar bears act as his dogs, pulling his sled and guarding his igloo's sleeping platform.[20] Fittingly, Aningat also fertilized barren women. Ammassalik women who could not conceive ate the flesh of polar bear penises, brought home by their husbands.

Concepts of masculine power and predation are interwoven in northern Native thought and belief, uncomfortably, perhaps, for non-Native sensibilities. Bears preying on women left in camp while the men are out on the sea ice are a recurring motif in Native women's stories and recorded dreams—as are legends about male enemies abducting women. The French anthropologist Jean Malaurie described the noteworthy practice of Greenlandic hunters giving polar bear teeth and claws to their wives to make them stay faithful. The token reminded a wife of her husband's courage and manhood, of his ability to provide better than a real or wished-for competitor would.[21] Food, sex, and survival also are linked in a Siberian Yup'ik cautionary tale of a stranger who saves a starving beauty by bringing her seal meat. Only after she becomes his wife does she realize that he is a polar bear bent on fattening and then killing her.

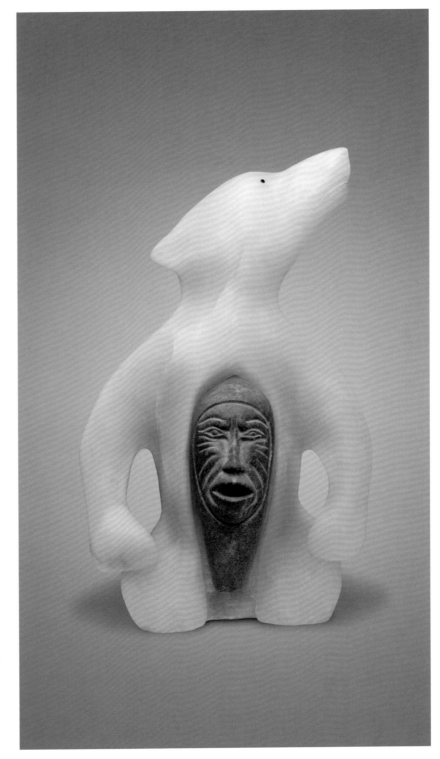

(*Left*) Hand-carved Santa—a "super-male" like the bear. The trim on his coat resembles polar bear fur, and the hirsute man dominates his mount. Both figures are associated with the North Pole as their home. Photo by David Bearden.

(*Right*) In *Shaman Transforming into Bear*, by Abraham Anghik Ruben, the boundaries between species are permeable and no hierarchy is evident. With their "superhuman" abilities, which could also harm, shamans sometimes were feared, just like the bear. Courtesy of Kipling Gallery Collection.

Bear shamans—who are at once super-bears and super-males, the most powerful, dangerous men—also personify this split personality. One name for the bear—*tulurialik*—translates as "who has fangs," and some shamans put carved ivory fangs into their mouth for their performances.[22]

A boy's first polar bear kill marked not only his transition into adulthood but also specifically, his achieving of sexual virility. According to the French Canadian anthropologist Bernard Saladin d'Anglure, "The bear, like the hunter, was valued for his predatory and reproductive qualities, that is, his powers of vision, rapid movement, and force that are also associated with sexual potency."[23] The equating of visual acuity with sexual dominance recalls aspects of the polar bear rug paintings and photos already discussed.

The idea of the bear as an exclusively male sexual predator, however, is far too simplistic. Among Greenland's Kalaallit, Tornarssuk—"the one who gives power," a polar bear deity or guardian spirit—sometimes appeared to female aspirants in a dream in half-human, half-bear form and had intercourse with them, thereby endowing them with shamanic intuition. The sex act in this case served as a transfer mechanism of spiritual power that transcended barriers of species and gender. While female shamans were more rare than male ones among the northern Native peoples mentioned here, their skills nevertheless matched those of male practitioners, and they were equally respected or feared.

Considering biological realities, Native northerners' choice of the polar bear as a multifaceted symbol for prowess, potency, and predation comes as no surprise. The sexual powers of female bears, while widely acknowledged, seem a less coherent and dominant theme, especially in non-Native contexts. In these regards, the bear that fiercely battles over females seems second only to another animal: the male of *Homo sapiens.*

A polar bear attacks a woman—a recurring theme of Inuit women's stories and dreams. This ca. 1965 drawing by Davidialuk Alasuaq of a real incident starkly contrasts with titillating images like those by Wardle or Putz. Here, the woman is armed and appears ready to defend herself. Courtesy of Bernard Saladin d'Anglure.

Archetype, Role Model, Eco Ambassador

I've discovered the polar bear as the primary character in my most personal language. . . . Whether walking on the tundra or through my imagination, polar bears influence my life with a power that serves as a trustworthy guide.

—BARBARA STONE, PERSONAL WEBSITE (2012)

UNLIKE THE CLASSIC FABLE, WHICH EMPLOYS ANIMALS TO SKEWER human behavior, a new "totemism" promises connections with Earth and its creatures, whose characteristics—actual or ascribed— it interprets to provide guidance. Each of these spirit helpers is thought to embody qualities a person desires. As in indigenous initiations, the helper often reveals itself in an encounter or dream. At other times, fueled by discontent with organized religion, people simply select it, consumer-style.

On lists of totem animals compiled by New Age "shamans"—who often do not belong to any identifiable Native group—the polar bear stands for qualities like "spirit communication," "overcoming adversity," and "rebirth." "Polar bear medicine wisdom" is about adapting and surviving in a hostile environment. Never mind that the "hostile" environment shaped this animal and keeps providing for it. "Polar bear wisdom" also teaches wanderlust, survival, introspection, power over life and death, the ability to navigate along Earth's magnetic lines, and how to use guile and your sense of smell. Here, the shaman's shifty associate has been neutered to become a benign, one-dimensional creature.

In such formulations, the bear's sensory acuity and primeval mode of existence, both of which we moderns have lost, raise it to an idealized level—it is holier than us, uncorrupted by progress. Seekers appropriate it, together with indigenous traditions (both in simplified forms), to feed their spiritual hunger. In the imagination of many, hunter-gatherers still share the bear's envelopment in nature. But by distorting Natives into ecological saints and burdening them with our failures, we deny them their basic humanity, as we deny bears their alien animalism.

New Age "healers" disseminate bogus or de-contextualized facts and anecdotal evidence that fits their agenda, like this, from a self-styled community for spiritual revolution: "When hunted, polar bear runs away from the hunter gradually and eventually forming a circle. Because the bear moves faster than the hunter, the bear eventually comes behind the hunter. Thus the hunter becomes hunted. There is a lesson to learn from this." Stories of circling, ambushing bears indeed can be found in the ethnographic literature—but what, one wonders, is the lesson to be learned, other than "always look over your shoulder, up north and in life"?

A few New Age proponents attribute negative qualities to the "ice bear." For them, it signifies "frozen, blocked and repressed emotions and the need to allow these feelings to flow and express themselves." The bear also brings "violent destruction to anything it can get its paws on."

Polar bears might not survive our tenure of Earth, but for seekers of enlightenment, they are "fearsome protectors of their young" and "aggressively forage for food in the water, town garbage heaps, or wherever they might find nourishment and protection. They fascinate us with their size, power, habits, and *ability to adapt and survive*" (emphasis added). In truth, unlike coyotes or ravens, polar bears are tuned to one habitat and likely to vanish before generalist species if their needs are not met. Even before industrial pollution and the climate crisis, polar bears died from disease and starvation; they were gored by walruses, and males killed in competition for females. Cubs fall prey to adult males, an intraspecific predation that journalists sometimes turn into loaded, hair-raising "cannibalism."[1] Already in 1597, in bare-bones, unemotional prose, Willem

This ceramic "Polar Bear Totem," by artist Crystal Morey, illustrates the identification with an animal alter ego that is typical of the new "totemism." In the original, indigenous form of this belief system, people saw themselves as descendants of a mythic animal ancestor. Courtesy of Crystal Morey.

Barentsz described polar bears eating their own kind: "The 29th of June, the sunne being south south-west, the two beares came againe to the place where the dead beare laie, where one of them tooke the dead beare in his mouth, and went a great way with it ouer the rugged ice, and then began to eate it."[2]

In 2008, at the Nuremberg zoo, a polar bear ate her two cubs, which were starving because she did not feed them. The zoo's managers were criticized for not intervening. When Nanook eats cubs as cuddly as Knut, loyalties are divided—we struggle with perceived cannibalism *and* infanticide. Rather than seeing such behavior as yet another example of adaptation, we condemn it as "nature at its most savage." One has to dig into scientific journals to read about cannibalism in other species. Herpetologists and other experts consider the behavior "not only common, but also important in the ecology of many species."[3] But what behavior scientists call "intraspecific predation" simply does not fit the agenda of most nature writers, or they are not familiar with it. Most conservation activists too live sheltered from any business red in tooth and claw. With food shortages in a changing environment, "shocking pictures" of bears eating bears and "even cubs" will become more common, though perhaps not less upsetting. Our terror stems in part from age-old taboos against consuming our kind, and in part from the fear of being eaten ourselves. We also are implicated in the bears' plight—our revulsion could simply deflect guilt. Of course, our society condones cannibalism in some contexts—feeding fishmeal to farm-raised salmon and allowing chickens to peck flesh from other living chickens as part of the "poultry industry." In a bear-eat-bear world, grizzly and polar bear males sometimes kill cubs by a different sire, for the resulting reproductive advantage. They then try to mate with the female, passing on their own genes instead. A biologist-hunter and two-time Alaska fish and game commissioner justified shooting a male polar bear as a corrective to natural selection. Because adult males cannibalize cubs, he thought, killing some should benefit the population.[4]

Ignoring blood and gore and starving polar bears, the websites and calendars of wildlife and environmental organizations commonly offer "nature porn"—shots of glowing, healthy, squeaky-clean polar bears, a fair share of them cubs, romping in immaculate snow, without an oil well in sight. This, of course, is a fallacy. PCBs and other organochlorines, as well as heavy metals such as mercury, concentrate at the top of Arctic food webs. Polar bears and many Inuit hunters and their families, because their diet is mostly marine mammals, ingest and store these toxins.[5]

A starving polar bear on Quebec's Caniapiscau River. Deep in black bear country, it was pursuing a porcupine. Photos like this are seldom publicized, not even by organizations that try to raise awareness of the species' perceived plight. Photo by Heiko Wittenborn. Courtesy of Miranda Taccia.

The "whiteness" of polar bears—symbolic of their purity and that of their environment—too is an idealization. The bears are born "white" but as they age their fur darkens, turning yellowish. Their coat is whitest in the winter, dirtier the more time they spend on land. In fact the perceived whiteness is only a trick of refraction, the same illusion that makes snow and ice appear white. In reality, each hair shaft is translucent and hollow, without pigment—an absence of color that, if metaphor is needed, should rather suggest Ahab's existential void. In a certain light some polar bears look grayish, and Scottish whalers called polar bears "brounies" (brownies).[6] When writers *do* note the off-white color of adult bears, they wholesomely call it "honey," "cream," "amber," or "ripe wheat," rather than "the color of coffee-stained teeth" or "old-paper sepia."

In zoos, where pool algae can invade hair follicles, the bears sometimes turn green. Zookeepers in the past preserved the coat's whiteness as one would bleach laundry, by pouring bluing into the bears' bath water. Circus trainers put a particular kind of sawdust in the ring to keep the bears white, and regularly hosed, scrubbed down, and then sprinkled them with sawdust before performances. Furriers bleached most of their polar bear hides to remove stains and yellow tinges. And some Norwegian suppliers towed the fresh hides behind their ships to keep them clean and undamaged.

Tackling visible industrial pollution, Defenders of Wildlife recently funded and zoo-tested polar bear washing tables, which trained responders can use to clean polar bears in case of an oil-spill on Arctic shipping lanes or at drill

At the Chicago Brookfield Zoo, a polar bear colored green by algae from the pool's water defies stereotypes of purity—and thereby visitor expectations. Photo by Asten Rathbun.

pads. Survival, not cosmetic reasons would necessitate this: after a spill, bears licking themselves or nursing would ingest toxic sludge.[7]

· · ·

Would images of grimy or skin-and-bones bears stuck on shore not urge us more strongly to reach for our wallets or change our behavior? When a corporation can raise two million dollars for the World Wildlife Fund and polar bears with a line of stylish pop cans and TV-watching, couch-potato cartoon bears, the answer seems to be *no.*

"We want to help the polar bear, a beloved Coca-Cola icon since 1922, by helping conserve its Arctic habitat," a company CEO said. "That's why we're using one of our greatest assets, our flagship brand, Coca-Cola, to raise awareness for this important cause." Concurrent with the loss of polar bear habitat and growing public interest in the bear, the company ramped up marketing and merchandising its humanized versions of the animal. However, rather than alerting us to the bears' problem (and implicitly, to ours), such inundations could have the opposite effect. Academic research of marketing unsurprisingly shows that the more abstract and anthropomorphized an animal character is, the less consumers think about the real animal and its natural context.

When Coca-Cola launched a special snow-white can featuring polar bears—a mother and her two cubs—for the 2011 holiday season, customers complained: some mistook it for the diet version; some said the pop tasted different than that in the red cans; others chose to boycott a business supportive of the "climate hoax."[8] Only a month after the cans' release, the firm switched back to its classic color scheme, a tradition of ninety years. Coca-Cola's campaign may have filled the company's coffers and introduced more people to mock polar bears through anthropomorphizing ads, but it has done little for real polar bears.

Another telltale intermingling of industry and a major environmental organization is the WWF's long affiliation with Shell. The petrochemicals giant was WWF's first corporate sponsor (in 1961), and the fund continued to accept money from BP and Shell for another four decades. In return, the WWF nominated Shell and three other oil companies for an environmental award.[9]

Banking on our fascination with other life-forms without whitewashing reality, some environmental organizations fight consumptive stupor with humorous or unsettling ad campaigns. They show polar bears as homeless bums or flayed mannequins that look like butchered steers, anatomical models that shed their hide to evade the heat.

Always, by Vasil Nedelchev—a painter's view of advertising and corporations. Employed in commercial campaigns, polar bears create substantial revenues. Courtesy of VisualCrafter.

The earth is heating up.
Sign the petition on the bigask.be and ask the Belgian government for a strong climate law.

Ad for a European environmental organization. Few dare to use polar bear images in such shocking ways, and this one, almost predictably, sparked controversy. Courtesy of Marc Paeps/TBWA Group.

In fact, an image of an emaciated polar bear taken in 2015 on a cruise to Svalbard was within days shared more than 50,000 times on the Internet. With sea-ice loss and the increasing accumulation of toxins in Arctic marine food chains, the ostensible health of the bears that appear in most conservation advertisements is only skin-deep. Considering the bear a "sentinel species" for humans and other large predators, Danish and Canadian scientists were alarmed to find human-made chemicals accumulating not only in polar bears' livers but also in their brains.[10] But how does one concretize an invisible threat?

Questions of how much of a decline polar bears face, of how many remain, of how we should guarantee their continued existence or curb the trade in their body parts (mostly skin rugs, fangs, and paws exported legally from Canada), are too complex to be examined in depth in this book. There can be no doubt that sea ice is diminishing fast, and that behavioral, physical, and genetic changes in bears and their seal prey are afoot. My focus here is on the polar bear as a flagship species for the conservation movement—and bugbear of conservatives—and the uses to which we put its imagery.

In the new millennium's politics, polar bears play the part whales played in the 1980s. From a theatrics-as-protest perspective, their shape lends itself better to impersonation than that of a rainforest or whale. Activists take advantage of this. Dressed as polar bears, they show up in the most unlikely places—the Kremlin, or Ottawa's Parliament Hill—as nonhuman "climate refugees."[11] In an act billed as "part protest, part performance," Greenpeace paraded a mechanical polar bear the size of a double-decker bus through central London, as part of its Save the Arctic campaign. Fifteen puppeteers operated Aurora the bear, which had an articulated head and neck, a mouth like an ice cave, and the real bear's "slightly lazy" ambling gait.

Greenpeace activists are not the only people who wear fake polar bear fur to discomfort the public. With her one-woman show *Ode to the Polar Bear*, the Inupiaq rapper and performance artist Allison Warden provides an indigenous take on climate change and development. Drawing on stories and experiences of her elders, she mourns the animal's passing and that of a way of life. During her monologue, she slips into various guises, including a polar bear's, transcending human-animal nature as did the shamans of old. Spectators of the show have reportedly burst into tears, as have those who watched a publicized video of a Hudson Bay polar bear cub dying of starvation next to its mother. Audiences of the theatrically scored, "hard to watch" scenes accused the filmmaker of standing by instead of feeding and "saving" that bear. But feeding wildlife is illegal in a national park, where the footage was taken.

In children's books about polar bears, which are flooding the market, the protective parent-offspring bond and the cubs' need to explore feature prominently, allowing the child to identify easily with the bears. More naturalistic illustrations and plots incorporate biological information, and there are retellings of Inuit polar bear myths. Children aged four are not deemed too young for doses of environmental education, though the message first must appeal to adults who buy such books. The children then learn why the polar bear's world is melting and how they and their parents, by conserving energy, can "whack a hole in the greenhouse." In Hans de Beer's *Little Polar Bear and the Whales*, Lars the bear saves some beluga whales from illegal hunters and from glaciers that threaten to block the bay. Unburdened by politics, there is *Dancing Larry*, "the Pinkwaters' lovable bear," who loves blueberry muffins and is on lifeguard duty at the pool. There is a "baby bear" wondering why it is white. And,

Polar bears in children's books have not always been cute, friendly, or educational. In A. Oberländer's *Bilderbuch*, 1928, two bears hijacked the balloon of Arctic aeronauts and descended upon Munich, causing a panic. Courtesy of Antiquariat Hilbert Kadgien.

There's a polar bear
In our Frigidaire—
He likes it 'cause it's cold in there.
With his seat in the meat
And his face in the fish
And his big hairy paws
In the buttery dish
He's nibbling the noodles.[12]

Funny, perhaps, the mental images these displaced bears provoke. Still, compared to the experiences of an Inuit child, they—or *Hush Little Polar Bear*, or time spent with white-teddy toys—differ significantly as an introduction to other-than-human lives. An Inuk might have grown up with a pet cub, and surely would have learned early not to make fun or speak ill of bears while also eating their meat and sleeping under bearskins. Books such as de Beer's *Little Polar Bear and the Whales* distort biological relationships, turning bears into allies of belugas. (The bears sometimes prey on these white whales, and not just on stranded ones.) Disparate childhood experiences thus shape culturally contrasting views of the bear in adults. In a barely disguised moral lesson in another children's book, a young bear learns from an older one that, if he is caught stealing food, he will be tranquilized and locked up in "polar bear jail." Tellingly, these two live in Churchill, where polar bears seasonally raid backyards and, formerly, garbage dumps, while crowding onshore until Hudson Bay freezes in late fall. The town does have a facility where wildlife officers hold adolescent-bear offenders before releasing them at "freeze-up" into the wild.

A bedtime story for grown-ups, T. Cooper's graphic novel and animated short *The Beaufort Diaries* (2010) follow a polar bear exiled from Alaska into "the wilds of Hollywood." In this riff on William Kotzwinkle's satirical parable *The Bear Went over the Mountain*, the protagonist also makes it big in "LA-LA Land," rising to stardom and hobnobbing with a famous real-life actor who has taken on global warming as his cause célèbre. "It's a sad state indeed," a movie star reviewing the book wrote, "when polar bears have nowhere to go but Hollywood after being forced from their rapidly diminishing natural habitat"—which might be their fate, metaphorically speaking, as they die in nature but survive celebrated onscreen. Reaching beyond naïve anthropomorphizing, the animal's personification in Cooper's tale functions as it once did in Aesop's and La Fontaine's: it mirrors our own society, our own foibles.

Biologically accurate, animal point-of-view narratives for children have an adult equivalent in writing that eschews the clinical discourse of science while giving insights into animal lives. The wildlife artist and Boy Scouts co-founder Ernest Thompson Seton pioneered this modern subgenre of narrative nonfiction, focusing on the animal's subjectivity. Sally Carrighar, a largely forgotten contemporary of Rachel Carson and Aldo Leopold, wrote in this style about polar bears like Henry Williamson's *Tarka the Otter* or Fred Bodsworth's *Last of the Curlews*, though without their conservationist tone. Her ten years in the Arctic yielded *Icebound Summer* (1953), a collage of wildlife portraits with a description of polar bears as sensible and true to their nature as it is timeless. In typical genre fashion, it emphasizes the bear's hunting prowess: "The bear was stalking a cub seal, below on the Norton Sound ice. . . . With a swinging pounce he was upon it—no, the young seal had dived. The bear scooped down with his paw, again and again, but the seal apparently had escaped. The bear ravenously wanted that tender meat. He drew back a short way and watched, alert and shrewd, doubtless expecting the seal to thrust its nose up through the slush for a breath."[13]

While adult fiction about polar bears remains rare, the frequency with which they appear in books and the media and their popularity in zoos aid wildlife conservation. To symbolically "adopt" a bear through Polar Bears International, you make a donation of up to 250 dollars, which funds research, activism, and education. Among the token gifts you'll receive in return is a soft and cuddly stuffed polar bear—"100% organic cotton and fair-trade produced"—that might just transport you back to your childhood.[14]

When climate change became a pressing political issue, zoos that had closed polar bear exhibits or were planning to do so because of their high costs reversed course, making sure polar bears were on hand. In part, this reflected zoo visitors' growing interest. But zoos also stepped up their breeding programs when the species was listed as threatened—many of their bears were well past the reproductive age. They soon increased their holdings also with abandoned cubs and "problem" bears removed from the Arctic.[15]

Like captive breeding programs and reintroduction efforts in general, interventions in the field raise the question of what constitutes wildness, or the bearness of polar bears. One of several emergency actions proposed to relieve starving bears has helicopters airlift food to the "most accessible" ones—at a cost of thirty-two thousand dollars per day. (Similar programs already exist for intensely managed animal species and populations such as the California condor, black bears in Washington, and brown bears in Eastern Europe.) Other last-ditch efforts biologists suggest include relocating bears farther north, where sea ice will last longer; moving more bears to zoos; and even euthanizing those unlikely to survive on their own.[16] Some Inuit who decry even the radio-collaring of polar bears as disrespectful to the animals and who are tired of "outsiders" meddling say to just let them be.

Already, polar bears used to humans and to associating humans with food have become nuisances in communities such as Kaktovik on Alaska's Beaufort Sea coast. Villagers there and elsewhere have killed polar bears in defense of life or property, sometimes on their doorstep. The temptation for locals to feed bears to attract them and the subsequent tourist dollars also is great.

Various organizations try to defuse encounters between polar bears and human residents. With the help of the WWF, Native Chukotkans in 2006 formed the Polar Bear Patrol, or Umky Patrol, to protect walrus haul-outs and reduce confrontations with bears in or near villages. The Umky Patrol uses old-fashioned spears instead of rifles, so as not to startle the walruses. (But it also carries night vision goggles and GPS equipment.) Alaska's North Slope Borough and the province of Manitoba have established similar patrols, which educate the locals and, thereby, protect polar bears. The patrols involve villagers in scientific research, escort children to daycare or school, monitor poaching, and generally keep everybody updated about polar bear sightings. In these projects, sponsoring agencies draw on the locals' traditional knowledge about wildlife and Arctic conditions.[17]

• • •

With the polar bear caught in the media's limelight, some Canadians began to consider it a more fitting national emblem than the beaver. In an attempt to oust the official signature animal—"the dentally defective rat"—one senator reminded her fellow citizens that a country's symbols are not constant and can change over time. The polar bear would be perfect for the part, with its "strength, courage, resourcefulness, and dignity." An opponent countered that "you can't beat a beaver for stoic hard work and industry," a perfect metaphor for the pioneering Canadian spirit. Such resistance shows the dif-

Two symbols of Canada's North: a "Mountie" sergeant and a polar bear, ca. 1920–27. A recent attempt by a politician to substitute the polar bear for the beaver as an expression of the nation's identity failed. Photo by Captain George E. Mack, courtesy of McCord Museum.

Cartoon of the British lion and its allies fighting Napoleon, 1808 (detail). The emperor leads the Russian bear by its nose, before the disastrous defeat of 1812. The embodiment of nations as animals has elements of the fable: satirical and stereotypical characterization. Courtesy of McGill University, Rare Book Collection.

ficulties of rebranding, with brand loyalty in this case entrenched for more than thirty-six years.

The political representation of countries not just *through* but also *as* animals draws upon stereotypes as well as fairytales and classic fables that helped codify the animal "character traits." The incarnation of Russia or the Soviet Union as a brown or polar bear dates at least back to the nineteenth century, which likened Czarist expansionism to the bear's "aggressive voraciousness." Western Europe's industrializing nations saw Russia as a shaggy, lumbering giant: foreign, predatory, archaic, and uncouth. The cartographic resemblance of a state to an animal could reinforce such projections. In his tale *Off on a*

Comet, Jules Verne compared Russia as seen from the stratosphere to a huge polar bear facing Asia, its left paw upon Turkey, its right on Mount Caucasus. Such caricature is even more pronounced in a cartoon by Gustave Doré from the 1850s in which the first Russian—bearded no less—is born from the union of a male polar bear and a female walrus. Closer to home, newspapers lampooned Secretary of State William Seward's 1867 purchase of Alaska or "Walrussia." A cartoon from that time shows a polar bear procession carrying icebergs, to cool down the ardor of Congress.

A store that sells fur garments and is also a taxidermy business, on Quebec City's Rue du Petit-Champlain, North America's oldest commercial district. The price of this polar bear skin was twelve hundred dollars. Photo by Julia Pelish.

• • •

When the senator pitched it as a new national symbol, the polar bear had already reinvigorated Canada's oldest trade, which the animal rights movement's stance against wearing fur had previously damaged. Since the bear's numbers were thought to have declined and restrictions on hunting it consequently increased, its value as status symbol rose, to a level comparable to its first appearance in Europe during the Middle Ages. Sports hunters now pay up to thirty thousand dollars to shoot a polar bear in Canada. In the last five years, the price of pelts alone doubled, with the best selling for twenty thousand dollars or more. Even in small amounts, legal polar bear hair, used in fly-fishing, is hard to obtain. Like real flies, lures made with the hollow hairs settle gently on water. There is no equivalent, and patches of "pre-treaty" skin with hair sell for six dollars per square inch in the United States.

All this encourages poaching, especially in Russia, where forty to two hundred bears are killed each year. Their skulls and skins enter the market with false Canadian documentation, the forging of which itself is a lucrative business. The resurgent demand for fur rugs, claws, carved masks with polar bear fur, and similar items comes largely from Russia and China, where a growing middle class spends money on status symbols that are passé in the West. South Koreans, on the other hand, buy dried polar bear gallbladders for "medicinal" uses, at three thousand dollars a piece.[18]

Backed by Russia and the members of the European Union (except for Denmark, with its historic ties to Greenland), the United States keeps trying to outlaw all trade in polar bear parts under the Convention on the Trade in Endangered Species (CITES). If international trade were to be banned, Inuit could still hunt polar bears under Canada's domestic law, though skins or other parts could no longer be exported.[19] Greenland has had a voluntary ban on polar bear exports since 2008, which does not mean much. Polar bears are still hunted throughout the Arctic, except on Norway's Svalbard archipelago. Alaska, Russia, and Greenland permit Native hunting; Canada permits hunting by Natives, non-Natives, and noncitizens. U.S. hunters can no longer import polar bear trophies from Canada, because the animal is now listed as threatened under the U.S. Endangered Species Act. Other nations allow trophies from Canadian hunts to be imported.

Canadian politicians say that initiatives to outlaw such trade or hunting are based more on emotion than on science and that the hunting quotas are sustainable. (Inuit and trophy hunters kill about six hundred polar bears per year.) In the feelings it awakens, this controversy resembles the "seal wars" of the 1970s and 1980s, when big-eyed, white "baby" harp seals clubbed on sea ice caused furor and even French sex symbols became activists. Impassioned appeals, however disguised, come from both sides. "A ban would affect our ability to buy the necessities of life, to clothe our children," an Inuit representative at the 2013 CITES conference said. "We have to protect our means of putting food on the table and selling polar bear hides enables us to support ourselves."[20] Perhaps by intention, this statement counts on our empathy, on our instinct to nurture and protect the *human* young and frail.

The same Native spokesman redirected the discussion toward the root cause of the polar bear's plight. He accused the United States of compensating for its lack of action on climate change and pollution of the Arctic from drilling and mining, of using the polar bear as a blunt tool, because it is "the perfect poster child."[21]

Art itself can no longer be apolitical or unaware of social currents, if its mission is to change public perceptions or to transcend established practices. The creators of the taxidermy exhibit *nanoq: flat out and bluesome*, Bryndís Snæbjörnsdóttir and Mark Wilson, sum up a rather recent shift in our attitudes toward polar bears: "During the last decade the image of the polar bear has moved in the public imagination from being an icon of strength, independence and survival in one of the most climatically extreme of world environments, to that of fragility, vulnerability and more generally of a global environmental crisis."[22] Their latest project, *Matrix*, focuses on the bears' maternity dens in Svalbard, "perfectly adapted model[s] for habitat in the arctic environment." The language of polar bear art has changed, as have its approaches. Drawing on wildlife biology and physics research, Snæbjörnsdóttir and Wilson plan to chart any changes in the architecture of polar bear dens that could signal the bears' adapting to new environmental circumstances, such as shortened winters and poor snow conditions. By translating their findings for a larger, non-academic public the artists hope to inspire contemplation and questioning of accepted knowledge or dogma.

With a different tack and a stronger slant, Ackroyd & Harvey created *Polar Diamond* (2009) after a trip to Svalbard. For this piece of conceptual art, the duo cremated a polar bear bone, which they obtained, with permission, from Svalbard, and artificially grew a diamond from the ashes. Their work sped up a process that in nature takes millions of years. It questions the price we pay for carbon. Ackroyd & Harvey think their diamond carries "an anticipation of loss, and the knowledge that rarity inevitably increases value." That of course applies to both diamonds and polar bears: the number of lowest-grade jewelers' diamonds has been estimated to be in the tens of thousands; polar bears number between twenty thousand and twenty-five thousand.[23]

Another conceptual piece deserves mentioning for its unusual fate. For his Ice Bear Project, the British wildlife artist Mark Coreth shaped an ice sculpture around a life-size, bronze polar bear skeleton. When the "flesh" melted, these bronze bones were revealed. As part of a WWF climate change campaign, the installation premiered in Copenhagen in 2009 before traveling to London, Sydney, and Montreal. In 2013, thieves with a big rig stole the skeleton—worth twenty-three thousand dollars—from Coreth's lawn. The police feared they would sell it as scrap metal to be melted down. Once again, a

The Icelandic artist Bjargey Ólafsdóttir painted this outline on Langjökull Glacier to draw attention to activists' demands that states agree to reduce the amount of CO_2 in the atmosphere from its current level of 400 parts per million to below 350 ppm. Photo by Christopher Lund.

political statement had been gutted by greed, for animal parts to be turned into cash.[24]

Contradictions abound. Matters quickly get complicated. Inspired by the Nazca lines and children's drawings, another Icelandic artist, Bjargey Ólafsdóttir, used organic red food dye to paint a gigantic polar bear outline on Langjökull Glacier, as part of a concerted effort by artists and environmentalists to call attention to the 2010 United Nations Climate Change Conference in Cancun.[25] It looked as if Earthlings had made a statement for extraterrestrials, showing them that they care about bears.

Less than half a year later, coast guard personnel killed a real polar bear stranded on Iceland's northern coast—as bears have since Norse times—because it might disappear into the fog, wander into more densely populated areas, and there pose a risk to the public. A fraction of said public was very upset by the killing. It suggested marooned bears be outfitted with radio-collars and monitored—and restrained only if they became dangerous. Or they could be tranquilized and transferred to the Reykjavík zoo. Or officials could catch, cage, and repatriate strays to Greenland, where, of course, they might also get shot, as part of that country's hunting quota for Natives.[26] The polar bear killing in Iceland in 2010, like one in 2008, garnered attention domestically and internationally. Many people thought it "unfortunate" that Icelanders were killing bears when most of the world (and some prominent Icelanders) felt that the bears needed special protection. A rich Icelandic businessman offered the use of his private jet, and to pay for the polar bear's relocation.

Like ideas, artful images can change lives and even save some. In 2001, one of Alaska's pro-development politicians raised a blank white poster board on the U.S. senate floor, like a modern-day Ahab poised for a strike. "This is what An-whar [ANWR] looks like nine months of the year," he said, trying to sway fellow senators to open a refuge to resource extraction. The Arctic National Wildlife Refuge he decried has the highest concentration of polar bear dens in Alaska. An opponent of drilling later held up a book with photos of winter scenes and polar bears emerging from their dens in the alleged white waste. The refuge remained one, for the time being.

A 2011 pie chart by the Canadian government lies at the opposite end of the emotional spectrum. In a kind of moral mathematics, it calculates the dollar value of polar bears: four hundred thousand dollars per bear. While the chart mentions "intrinsic" and "cultural, artistic, and spiritual values for Aboriginals," only the bears' economic worth is given in dollars—it takes up two thirds of the pie chart. "Intrinsic value," a mere sliver of the pie, is the "bears' non-utilitarian role in the ecosystem and their right to exist."[27] In all fairness it must be said that the report also determined how much Canadians would *spend* to preserve the charismatic species that graces stamps, coins, and, as polar bear–shaped license plates, cars. Canadians were willing to pay what was then the price of an iPad—508 dollars per household—to avoid losing the country's polar bear population, estimated at fifteen thousand. Considering the price of a trophy hunt or a skin, a dead bear is valued much more highly by a few people than a live one is by many. The less "attractive," more "alien," but no less threatened St. Lawrence Estuary beluga whale was worth a fifth of a polar bear to the average Canadian. Even wildlife researchers are not immune to ranking North America's bear species according to their cultural, social, and economic value. For many biologists, brown bears are a notch above black bears. And polar bear biologists think their subject is "the cat's meow."[28] A bear population's numbers and status—"threatened" versus "common"—and the funding available for studying it doubtlessly in-

Polar bears prowling in Churchill are trapped and detained at a special holding facility, the polar bear compound or "jail." Here, Manitoba wildlife managers steady a net with a captured female bear while the helicopter ascends to return her to the wilds. Photo by V. C. Wald.

fluence this attitude. But more significant, perhaps, is an ever-elusive quality: the animal's perceived "charisma."

Like the bear of the Viking traders, the emblem of nature conservation is precious as a commodity and as a pawn in political maneuvers. Even if we never reach the point where polar bears are fed bear kibble from helicopters, bears today, managed and marketed, no longer seem quite "pure" or genuinely wild. While the blending of consumer logos and wildlife might strike some people as odd, it is also no longer limited to the corporate sector. The president of Polar Bears International, a former marketing director, is dedicated to turning the bear into a recognizable environmental brand, "spinning" its image on guided tours outside Churchill. Still, overexposure and a desensitized public could weaken the message and the "Lord of the Arctic" fade to a new cliché. Some critics think polar bears have already begun to disappear in the white noise of our culture. "The polar bear has lost a lot of its cachet," the writer Jon Mooallem said in an interview. "It's become too political. It doesn't really resonate with environmentalists anymore and it ticks off everyone else. What's amazing is that it's just a freaking bear, yet it's become as divisive a figure as [radio talk show host] Rush Limbaugh."[29]

Mooallem summed up the dilemma of image: "In the twenty-first century, how species survive, or go to die, may have to do more with Barnum than with Darwin."[30]

It may have to do even more with Konrad Lorenz, Marshall McLuhan, and Jean Piaget.[31] With our tendency to mess things up and then try to fix them—culminating at present in desperate schemes of geo-engineering—we find it hard to accept that perhaps the polar bear's time is running out. And that ours could be too.

In *We Dreamt Deaf*, a taxidermy sculpture by the Aleut-Tlingit artist Nicholas Galanin, a polar bear is quasi-resurrected from its rug existence. The underlying concept meshes with the once widespread Native belief that some life force remains in the bear after its death, even in parts of the body. Courtesy of Nicholas Galanin.

Another Seaside Attraction

The introduction of late years of the use of the skins of the larger animals, such as the Polar bear . . . as decorations in the furnishing of large apartments, has led to an increased commerce in these skins, which are unquestionably beautiful, not only as mats and rugs, but also for wall decoration. . . . When good taste intervenes and vulgarity is avoided, handsome fur rugs and skins, and even stuffed animals produce a fine effect.

—RICHARD DAVEY, *FURS AND FUR GARMENTS* (1895)

TO EXPLORERS, WHALERS, AND SEALERS, THE POLAR BEAR WAS just one more northern attraction, its skin and meat by-products, so to speak, of their main line of work. To present-day polar bear tourists and big game hunters—and quite a few journalists, filmmakers, and biologists—it is the predominant and sometimes exclusive reason for a visit to the Arctic.

No discussion of polar bear tourism can ignore Churchill, Manitoba, the self-styled Polar Bear Capital of the World. Its international cachet and the sheer volume of visitors it attracts offer an indispensable spectrum of values and attitudes to the student of polar bear lore. A town of eight hundred dwarfed by the vast tundra and Hudson Bay, Churchill grows threefold for about six weeks every fall, swelled by tourists who flock there just as the snow geese prepare to head south. As soon as the bay freezes over in November, scores of bears that were hungrily pacing on shore disappear in search of fat seals, marking the end of tourist season.

Easy access made Churchill's the most-studied and best-known polar bear population in the world. Bears still outnumber townspeople there, but according to wildlife biologist Andrew Derocher, bear numbers have dropped from twelve hundred to nine hundred over the past three decades, with much of the decline occurring in the last decade. Consequently, the tone of reporting about Churchill shifted between the sensationalist 1982 National Geographic TV documentary *Polar Bear Alert*—which emphasized dangerous bear encounters and first put the town on tourists' radar—and around 2005, when freeze-up started to happen later and later, bears were seen starving, and the discussion about global warming took off.[1]

With elephantine, bear-proof expedition-style tundra buggies (or "Polar Rovers") and mobile lodges resembling sleeper train cars or mining camps on wheels, the bear-watching outfit Natural Habitat Adventures in Churchill can "get you closer to more polar bears, in exceptional comfort and safety, than any other option out there"—for a handsome thousand dollars per day. (Even the smaller buggies carry lunch and are outfitted with a bathroom, heater, and observation deck.) An eight-day photographic expedition in their mobile, gravy-train "Tundra Lodge" will set you back eight thousand dollars. The trip, accompanied by renowned wildlife photographers, offers "the ultimate in proximity."

In the highly organized version of Churchill polar bear tourism, there is no touching, no feeding, and no chasing of bears. Buggy drivers won't even approach resting bears. The bears might be nothing but white dots on the horizon or they might be so close that visitors can smell their fishy breaths. According to one guest, "You probably need to go on a dozen tours and take tens of thousands of photos in order to make a few lucky shots, producing true

The "Tundra Lodge" is a mobile bear observatory parked in the Churchill Wildlife Management area. It boasts a dining unit, a computer lounge with Internet access, and a webcam for live online footage of the annual polar bear migration. Photo by Valerie Abbott.

ANOTHER SEASIDE ATTRACTION

gems one could be proud of. This makes sense to professional photographers and cameramen whose bear tours are paid for by a journal or TV studios. But most people go on a tour once, twice at most." For the same wildlife watcher, the Churchill operations are decidedly too low-tech. To spot bears, buggy drivers and tour guides solely rely on "primitive optical equipment," spotting scopes and binoculars. There is no system in place to track bears in the area, this modern-day Henry Hudson complains, suggesting that, "just one light drone with IR camera would pay off."[2]

In nearby Ontario, more active travelers venture out into Hudson Bay and its estuaries in motorized canoes in the care of local guides armed with rifles or shotguns as an "insurance policy" against "hostile" bears. "I can barely keep my eyes open," a client of Hudson Bay Polar Bear Park Adventures blogged. "My legs ache, and my face is wind-burned after our long trip to the bay today. But the thrill of seeing polar bears in the wild far outweighs any discomfort or weariness I feel."

"I tend to judge my adventures on what I learned, the day-to-day experiences, and the memories I store away in my mind," another participant states. "Added to this are the pictures that capture the moments." And indeed, the documentation of the experience can become paramount, almost as important as the encounter itself. The daily dispatches from the front lines of wildlife watching are perceived as a difficult task, almost an obligation: "Although the teepee [at camp] is far more luxurious than any of our tents, there is only one amenity here that is of interest to us: the electrical outlet. We now have an unbridled supply of electrons to power all our hi-tech needs," foremost of which is the charging of batteries for computers, phones and cameras. "We have used two hours of phone time already today," this traveler worries, "sending a backlog of nearly thirty photographs that we couldn't send before."[3]

The ecotourist's bear sighting and the snapshot that freezes it are the equivalent of the trophy hunter's kill and consequent photo-documentation. Without this proof both might consider the venture a bust. Eight decades ago, forester-ecologist Aldo Leopold, pioneering a land ethic and conservation aesthetic, already outlined traits that *all* trophies share: "The trophy, whether it be a bird's egg, a mess of trout, a basket of mushrooms, the photograph of a bear, the pressed specimen of a wild flower, or a note tucked into the cairn on a mountain peak, is a *certificate*. It attests that its owner has been somewhere and done something—that he has exercised skill, persistence, or discrimination in the age-old feat of overcoming, outwitting, or reducing-to-possession."[4]

The pleasures trophies provide, according to Leopold, lie in the seeking as well as the getting, and their value far exceeds their nominal worth. A social species like *Homo sapiens* also enjoys the "sharing." Disseminating accounts of the experience via photos and stories or blog posts almost instantly and long-distance, bear-watchers accrue status. Bucket lists of destinations and animal species rival those of trophy hunters' worldwide safaris. As one Churchill visitor put it, "One thing that happens when you first see a polar bear is that, in that instant, you become suddenly cooler and more interesting than almost anyone you know. You may be less attractive than your friends, or have less money than your enemies, but as soon as you see those giant paws with your own eyes, you've done something they haven't and probably never will. It means that you've gone to extremes, that you have the courage of conviction to spend a lot of money to go someplace that seems really important."[5] Just as often, trip accounts simply are meant to share impressions. People at home who cannot afford such a trip for lack of money or time get to live the wilderness experience vicariously.

The difference between watching polar bears in a zoo and watching polar

Polar bear hunt by Ludwig Beckmann, 1879, from the German journal *Die Gartenlaube*—a "kill shot" engraving, before photography became widespread. Orphaned cubs often were kept as pets before being donated to zoos. Courtesy of Bildbasis.

bears in the wild—even those habituated to the presence of people—is that the wild bears are thought to engage in their normal pursuits, their unknown and largely unknowable agendas. This uncorrupted presence is central to the visitor experience. The bear's independence from us makes it magnificent, restoring a kind of dignity we take from it in the circus and zoo.[6] People don't want to travel thousands of miles to watch polar bears raiding yesterday's garbage. Though it smells worse, a bowhead carcass crowned with polar bears is a different story; it is seen as part of the "natural" environment, even if Native whalers killed and landed the whale. Even with filthy bears, that bone pile becomes extremely photogenic.

In addition to proximity, wildlife watchers crave the animal's direct look. In many museum dioramas, at least one of the taxidermy exhibits in a group has been mounted so as to make eye contact. In the gaze of a large mammal, the viewer feels known, beheld by an alien intelligence, connected to her surroundings. "The eyes of an animal when they consider a man are attentive and wary," John Berger writes in *About Looking*, but "the same animal may well look at other species the same way. He does not reserve a special look for man. But by no other species except man will the animal's look be recognized as familiar. Other animals are held by the look. Man becomes aware of himself returning the look."[7] Eye contact that results in moments of intimacy with wildlife is of course a fallacy, a mere substitute for a deeper, more meaningful relationship, which could come at the cost of insomnia, an arm or a leg, or a life, or after years of dedicated study.

While some tourists humbly consider each bear sighting a special gift or payback for karmic points earned, for many it is an expectation. They have paid dearly for it, after all. Only few travelers express even slight unease at their intrusion into the bear's domain. "Our presence was interference," Barry Lopez recalls in *Arctic Dreams*. "We approached as slowly as before, and he turned to glower, treading water, opening his mouth—the gray tongue, the pale violet mouth, the white teeth—to hiss. He paddled away abruptly to a large floe and again catapulted from the water, shook his fur out, and started across the ice to open water on the far side. We let him go. We watched him, that undeterred walk of authority."[8]

The distance to within which a tourist manages to approach serves as a measure for the value of the experience—the closer, the better. Despite tourist information brochures, local ordinances, guide workshops, and commercial-use permits for tour operators that incorporate guidelines and protocols for safely viewing and coexisting with bears, the potential for conflict remains. Given the nature of the business and the environment, compliance with guide-

A bear feeds on a whale carcass on Svalbard's west coast, watched by tourists. Proximity to the wildlife they have come to observe ranks high on visitors' lists of desirable conditions. Photo by Oscar Westman, courtesy of Vega Expeditions.

lines is difficult to monitor. Tour guides can push to the limits in an attempt to give clients their money's worth: twenty feet or less. This not only endangers people and bears, but also stresses the animals. In Churchill, polar bears reputedly have been baited, which is illegal. The cage used in filming *Polar Bear Alert* was doused in seal oil to attract and excite bears, and on other occasions bears have been fed lard, which does not show up on photographs taken in snowy conditions.[9]

The effects of wildlife watching on polar bears and the need for more effectively managing visitation have barely been studied. Attacks on humans and resulting injuries inside national parks or polar bear preserves so far have been rare. The 2011 death of the boy on a British Schools Exploring Society youth expedition in Svalbard I've mentioned, and other attacks on tourists in Svalbard and Canada, are largely exceptions. But as visitor numbers grow, so does the likelihood of human-bear conflicts and casualties.

The typical polar bear tourist in Churchill is middle-aged to older, well educated, and financially successful. Slightly more males than females visit; nearly half are forty-five to sixty-four years old and earn one hundred thousand dollars per household. Fully 88 percent have a post-secondary degree

ANOTHER SEASIDE ATTRACTION

or diploma and, as polar bears have become hostages in the culture wars, it seems likely that among American visitors, Democrats outnumber Republicans.[10] Summarizing their motives, one can say that the things that matter most to Churchill's bear-watchers are exclusivity, photo trophies, "spiritual moments," and the experiential nature of the trip, as well as learning and natural history interpretation.

Wildlife viewing constitutes one of the fastest growing outdoor activities in the world, and the demand for bear-watching opportunities in particular has skyrocketed in recent years. Tour operators now offer trips to a number of polar bear destinations, including Barrow and Kaktovik in Alaska; Ivvavik National Park in the Yukon; four National Parks in Nunavut; Polar Bear Provincial Park in Ontario; Wapusk National Park in Manitoba; the Svalbard Archipelago; and Wrangel Island and Franz Josef Land, off the coast of eastern and western Siberia, respectively. Bear-watchers and trophy hunters come in search of rejuvenation, looking for "authentic experiences" outside the "incessant rhythms," anxieties, and limitations of their daily lives.[11] This drive should not be underestimated. An investment banker and owner of a quirky Washington, D.C., bar died in an Oslo hospital after becoming ill from acute leukemia while traveling north of the Arctic Circle to see endangered polar bears.

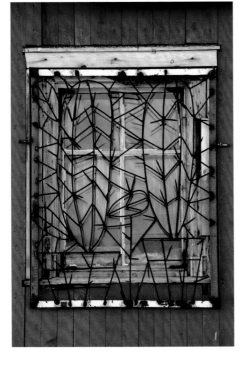

Polar bear–proof window on Wrangel Island, Chukotka, which is rarely visited by tourists. John Muir, who traveled there in 1881 and witnessed an attempt to claim the island for the United States, described sports hunters on board killing some bears. Photo by Ngaire Hart.

Concerns over vanishing landscapes, cultural heritage, and threatened species that the media keep publicizing have given rise to an ecotourism trend variously known as "disappearing tourism," "doom tourism," or "last chance tourism."[12] Bird-watchers with "life lists" chase rare species to the ends of the earth. The polar bear's relative rarity and the specter of its becoming more rare or even extinct account in part for the motivation to spend income on a nonessential pursuit. Polar bear viewing can be one component in a tour package that also includes stops at old gold-mining camps, defunct whaling stations, or Native communities; northern lights are another big draw, and the bear-watching sometimes is scheduled for only a day or two of the vacation. In part, this reflects the restlessness of modern tourists but also the exorbitant cost of such trips. Clients want a good return on their investment, and once the bears have been checked off their to-see and to-do lists (as they quickly are, in polar bear hotspots), it is time to move on.

Unfortunately, those who follow the call to the polar bear ranges only accelerate negative impacts—often unconsciously—by leaving bigger carbon footprints, and by changing the fabric of the human communities they visit, and by contributing to the habituation of bears.

In Canada, polar bear viewing excursions, like trophy hunting trips, often are staged from Native villages, which provide local guides. Occasionally, cultural attitudes regarding the bear come to loggerheads. In 1992, tourists on a three-week polar bear expedition were outraged when their Inuit guides legally shot five polar bears to feed the sled dogs. The public outcry that followed the incident caused the WWF to revoke their support of the tour operator.[13] Natives who have followed a subsistence way of life for millennia resent interference from outsiders intent on stigmatizing the wearing of fur or the killing of animals. At the same time, the cash that visitors spend contributes to local people's larders.

Subsistence hunters and polar bear-watchers at cross-purposes are nothing new. The director of the silent movie classic *Nanook of the North*, Robert J. Flaherty, described a polar bear sighting during an expedition on which he hoped to get good footage. While Flaherty tried to position himself and his camera, his Inuit guides eagerly fired upon the bear, spoiling the filmmaker's chance for "a most interesting picture." In the finished *Nanook*, no living polar bear appears, even though Allakariallak—who played the main character—insisted that one should, and a polar bear scene was expected of Arctic documentaries of the time. Pitching the idea beforehand, Allakariallak had excitedly pantomimed such an encounter on Flaherty's cabin floor, with nimble sidestepping and a fiddle bow substituting for a harpoon. A trip Flaherty made specifically to film such a reenacted foot hunt for a bear in her den proved to be difficult, dangerous, and ultimately futile. The men, who travelled six hundred miles in eight weeks and lost two dogs through starvation, were lucky to escape alive.[14]

In addition to selling hunting permits and working as guides, Native people gain other benefits from polar bear tourism, as through the souvenir trade. After Nome was founded in the Alaska gold rush of 1899–1900, King Island Inupiat began summering near the town, selling intricate ivory carvings and sealskin sewing to tourists and townsfolk. In the present, booming market, polar bear effigies sold to tourists and galleries are hard currency, with demand shaping supply. Some Inuit artists specialize in "dancing bears," which they carve from serpentine, soapstone, or other materials. These sculptures are sought after and have become a kind of pop art of the Inuit art world. The sculptor generally portrays the bear upright with a hind leg raised, as if balancing on one leg, or with one of the front paws on the

Decorative, carved polar bear jaw by Manasie Akpali-apik. Inuit artists create such jawbones specifically for tourists and collectors. Like dancing bear sculptures, they were not part of the traditional material culture. Courtesy of Waddington's Auctioneers and Appraisers.

ground and the hind legs up in the air, in the one-armed handstand of an acrobat. The skill required in making these freestanding figurines increases their price.

Not every Nunavut village produces joyously jigging bears, and some art critics doubt that they are a traditional motif, an assertion that hinges on definitions of tradition. The same is true of Inupiaq scrimshaw work and cribbage boards with polar bear designs—inspired by the crafts of nineteenth-century sailors—and of Greenlandic *tupilaq* statuettes. Bering Strait souvenir *oosiks* capped with carved walrus or polar bear heads likewise cater to outsiders' tastes and ideas.

The symbolic appropriation of the trophy bear, a pricey token of dominance, begins with the hunter's trophy shot, the photographic proof of his (or more rarely, her) deed. The display, which is rooted in mid-seventeenth-century hunting still lifes, has always been fairly ritualized. Nowadays, the hunter often poses behind the bear with his weapon—high-powered rifle or compound bow—to make the animal appear larger. Modern trophy hunters sometimes use muzzle-loaders, and one rushed huntsman in 2007 shot a charging polar bear with the ramrod still inside the barrel. His rifle exploded. The ramrod went "clean" through the bear and stuck in the ice behind it, the guide excitedly recalled. In some people, polar bears bring out the atavistic, and the hunt becomes a reenactment of Last Frontier fantasies. On a 1926 Greenland expedition sponsored by the American Museum of Natural History (and led by George Putnam, the future husband of Amelia Earhart), a crewmember dressed in fringed buckskin killed a polar bear with a bow and arrows. Playing "Arctic rodeo," a Wyoming dude ranch cowboy and Yellowstone Park ranger on the trip then roped the two cubs, which were shipped to the Bronx Zoo.[15]

In the most noticeable difference in trophy shots then and now, the classic foot-on-carcass pose popular in the late nineteenth century has today become rare. Perhaps it is too clichéd or controversial. The hunter in the image nowadays kneels, as if in humbleness. Like the exaggeration of the bear's and the environment's fierceness in exploration narratives, emphasis on the beast's bulk (through this trick of perspective)—or in verbal accounts, on its reluctance to die—makes the hunter appear even more valorous. As the cultural anthropologist Garry Marvin remarked, the bear also is never posed on its own, "as a photograph of the dead polar bear without the agent of its death would make no sense." Marvin provides an angle beyond conservation concerns for explaining the unease that some viewers of trophy photos experience. The coziness between hunter and bear feels unnatural. "There should not be an easy intimacy between humans and polar bears." Many Native people would agree.[16] Marvin, however, ignores an important aspect of proximity in this staged scene. Killing—like sex, another of the most elemental ways of interacting with an-

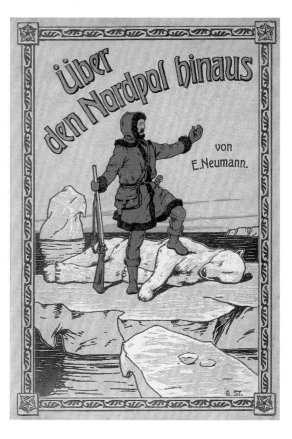

The cliché pose of the conqueror. Cover of Ernst Neumann's *Über den Nordpol hinaus* (*Beyond the North Pole*), 1921. Putting one's foot on the back of the vanquished is no longer common among trophy hunters and even less so among warriors. Author's collection.

Bear and caribou taxidermy mount. The taxidermist strove to create a lifelike scene, almost a photographic snapshot. For trophy hunters, such scenes keep memories of their quests alive. Photo by Olivier de Lapeyriere, courtesy of Cornette de Saint Cyr.

other being—bridges the gap that isolates us as individuals; in the hunt we overcome our apartness in the natural world, our separateness as a species. Intimate knowledge gained from the twinned acts of looking and killing marks Audubon's bird studies and informed many naturalist-collectors of his time.[17]

A hunter's "kill shot," like the taxidermic trophy, serves as mnemonic device, instrumental in reviving and prolonging but also in broadcasting the event. The formative experience is not limited to the actual moment of ending the bear's life but includes the preliminaries: rugged camp life, enduring the weather and barren white sea, seeking and stalking the bear. Some outfitters now give clients a souvenir DVD documenting the entire hunt. But taxidermists strive for more than just physical accuracy. They are in the business of "turning outdoor memories into wildlife art," as one studio's website puts it. Like CGI artists and animators, they seek to replicate lifelike poses and thereby, the bear's "wild personality." Another practitioner, whose workshop once processed one thousand bears per year, sees taxidermy as firmly rooted in the tradition of human creative enterprises: "Man has always tried to save beautiful animal trophies, by sun-drying, by drawing pictures with burnt sticks on the walls of his cave, or carving tools or implements from the horns. We are just carrying on."[18] The creation of animal effigies and cave "art" of course were embedded in rituals that were essential for the functioning of the group, a small band of nomadic hunters. In that respect, any comparison with the hobby of trophy hunting falls short.

In the jargons of trophy hunters, government agencies, and many scientists, polar bears become a "renewable resource" managed for "sustained yield." They are "harvested" or "taken." The on-site trophy photo is sometimes the "harvest shot." In official reports, sport hunting qualifies as a "consumptive form of wildlife tourism" (as opposed to "nonconsumptive" bear-watching). In less formal settings, the language is less restrained. The bear now is "a big sucker." Hunters "get," "drop," "finish off," "put a couple of shots into," or "plant a bullet" in "their" bear. One, a physician who traveled with John Muir on the U.S. revenue cutter *Corwin*, thought a polar bear's slaughter "about as enlivening as shooting a sheep."[19] Some writers, however, comment on the bear's ability to absorb bullets without noticeable effects and, with typical hyperbole, recall wounded bears that escaped "with enough lead in their body, it would seem, to sink them."[20]

Occasionally, trophy hunters experience something like regret. "The hunt was exhilarating," one said. "I had mixed emotions. That bear was such a magnificent creature. But I felt privileged to do it." Historically, shooting a bear in the water was considered the poorest of sports: "In fact, it is no sport at all, for the element of danger, which makes the pursuit of savage animals so attractive, is altogether wanting."[21]

"My friends and guests who visit for the first time stand in awe and envy of my polar bear," one hunter writes of his taxidermy trophy. The animal has not only been appropriated—*my* polar bear—but also, like the wildlife watcher's bear, has become a status symbol. Out of thousands of bears, "that noble beast" earned the hunter's "undying respect and gratitude" by making his "lifetime dream" come true. The bear has been instrumentalized here, as it is for the Inuit hunter: a defining aspect of male biographies and personalities. The "archetypal hunt," according to this devotee, never ends.[22]

Visual metaphors are at play. Images are silent (and death is the ultimate silence), privileging the painter or hunter-photographer, denying the subject a voice. Art critic John Berger hints at the bear's anonymity, its speechlessness, but also at the thrill of its slaying, the same factors that ease killing in modern warfare. Seen through the scope of a .338 Winchester, "The animal's lack of common language, its silence, guarantees its distance, its distinctness, its exclusion from and of man. Just because of this distinctness, however, an animal's life, never to be confused with a man's, can be seen to run parallel to his. Only in death do the two parallel lines converge and after death, perhaps cross over to become parallel again: hence the widespread belief in the transmigration of souls."[23] Regardless of whether or not the hunter subscribes to such transmigrations, a part of the animal's life force flows into him with the killing.

Invigoration of this kind does not come cheap. Advertised as by far the toughest hunt on earth, "not for the weak of heart," and with "nothing between you and the elements but a canvas tent and the clothes on your back," a Spartan vacation in search of manhood will set you back twenty to twenty-five grand (in U.S. dollars), including travel and gear. For the price of a hundred-night, luxury world cruise, "You can be among the few who have braved Canada's Northwest Territories in quest of the North's most spectacular bear." Only the Marco Polo sheep, the tiger, and perhaps the jaguar rival this trophy animal in terms of prestige.[24]

The economic benefits of trophy polar bear hunting to Inuit communities are a contested issue. With animal rights and conservation activists in one corner and anthropologists and government officials in the other, reports differ. According to some social scientists, community-based, Inuit-guided polar bear trophy hunting "contributes to wildlife management and sustainable economic and community development in the Canadian Arctic."[25] Environmentalists counter that Native communities' economic benefits from trophy hunting are negligible and concentrated in the hands of the few individuals

Baffin Island Inuit offer men of the Navy Oceanographic Office a polar bear hide, in 1955. They tried to sell it as a souvenir, for cash needed for subsistence activities. Gasoline, guns, boats, and ammunition require substantial investments in communities with few year-round jobs. Photo by William McTigue.

directly involved in the guiding. They also claim that trophy hunting of polar bears in Canada has no "deep history" and only took off after hunting was banned in other countries as part of conservation agreements.[26]

The noted polar bear biologist Ian Stirling conceded that trophy hunters first set their sights on the White Bears in significant numbers in Alaska during the 1950s. Planes and helicopters were used for spotting bears and for transporting hunters to them. Bear populations became even more accessible in the 1960s through snowmachines, and enough bears were killed to endanger some subpopulations. This development sparked global concern and eventually led to the 1973 International Agreement on the Conservation of Polar Bears and Their Habitat.[27]

A substantial amount of money must be added to the cost of the trophy post-hunt for the bear's resurrection as a taxidermy mount—it is no wonder that outfitters and taxidermists joke that all their clients are doctors or dentists. (Many, it has to be said, make significantly less money, saving for decades for this once-in-a-lifetime endeavor.) The types of mounts and services offered can be bewildering to the layperson, the choices and prices like shopping at

Polar bear hides on a wall in Tromsø, northern Norway, in the late 1960s, hung up for sun bleaching. Tromsø tanneries bought hides from trappers and weather-station personnel who wintered on Svalbard and sold them to tourists. Photo by Thor Larsen, courtesy of Norwegian University of Life Sciences.

ANOTHER SEASIDE ATTRACTION

Saks. Life-size mounts are 7,200 dollars up to sixty inches, and extra per each additional inch; head mounts are 1,200 to 1,500 dollars; rugs with the head, 275 dollars per square foot. Skulls will be cleaned and bleached for $175 each (prices in Canadian dollars). Hunters can choose to have a hide simply tanned or else made into a rug, with the bear's feet and head or without, with or without padding and different felt borders. There are head mounts, shoulder mounts, full (life-size) mounts, and choices between open or closed mouth—open involves a surcharge because it requires more labor to show tongue, teeth, and gums.[28] Nonhunters or hunters who cannot afford the commercial hunt but would like to spuce up their living room with a life-size polar bear can buy one online, for about fifteen thousand dollars for a six- to seven-foot animal, which is not very tall.

Again, size is a big deal. There are legendary bears, like the one Oregonian Arthur R. Dubs shot in 1961, in Kotzebue Sound, a white colossus that weighed more than a Volkswagen Beetle and, as a full mount, stood eleven feet and one and one half inches. Another, which publishing mogul Robert E. Petersen killed in 1965 (with a handgun no less), now stands in the NRA museum. It is twelve feet eight inches tall—on a basketball court, this bear would look *down* at the hoop.

True or not, the narrative accompanying any trophy is appropriately heroic. A *Life* magazine article described how Dubs spotted the bear while flying

A creative way to visualize a record-size polar bear, like the one at the NRA museum, which looms almost thirteen feet. 2015 photo-composite, courtesy of Ben Hillman.

out of the Chukchi Sea village Kotzebue and how he "bagged it" just inside the Russian line between Big and Little Diomede Islands, "under the nose of Russian jet fighter patrols."[29] The Boone and Crockett Club—which developed a system of measuring and ranking game animals—lists a different polar bear as the world's biggest, judging by skull measurements rather than overall size.

In his book *The North Pole* (1910), Robert E. Peary preserved the image—and later the body—of another bear of the ice, as physical evidence of history: "Just after breakfast the Eskimos came in with a polar bear, a female yearling six feet long, and I determined to have it mounted for Marie's birthday bear. It should be standing and advancing, one paw extended as if to shake, the head on one side and a bearish smile on the face."[30] Peary did not waste the meat either, dining on some juicy bear steaks, using a special tablecloth, his best cups and saucers, and new spoons. He liked to refer to wildlife photography, one of his hobbies in the Arctic, as "frozen taxidermy." An anthropology student dropout, Donald Baxter MacMillan, was on board with Peary, and perhaps even shared in the 1909 polar bear dinner. As we saw in an early chapter, he later organized his own expedition and donated to his college a polar bear he had shot and which the American Museum of Natural History had prepared—the bear that became Bowdoin's mascot. Post-hunt celebrations with companions, and trophies passed on as heirlooms are facets of modern trophy hunting also, as described by the hunter who killed the famous grizzly–polar bear hybrid in 2006. Jim Martell who was asked to lend his trophy to museums (part polar bear, it cannot be sold) was planning a "bear party" to show off his one-in-a-million evidence for an ursine one night stand.

Thus the tradition continues.

Depending on personal philosophies, taxidermy can be "a magical mix of science, art, and theater" or the assembly of "pelted prosthetics." In the early twentieth century, exhibits were stuffed with straw. Clay muscles sculpted onto the original skeleton yielded more realistic manikins that quickly became popular. Nowadays, a plaster of Paris mold is made and from it a papier-mâché model upon which the animal skin then is mounted. According to a journalist who extensively researched and even practiced in this sometimes-bizarre microcosm, no profession is either as loved or as hated, which puts taxidermy cheek to jowl with trophy hunting and trapping. "People who love taxidermy will risk imprisonment to import a polar bear," the woman journalist wrote of this passion.[31]

One can gain insights from people besides Peary about the pleasure of freezing lives to a standstill. The Smithsonian's chief taxidermist, William Hornaday, whose account of the near-extermination of the bison became a

ANOTHER SEASIDE ATTRACTION

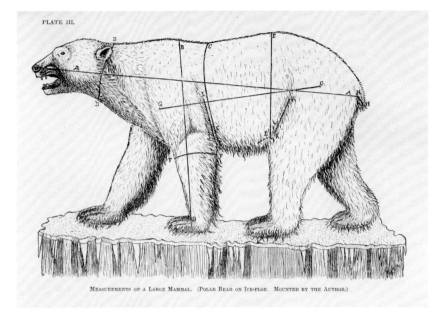

PLATE III.

MEASUREMENTS OF A LARGE MAMMAL. (POLAR BEAR ON ICE-FLOE. MOUNTED BY THE AUTHOR.)

Measurements for a taxidermic polar bear on an "ice-floe," mounted by William T. Hornaday, director of the New York Zoological Park. From his 1894 book *Taxidermy and Zoological Collecting*. Unlike Hagenbeck, Hornaday thought proximity to the bears essential for a good visitor experience. Courtesy of Smithsonian Libraries.

nightmarish classic, is one of them. "The sight of a particularly fine animal," he wrote in his taxidermy manual, "either alive or dead, excites within me feelings of admiration that often amount to genuine affection; and the study and preservation of such forms has for years been my chief delight." The man who, according to his most recent biographer, probably killed more endangered animals than anyone else at the time thought to make them "comparatively immortal" in the act of stuffing them. He regarded taxidermy as a form of conservation: posterity would be able to experience and learn about these species through his work. One gets the impression that at that point in Hornaday's career, living and dead animals equally mattered to him and that, ultimately, a specimen in either state was to him only a means to a pedagogical end. Eventually, though, this trophy-hunting collector became a pugnacious zoo director and ardent conservationist.[32]

◆   ◆   ◆

If the medieval menagerie can be considered the predecessor of the modern zoo and the Roman arena that of the modern circus, the cabinet of curiosities must be seen as the model for natural history museums and their educational taxidermy exhibits.

There were no public museums until the eighteenth century, and scientific collections evolved from the private treasure chambers of nobles and royals.

The only natural objects found in such collections were fabulous or extremely rare. Jean de France—the Duc de Berry (1340–1416), a manic collector—had a wonder cabinet that held sea monsters, griffins' talons, and a giant's jaw, as well as genuine objects such as ostrich eggs, teeth from a "horse of the Nile" (a hippopotamus), and the skin of a polar bear "with his head." Not until Linnaeus and Lamarck, three hundred years later, would collections be used to generate rigorous scientific classifications.[33]

The Danish physician and linguist Ole Worm created one of the first antecedents of the modern museum, representative of the seventeenth century's interest in science and the diversity of the world. An engraving of the Museum Wormianum, this cabinet of curiosities in his home, shows scientific instruments, ethnographic objects, and samples of the natural world, including a snarling polar bear cub hanging from the ceiling. While many contemporary scientists relied solely on books, Worm wanted to experience objects that interested him and to reflect on how their meanings changed outside their natural contexts. In his time, biological specimens and ethnographic artifacts were still lumped together as "natural history" collections. Worm was also a professor of natural philosophy (the precursor of modern science) in Copenhagen and used his hoard to teach students.[34]

In the bourgeois and aristocratic homes of the nineteenth and early twentieth centuries, mounted polar bears or polar bear rugs—like the trophy Nelson may have wanted for his father—served representational rather than educational purposes. As such, they functioned as an outgrowth of and signifier for the colonial enterprise.

Guarding the entrance of the East Anglian Somerleyton Hall, two giant upright polar bears greet the visitor to this mansion, now open to the public. They are souvenirs from the first Lord Somerleyton's 1897 excursion to Spitsbergen. As a youngster, the lord ventured north in a nobleman's rite of passage, shooting and capturing fifty-five polar bears. He brought two back to England alive, one of which survived for several years, possibly at the Regent's Park Zoo.[35]

One of the stuffed Somerleyton bears was chosen for an unequaled exhibit, Bryndís Snæbjörnsdóttir and Mark Wilson's *nanoq: flat out and bluesome*, perhaps the most unusual conceptual group of artifact-specimens ever assembled. The artist-curator pair discovered the provenance and retrieved the histories of every full-mount polar bear in the United Kingdom. They reexhibited all thirty-four—twenty-four via photos of them taken on site, as well as ten of the mounted originals—in new surroundings: Bristol's Spike Island. Some, like the Somerleyton bears, came from Arctic expeditions,

A re-creation of Ole Worm's cabinet of curiosities, a seventeenth-century predecessor of natural history museums. Rosamond Purcell created this replica from surviving specimens and an engraving that was the frontispiece for *Museum Wormianum*, the original catalogue of Worm's collection. Photo by Jens Astrup, courtesy of Natural History Museum of Denmark.

Entrance of Lord Somerleyton's manor, with one of two bears he shot in 1897 in Spitsbergen guarding the door and impressing visitors. He brought back two live bears also, and at least one probably ended up at London's Regent's Park Zoo. Courtesy of Mark Wilson.

others from animals euthanized in British zoos; put together, they stand as sad relics of a "culture of longing" that in some respects resembles our own.[36] The roster of the *nanoq* bears' provenances contains a veritable who's who of Arctic exploration. One was shot during the Jackson-Harmsworth Expedition that met *Fram* survivor Fridtjof Nansen; another came from a search party for Franklin, and a third, from Peary's attempt to succeed where Franklin had failed.

In death, the bears on display at Spike Island lost their individuality, which the artists restored by giving them post-mortem "biographies"—the titular "cultural life of dead animals" of the exhibition's catalogue. While these bears thus are commemorated, the collection of corpses and their images also formulates a subtle critique of trophy hunting and natural history collections. The glass display cases and lighting only emphasize the artificiality of these bears. They appear imprisoned, removed from the specific circumstances of their lives; *nanoq* also reprises a major theme in exploration narratives, of equating Britain with culture and the Arctic—incarnated as White Bears—with nature.

ANOTHER SEASIDE ATTRACTION

Exhibition of *nanoq: flat out and bluesome* at Spike Island, Bristol, by Bryndís Snæbjörnsdóttir and Mark Wilson, 2004. The artists located every taxidermized polar bear in the United Kingdom and documented the bears' cultural "afterlife." Photo by Alan Russell.

• • •

Our own culture of longing drives us to seek things tangible and intangible in the less and less ice-bound Far North. A person's motives for going may differ or even clash with those of other visitors to the Arctic. But the presence of "charismatic" and especially large carnivorous wildlife makes all of us equally vibrant and alert. We feel deeply amazed at our own creaturely nature, and alive. It is easy in such situations to project qualities onto wildlife, qualities that we'd like to find in ourselves. *They* are brave, trusting, curious, fierce, nurturing, loyal, powerful, or sublime. *They* lead simple lives tuned to the sea and the land, unworried about the future. Like yetis, unicorns, or dragons of yore, polar bears fill varying needs, and have done so for at least eight thousand years: "they become precisely what we ask of them, their spine-tingling roars or puppy rambunctiousness speaking to our concerns."[37]

Even before its first contact with European naturalists, the White Bear defied easy categorization. Coupling with grizzlies, giving birth to mixed offspring, mingling with walrus and whales, it continues to evade definition. It's a creature of edges, one that "hunts the ice margins, the surface of the water,

and the continental shore."[38] It pigeon-toes the line between physical and metaphysical realms. The only thing that can be said with certainty is that the polar bear has been and is many things to many people. Across cultures and time, its whiteness invited projection, and we eagerly saddled it with our fears, fantasies, and ambitions. Like the blank spots on explorers' maps, it keeps us forever guessing its true nature. It is our chance to redeem ourselves or at least, to face our shortcomings. Without it, the world would be less colorful, less complete.

The bear we call "white" reflects all wavelengths of visible light and therefore could be considered all-colored. *Cabeza de Oso Polar*, a head mount sculpted in plasticine by Luciana Novo, 2011. Courtesy of Luciana Novo.

NOTES

A BEAST FOR THE AGES

1   Lars Normann Sørensen, *Henry Rudi, Isbjørnkongen* (Oslo: Gyldendal, 1958). For current population numbers, see IUCN Species Survival Commission, Polar Bear Specialist Group, "Summary of Polar Bear Population Status per 2014," http://pbsg.npolar.no/en/status/status-table.html.

2   Oran R. Young and Gail Osherenko, eds., *Polar Politics: Creating International Environmental Regimes* (Ithaca, NY: Cornell University Press, 1993), 105.

3   For specifics, see the agreement: United Nations Environment Programme, "Agreement on Conservation of Polar Bears," http://sedac.ciesin.org/entri/texts/polar.bears.1973.html.

4   Damian Carrington, "Bid to Halt Polar Bear Trade Fails," *The Guardian*, March 7, 2013, www.theguardian.com/environment/2013/mar/07/halt-polar-bear-trade-fails; National Resource Defense Council (NRDC), "Polar Bear SOS!" https://secure.nrdconline.org/site/Advocacy?cmd=display&page=UserAction&id=2975.

5   *Liber de bestiarum natura*, ca. 1200 CE. Aberdeen University Library, University of Aberdeen, Scotland, Univ. Lib. MS 24, folio 7, recto, http://bestiary.ca/manuscripts/manu100.htm.

6   Jackie Morris, "Jackie Morris's Snow Animals: In Pictures," *The Guardian*, December 6, 2015.

7   For a good overview of the field of anthrozoology, see Margo DeMello, *Animals and Society: An Introduction to Human-Animal Studies* (New York: Columbia University Press, 2013).

8   Paul Shepard, *The Others: How Animals Made Us Human* (Washington, DC: Island Press, 1997), 5.

9   Ellen Meloy, *Eating Stone: Imagination and the Loss of the Wild* (New York: Pantheon, 2005), 15–16.

10 Georges-Louis Leclerc, Comte de Buffon, *Histoire Naturelle de Buffon*, vol. 5 (Paris: Hacquart, 1801), 154.

11 Waldemar Bogoras, *The Chukchee*, Memoirs of the American Museum of Natural History, vol. 9 (New York: Johnson Reprint Corporation, 1909), 283, 326.

12 Excellent overviews of polar bear biology are Derocher, *Polar Bears*, and Stirling, *Polar Bears*.

13 "Polar Bear FAQs," Polar Bears International, www.polarbearsinternational.org/about-polar-bears/faqs.

THE LIFE AND DEATH OF A SUPERSTAR

1   Nicholas Kulish, "In Death as in Life, Knut the Polar Bear Demands Attention," *New York Times*, January 5, 2012. The marker bears Knut's paw print and was placed next to the grave of Knut's handler, Thomas Dörflein.

2   Kate Connolly, "Rejected at Birth, Knut Becomes Berlin Zoo's Bear Essential," *The Guardian*, March 23, 2007. Articles about Knut are simply too numerous to list here. For a good summary and critical assessment of the minibear mania, I suggest Moira Weigel, "The Knut and Tom Show," *n+1*, December 18, 2008, https://nplusonemag.com/online-only/online-only/knut-and-tom-show/.

3   Christel Kucharz, "Knut's Keeper Confesses: 'Sometimes I Could Hurl Him against the Wall,'" *Spiegel Online International*, April 11, 2007, www.spiegel.de/international/zeitgeist/knut-s-keeper-confesses-sometimes-i-could-hurl-him-against-the-wall-a-476566.html.

4   "Carpe Diem: Knut Caught Munching 10 Live Fish," *Spiegel Online International*, April 7, 2008, www.spiegel.de/international/zeitgeist/carpe-diem-knut-caught-munching-10-live-fish-a-545790.html.

5   Michael Slackman, "For Mourners of Knut, a Stuffed Bear Just Won't Do," *New York Times*, April 11, 2011.

6   Andrea Zammert, "Knut Mania Sweeps the Globe," *Bloomberg Businessweek*, May 8, 2007.

7   "Polar Bear Turned Cash Cow: Knut the Business-Bear," *Spiegel Online International*, May 11, 2007, www.spiegel.de/international/zeitgeist/polar-bear-turned-cash-cow-knut-the-business-bear-a-482368.html.

8   T. A. Badger, "When It's Bear vs. Tourist, Alaskans Prefer the Bear," *Miami Herald*, September 29, 1994. N. R. Kleinfield, "Farewell to Gus, Whose Issues Made Him a Star," *New York Times*, August 28, 2013. Amy Dee Ste-

phens, "Carmichael the Polar Bear," *Zoo Sounds*, Spring 2012, available at *Amy Dee Stephens: On Writing*, https://amydeestephens.wordpress.com/2012/06/01/carmichael-the-famous-polar-bear/. Elliot Chaze, "Velox the Bear, Scornful of Bars," *Owosso-Argus Press*, December 22, 1949.

9   "Obituary: Knut's Keeper Remembered," *Spiegel Online International*, September 23, 2008, www.spiegel.de/international/germany/obituary-knut-s-keeper-remembered-a-579927.html.

10 John Berger, *About Looking* (New York: Vintage, 1992), 28.

11 Highland Wildlife Park (Kingussie, Scotland), press release, November 3, 2010. Leslie Kaufman, "To Save Some Species, Zoos Must Let Others Die," *New York Times*, May 27, 2012.

12 Natalie Angier, "The Cute Factor," *New York Times*, January 3, 2006. Angier, who coined the phrase, applied it to the panda, but it applies equally to polar bear cubs.

THE BEAR AS EARLY COMMODITY

1   William George Aston, ed., *Nihongi: Chronicles of Japan from the Earliest Times to A.D. 697*, vol. 1 (London: Kegan Paul, Trench, Trübner and Co., 1896), 257, 263. Yoshikazu Sato, Hidetsugu Nakamura, Yuka Ishifune, and Noriyuki Ohtaishi, "The White-Colored Brown Bears of the Southern Kurils," *Ursus* 22, no. 1 (2011): 84–90.

2   Alexander Stubbing, "Polar Bears and Iceland: An Overview, History and Proposed Response Plan," MA thesis, University of Akureyri, 2011, 13. In the brutal winter of 1880–81 alone, about eighty polar bears were stranded on Iceland's northern coast; Ævar Petersen, email message to author, Jan. 9, 2014.

3   Niels Horrebow, *The Natural History of Iceland* (London: A. Linde, D. Wilson, et al., 1758), 38, 43.

4   *Morkinskinna: The Earliest Icelandic Chronicle of the Norwegian Kings (1030–1157)* (Ithaca, NY: Cornell University Press, 2000), 211–15. For a more thorough analysis of this tale, see Miller, *Audun and the Polar Bear.*

5   George Webbe Dasent, "The Cat on the Dovrefell," in *Popular Tales from the Norse* (Edinburgh: Edmonston and Douglas, 1888), 80. For some speculations about the story's factual basis, see *Saga Book of the Viking Society*, vol. 13 (London: Viking Society of Northern Research, 1946–1953), 92–95.

6   Georg Nyegaard, email message to author, Nov. 28, 2014. Thomas H. McGovern, "Contributions to the Paleoeconomy of Norse Greenland," *Acta Archaeologica* 54 (1985): 73–122.

7   John Caley, Sir Henry Ellis, and Bulkeley Bandinel, *Monasticon Anglicanum: A History of the Abbies and Other Monasteries, Hospitals, Frieries, and Cathedral and Collegiate Churches, with Their Dependencies, in England and Wales* (London: Longman, 1819), 96. Olaus Magnus, *Historia de gentibus septentrionalibus* [*Description of the Northern Peoples*], ed. Peter Foote (Rome, 1555; repr. London: Hakluyt Society, 1998), 621.

8   National and University Library of Iceland, "Íslandia," http://islandskort.is/is/map/show/2.

9   Fridtjof Nansen, *In Northern Mists: Arctic Exploration in Early Times*, vol. 2 (London: Ballantyne, 1911), 177.

10 G. J. Marcus, "The Greenland Trade-Route," *The Economic History Review*, new series, 7, no. 1 (1954): 71–80.

11 Donald, F. Logan, *The Vikings in History* (New York: Routledge, 2013), 71. Birgitta Wallace, "Scandinavia in 'Chapters 24–25, 32–33, and 38,'" *Where is Vinland?* www.canadianmysteries.ca/sites/vinland/vikinglife/4115en.html.

12 Joseph Fischer, *The Discoveries of the Norsemen in America with Special Relation to their Early Cartographical Representation* (St. Louis: B. Herder, 1903), 102, 104.

13 "*Ursus albus sicut nivea magnitudinis insolite*" in the original. Werner Paravicini, "Tiere aus dem Norden," *Deutsches Archiv für die Erforschung des Mittelalters* 59, no. 2 (2003): 578–79.

14 Edward Turner Bennett, *The Tower Menagerie: Comprising the Natural History of the Animals Contained in that Establishment; with Anecdotes of Their Characters and History* (Chiswick: Charles Whittingham, 1829), xiv. Daniel Hahn, *The Tower Menagerie: The Amazing Six Hundred Year History of the Royal Collection of Wild and Ferocious Beasts Kept at the Tower of London* (New York: Tarcher, 2004), 43. Phillip Drennon Thomas, "The Tower of London's Royal Menagerie," *History Today* (August 1996): 30.

15 Richard Davey and T. S. Jay, *Furs and Fur Garments* (London: International Fur Store, 1895), 49.

16 Samuel Purchas, *His pilgrimes In fiue bookes*, vol. 3 (London: Henry Fetherstone, 1625), 502.

17 Gerrit de Veer and Koolemans Beijnen, *The Three Voyages of William Barents to the Arctic Regions: 1594, 1595, and 1596* (London: Hakluyt Society, 1876), 15.

18 Garry Marvin, "Perpetuating Polar Bears: The Cultural Life of Dead Animals," in *nanoq: flat out and bluesome: A Cultural Life of Polar Bears*, ed. Bryndís Snæbjörnsdóttir and Mark Wilson (London: Black Dog Publishing, 2006), 157–65.

19 Louise McConnell, *Dictionary of Shakespeare* (Teddington, Middlesex: Peter Collin, 2001), 135.

20 Barbara Ravelhofer, "'Beasts of Recreacion': Henslowe's White Bears," *English Literary Renaissance* 32, no. 2 (2002): 287–23. Teresa Grant, "Polar Performances: The King's Bear Cubs on the Jacobean Stage," *Times Literary*

Supplement, June 14, 2002. Teresa Grant, "White Bears in *Mucedorus, The Winter's Tale,* and *Oberon, the Faery Prince,*" *Notes and Queries* 48 (Sept. 2001): 311–13. Some Shakespeare scholars no longer classify *Mucedorus* as part of the bard's oeuvre.

21 Dennis Biggins, "'Exit Pursued by a Beare': A Problem in The Winter's Tale," *Shakespeare Quarterly* 13, no. 1 (1962): 3.

22 John Taylor, *Bull, Beare, and Horse, Cut, Curtaile, and Longtaile. With Tales, and Tales of Buls, Clenches, and Flashes. As also here and there a touch of our Beare-Garden-sport; with the second part of the Merry conceits of Wit and Mirth. Together with the Names of all the Bulls and Beares* (London: M. Parsons, 1638).

23 McConnell, *Dictionary of Shakespeare,* 167. Erica Fudge, *Perceiving Animals: Humans and Beasts in Early Modern English Culture* (Champaign: University of Illinois Press, 2002), 15.

24 Joseph Quincy Adams, *Shakespearean Playhouses: A History of English Theatres from the Beginnings to the Restoration* (Ithaca, NY: Cornell University, 1917), 130.

25 Walter M. Dunne, *The Diary of John Evelyn,* vol. 2 (Washington and London: M. Walter Dunne, 1901), 53–54. To this day, financial trends are "bear" or "bull" markets, named for the allegedly contrasting fighting styles of these animals: grumpily guarded versus blindly charging.

26 Purchas, *His pilgrimes,* 561.

27 Robert Chambers, *The Book of Days: A Miscellany of Popular Antiquities in Connection with the Calendar, Including Anecdote, Biography, and History, Curiosities of Literature and Oddities of Human Life and Character,* vol. 1 (Edinburgh: W. and R. Chambers, 1863), 409. *Ye Olde White Bear* still is in business. The animal—a non-drinker that metabolizes water from the fat in its diet—has never ceased to entice drinkers. Today, both beer bottles and pubs bear its image or name.

28 Ravelhofer, "'Beasts of Recreacion,'" 293.

29 Bennett, *Tower Menagerie,* xiii.

OBJECT OF SCIENTIFIC CURIOSITY

1 Patricia Tyson Stroud, *The Emperor of Nature: Charles-Lucien Bonaparte and His World* (Philadelphia: University of Philadelphia Press, 2000), 115.

2 Louise E. Robbins, *Elephant Slaves and Pampered Parrots: Exotic Animals in Eighteenth-Century Paris* (Baltimore: Johns Hopkins University Press, 2002), 79, 88.

3 Other contributions by Buffon were significant. In the course of his proto-Darwinian theorizing, he discovered the first principle of biogeography, noticing that despite similar environments, different regions have distinct plants and animals. Georges-Louis Leclerc, Comte de Buffon, *Histoire naturelle, générale et particulière,* vol. 18 (Paris: Imprimerie royale, 1767–68), 18–38.

4 James Cook, *The Voyages of Captain James Cook Round the World* (London: Jacques and Wright, 1825), 90, 352.

5 Thomas Pennant, *Arctic Zoology,* vol. 1 (London: Henry Hughs, 1784), 53–57.

6 George F. Lyon, *The Private Journal of Captain G. F. Lyon* (London: John Murray, 1824), 376. For a closer look at the alleged nose covering, I recommend Harington, "The Bear behind the Paw." After reviewing the literature, this wildlife biologist concluded that most reports could not be substantiated. A few eyewitness accounts seemed reliable, but Harington wondered why none came from outside the North American Arctic—which could indicate a cultural rather than a biological phenomenon.

7 *The King's Mirror,* trans. Laurence Marcellus Larson (New York: American-Scandinavian Foundation, 1917), 141–44.

8 Olaus Magnus, *Historia de gentibus septentrionalibus* [*Description of the Northern Peoples*], ed. Peter Foote (Rome, 1555; repr. London: Hakluyt Society, 1998), 621.

9 Edward Topsell, *The History of Four-footed Beasts* (London: Jaggard, 1607), 36.

10 Charles Wendell Townsend, ed., *Captain Cartwright and his Labrador Journal* (Boston: Dana Estes & Company Publishers, 1911), 178–79.

11 William Scoresby, *Journal of a Voyage to the Northern Whale-Fishery: Including Researches and Discoveries on the Eastern Coast of West Greenland, Made in the Summer of 1822, in the Ship Baffin of Liverpool* (Edinburgh: Archibald Constable, 1828), 518.

12 Valerian Albanov, *In the Land of White Death: An Epic Story of Survival in the Siberian Arctic* (New York: The Modern Library, 2000), 81. Where the ice is extremely thin, bears belly-slide to reduce the risk of breaking through (by distributing their weight).

13 William Scoresby, *Journal of a Voyage,* 110.

14 Traction actually comes not from hair on the soles (there is none) but from the nubby profile of the black-skin footpads. Buckland was referring to hair on top of the foot and between the toes.

15 Frank Buckland, *Animal Life: Notes and Jottings from Animal Life* (London: Smith, Elder, and Co., 1886), 255.

16 William Scoresby, *Journal of a Voyage,* 517.

17 J. B. Tyrrell, ed., *David Thompson's Narrative of His Explorations in Western America* (Toronto: Champlain Society, 1916), 23.

18 John George Wood, *Homes without Hands: Being a Description of the Habitations of Animals Classed According to Their Principle of Construction* (New York: Harper and Brothers, 1866), 39.

19 William Scoresby, *Journal of a Voyage,* 519.

20 Alexander Leslie, *The Arctic Voyages of Adolf Erik Nordenskiöld: 1858–1879* (London: Macmillan and Co., 1879), 144, 287.

21 Fridtjof Nansen, *In Northern Mists: Arctic Exploration in Early Times*, vol. 2 (New York: Frederick A. Stokes Company, 1911), 112.

22 Hans Egede, *A Description of Greenland* (London: Longmans, 1818), 84.

23 Oliver Goldsmith, *A History of the Earth, and Animated Nature*, vol. 3 (Philadelphia: Thomas T. Ash, 1823), 179.

24 Adolf Erik Nordenskiöld, *The Voyage of the Vega Round Asia and Europe*, vols. 1–2 (London: Macmillan and Co., 1881), 137. Julius Payer, *Die österreichisch-ungarische Nordpol-Expedition in den Jahren 1872-1874: Nebst einer Skizze der zweiten deutschen Nordpol-Expedition 1869-1870 und der Polar-Expedition von 1871* (Wien: Alfred Hölder, 1876), 139.

25 John William Draper, *A History of the Intellectual Development of Europe* (New York: Harper Brothers Publishers, 1864), 535. For polar bear archaeological and paleontological finds outside their current range, see O. Ingólfsson and Ø. Wiig, "Late Pleistocene Fossil Find in Svalbard: The Oldest Remains of a Polar Bear (*Ursus maritimus* Phipps, 1744) Ever Discovered," *Polar Research* 28, no. 3 (2009): 455–62.

26 James Lamont, *Seasons with the Sea-horses: Sporting Adventures in the Northern Seas* (London: Hurst and Blackett, 1861), 273–74. Charles Darwin to James Lamont, Feb. 25, 1861, Darwin Correspondence Database, www.darwinproject.ac.uk/entry-3071.

   Here is Darwin's bear passage in full: "In North America the black bear was seen by Hearne swimming for hours with widely open mouth, thus catching, like a whale, insects in the water. Even in so extreme a case as this, if the supply of insects were constant, and if better adapted competitors did not already exist in the country, I can see no difficulty in a race of bears being rendered, by natural selection, more and more aquatic in their structure and habits, with larger and larger mouths, till a creature was produced as monstrous as a whale." Charles Darwin, *On the Origin of Species: Or the Preservation of Favoured Races in the Struggle for Life* (London: John Murray, 1859), 184.

27 In part, the confusion could stem from penguins having been mistaken for auks—the black-and-white, upright, stubby-winged Arctic diving birds.

28 David Crantz, *The History of Greenland: Including an Account of the Mission Carried on by the United Brethren in That Country* (London: Longman, 1820), 123.

29 Egede, *Description of Greenland*, 60. Egede became known as the "apostle of Greenland," for his effort (be-ginning in 1721) to find and convert any Norse left there after the colony lost contact with Europe, sometime in the Middle Ages. He ended up settling with the Kalaallit and missionizing among them. Mark Nuttall, ed., *Encyclopedia of the Arctic* (New York: Routledge, 2005), 544–45.

30 Wood, *Homes without Hands*, 55–57.

31 Nordenskiöld, *Voyage of the Vega*, 141.

32 Samuel Hearne, *A Journey from Prince of Wales's Fort in Hudson's Bay to the Northern Ocean in the Years 1769, 1770, 1771, 1772* (Toronto: Champlain Society, 1911), 418. Hearne was the first European to traverse northern Canada, finding an overland route to the Arctic Ocean. Preble edited and annotated Hearne's journals.

33 Joaquin Miller, *True Bear Stories* (Chicago and New York: Rand, McNally and Co., 1900), 154–55.

34 Hearne, *Journey from Prince of Wales's Fort*, 418.

35 Peter Freuchen, *Vagrant Viking: My Life and Adventures* (New York: Julian Messner, 1953), 4. A onetime diplomat, film star, resistance fighter, and quiz show winner, this bearded, bearish socialist was one of the Arctic's most colorful characters.

36 Wood, *Homes without Hands*, 58.

37 Scoresby, *Journal of a Voyage*, 520–21.

38 J. B. Tyrrell, ed., *Journals of Samuel Hearne and Philip Turnor: Between the Years 1774 and 1792* (Toronto: Champlain Society, 1968), 418.

39 Egede, *Description of Greenland*, 59. Scoresby, *Journal of a Voyage*, 517. John James Audubon, *The Viviparous Quadrupeds of North America*, vol. 2 (New York: V. G. Audubon, 1851), 282.

40 Nordenskiöld, *Voyage of the Vega*, 140.

41 Salomon August Andrée, Nils Strindberg, and Knud Fraenkel, *En ballon vers le pôle: Le drame de l'expédition Andrée d'après les notes et documents retrouvés à l'île Blanche publiés par la Société suédoise d'anthropologie et de géographie* (Paris: Librairie Plon, 1931), 172.

42 Alfred Edmund Brehm, *Brehm's Life of Animals: A Complete Natural History for Popular Home Instruction and for the Use of Schools*, vol. 1 (Chicago: A. N. Marquis and Co., 1895), 259.

43 Nordenskiöld, *Voyage of the Vega*, 138.

44 Sean T. Peake, *The Travels of David Thompson: The Hudson's Bay Company 1784–1797, the Missouri, Mississippi, and Lake Superior, 1797–1798* (Bloomington, IN: iUniverse, 2011), 13. "A Herd of Polar Bears," *New Zealand Herald*, June 2, 1905.

45 "Bear Shot in N.W.T. Was Grizzly-Polar Hybrid," *CBC News*, April 30, 2010. For the 2006 hybrid, see Alicia P. Q. Wittmeyer, "Rare Hybrid Bear Coming to Reno Hunting Show," *Tahoe Daily Tribune*, January 18, 2007.

46 Regarding tangled lines of descent: a subspecies of brown bear at home on islands in Southeast Alaska carries genetic material inherited from female polar bears. James A. Cahill, Richard E. Green, Tara L. Fulton, Mathias Stiller, Flora Jay, Nikita Ovsyanikov, et al., "Genomic Evidence for Island Population Conversion Resolves Conflicting Theories of Polar Bear Evolution," *Plos Genetics*, March 14, 2013.

47 George A. Feldhamer, Bruce C. Thompson, and Joseph A. Chapman, *Wild Mammals of North America: Biology, Management, and Conservation* (Baltimore: Johns Hopkins University, 2003), 587. In 1781, the first recorded usage of the English "polar bear" appeared in T. Pennant, *History of Quadrupeds* (London: B. White).

48 "Naming Hybrid Big Cats," Messybeast Portal, Hybrid and Mutant Animals, messybeast.com/genetics/hybrid-names .htm.

FROM WHITE TERROR TO TROPHY OF MODERNITY

1 Tom Kelly, "The Half-Ton Killer That Sees Man as Its Prey," *Daily Mail*, August 6, 2011.

2 Harriet Arkell, "So THAT's What It's Like to Be Eaten by a Polar Bear!" www.dailymail.co.uk/news/article-2257088/ Starving-polar-bear-attacks-BBC-cameraman-pod-Arctic-Norway.html.

3 Thomas Hood, *Odes and Addresses to Great People* (London: Baldwin, Cradock and Joy, 1825), 95.

4 Kenneth Burke, *Permanence and Change: An Anatomy of Purpose* (Berkeley: University of California, 1984), 272.

5 Stephen Herrero, *Bear Attacks: Their Causes and Avoidance* (Guilford, CT: Lyons Press, 2002). I do not mean to downplay the risk of traveling in polar bear country. For a positively harrowing account of a mauling, see Jake Abrahamson, "The Man Who Survived a Polar Bear Attack," *Sierra*, February 2015, www.sierraclub .org/sierra/2015-1-january-february/feature/man-who -survived-polar-bear-attack.

6 Viðar Hreinsson, ed., *The Complete Sagas of Icelanders, Including Forty-nine Tales* (Reykjavík: Leifur Eiríksson, 1997).

7 Gerrit de Veer and Koolemans Beijnen, *The Three Voyages of William Barents to the Arctic Regions: 1594, 1595, and 1596* (London: Hakluyt Society, 1876), 15.

8 Hendrik Tollens, *The Hollanders in Nova Zembla, 1596 to 1597* (New York: Putnam and Sons, 1884), 106.

9 Ibid., 70–71.

10 Herman Melville, *Moby-Dick, or, The White Whale* (New York: Harper and Brothers, 1851; Boston: St. Botolph Society, 1920), 186.

11 Ibid., 180.

12 W. M. Dunkle, *Naval Arctic Operations Handbook*, part 1 (Washington, DC: Department of the Navy, 1949), 111.

13 William Martin Conway, *No Man's Land: A History of Spitsbergen from Its Discovery in 1596 to the Beginning of the Scientific Exploration of the Country* (Cambridge: Cambridge University Press, 1906), 208–10.

14 "Spirit bears" account for only 10–25 percent of the Kermode subspecies of black bear *(Ursus americanus kermodei)*, which has an estimated total population of four hundred to one thousand animals. Their rareness stems from the fact that the gene for white fur is recessive; sometimes a black mother will have a white cub. Kermit Ritland, Craig Newton, and H. Dawn Marshall, "Inheritance and Population Structure of the White-Phased 'Kermode' Black Bear," *Current Biology* 11, no. 18 (2001): 1468–72.

15 Petra Werner, "Die Menagerie des Landgrafen Karl: Ein Beitrag zur Einheit von Natur und Kunst im Barockzeitalter," PhD diss., Universität Kassel, 2013, 41.

16 Born in Heidelberg, Roos was part of a family of four generations of animal painters, and had a penchant for portraying the White Bear. At least four images of that subject by him still exist. Evelyn Lehmann, *Das große Kasseler Tierbild: Das barocke 'Tierstück' von Johann Melchior Roos, die Klassiker Menagerien und einiges mehr über Mensch und Tier* (Petersberg: Michael Imhof Verlag, 2008).

17 Christa N. Selnick, "White Sow, White Stag, and White Buffalo: The Evolution of White Animal Myths from Personal Belief to Public Policy," MA thesis, Georgetown University, 2012, 45. The British Columbia government extended its ban on the hunting of spirit bears from the coast to the entire province a few years ago, mostly because of the bear's rareness and its worth as a tourist attraction.

18 Charles Kingsley, *The Life and Works of Charles Kingsley* (London: Macmillan and Company, 1902), 58.

19 Jules Verne, *The Fur Country* (Rockville, MD: Wildside Press, 2003), 256.

20 Alexander Leslie, *The Arctic Voyages of Adolf Erik Nordenskiöld, 1858–1879* (London: MacMillan and Co., 1879), 254.

21 Sophie Gilmartin, '*The Cravings of Nature': Landseer's Man Proposes, God Disposes and the Franklin Expedition* (Egham: Royal Holloway University of London, 2008), 3.

22 Ann Sylph, email to the author, July 22, 2013; Laura MacCulloch, "Edwin Landseer, *Man Proposes, God Disposes*, 1864," Royal Holloway University of London, May 5, 2013, www.rhul.ac.uk/archives/itemofthemonth/items/may2013 .aspx.

23 R. Potter, ed., "From Dr. John Rae's Report to the Hudson's Bay Company," Rhode Island College, www.ric.edu/faculty/rpotter/cann.html.

24 Charles Dickens, "Sir John Franklin and His Crews," *Household Words* 11 (1855): 16.

25 Robert Southey, *The Life of Nelson* (London: John Murray, 1813), 11. John Sugden, *Nelson: A Dream of Glory, 1758–1797* (London: Jonathan Cape, 2004), 75. For a good analysis of the painting's historical and philosophical context, see Diana Donald, "The Arctic Fantasies of Edwin Landseer and Briton Riviere: Polar Bears, Wilderness and Notions of the Sublime," *Tate Papers* 13 (2010), www.tate.org.uk/research/publications/tate-papers/13/arctic-fantasies-of-edwin-landseer-and-briton-riviere-polar-bears-wilderness-and-notions-of-the-sublime. Also valuable were Ron Broglio's unpublished lecture notes, "Edwin Landseer and Animality: Culture and History at a Limit," 2011, and Lewis-Jones, "Nelson and the Bear."

26 Adolf Erik Nordenskiöld, *The Voyage of the Vega Round Asia and Europe* (London: MacMillan and Company, 1882), 111. William Scoresby, *Journal of a Voyage to the Northern Whale-Fishery: Including Researches and Discoveries on the Eastern Coast of West Greenland, Made in the Summer of 1822, in the Ship Baffin of Liverpool* (Edinburgh: Archibald Constable, 1828), 110.

27 J. E. Honderich, "Wildlife as a Hazardous Resource: An Analysis of the Historical Interaction of Humans and Polar Bears in the Canadian Arctic," MA thesis, University of Waterloo, Ontario, 1991, 134. Julius von Payer, *New Lands within the Arctic Circle: Narrative of the Discoveries of the Austrian Ship Tegetthoff in the Years 1872–1874* (Cambridge: Cambridge University Press, 2012), 212, 220.

28 Andrej Argentov, "Lower Kolyma Area," *Proceedings of the Russian Geographical Society* 15 (1880): 449–51.

29 Ilya Sel'vinskii, "Umka belyi medved" ["Umka the White Bear"], in *Sobranie sochinenii v shesti tomakh* [*Collected Works in Six Volumes*], vol. 4. (Moscow: Goslitizdat, 1973), 49–50. Yuri Slezkine, *Arctic Mirrors: Russia and the Small Peoples of the North* (Ithaca, NY: Cornell University Press, 1994), 297.

30 Alexander Leslie, *Arctic Voyages*, 90.

31 Arthur Conan Doyle, *Sir Arthur Conan Doyle: Memories and Adventures* (Ware, Hertfordshire: Wordsworth Editions Limited, 2007), 36.

32 Rasmussen, *The Bear in the Ice Hole*, 1–7.

33 W. S. Champ, "A Polar Bear Story," *National Geographic Magazine* 17 (1906): 35–36.

34 Frank Buckland, *Animal Life: Notes and Jottings from Animal Life* (London: Smith, Elder, and Co., 1886), 258. Spencer Walpole, "Mr. Frank Buckland," *Popular Mechanics* 18 (1881): 812–20.

35 John Muir, *The Cruise of the Corwin: Journal of the Arctic Expedition of 1881* (Boston: Houghton Mifflin, 1918), 161. Carl Hagenbeck, *Beasts and Men: Being Carl Hagenbeck's Experiences for Half a Century among Wild Animals* (London: Longmans, Green, and Company, 1912), 53.

36 Arnold Pike, "Arctic Hunting," in *Big Game Shooting*, vol. 2, ed. Clive Phillips-Wolley (London: Longmans, Green, and Co., 1894), 16, 20.

37 Theodore Roosevelt, *The Works of Theodore Roosevelt: Hunting Trips of a Ranchman* (New York: Charles Scribner's Sons, 1906), 143.

38 Walter Wellman, "An Arctic Day and Night," *McClure's Magazine*, April 1900.

39 Paul Rainey, *Cosmopolitan* 50 (1910): 91–103.

40 "Four Years in the White North: Donald B. MacMillan's Crocker Land Lecture," Bowdoin College, Peary MacMillan Arctic Museum and Arctic Studies Center, 2001, http://www.bowdoin.edu/arctic-museum/exhibits/2001/four-years.shtml.

41 William Carlos Williams, *The Collected Poems of William Carlos Williams*, vol. 2 (New York: New Directions Publishing, 1991), 395.

42 Charles T. Feazel, *White Bear: Encounters with the Master of the Arctic Ice* (New York: Ballantine Books, 1990), 42.

43 I owe Mark Neumann the idea of "geographies of fantasy," a perspective he so aptly applied to texts about the Grand Canyon. Mark Neumann, *On the Rim: Looking for the Grand Canyon* (Minneapolis: University of Minnesota Press, 2001), 177.

ZOO BEAR AND CIRCUS BEAR

1 Vernon N. Kisling, ed., *Zoo and Aquarium History: Ancient Animal Collections to Zoological Gardens* (London and New York: CRC Press, 2000), 77, 133. In 1664, Tsar Aleksei Mikhailovich received his first polar bears, and this pair was most likely kept at his summer mansion near Moscow—but these animals were exclusively for the entertainment of the monarch and his coterie of boyars.

2 Maureen Cassidy-Geiger, ed., *Fragile Diplomacy: Meissen Porcelain for European Courts Ca. 1710–63* (New Haven, CT: Yale University Press, 2007), 66.

3 *The Scots Magazine* 74 (September 1812): 652. A cub in Leith, brought there by whaling captain William Scoresby—the first live polar bear in Scotland—had been housed in a cage made from a hogshead barrel while traveling. It was washed daily with pails of seawater and, while in Leith, fed on "bullock liver or garbage of fish." One of the bears at the Paris menagerie subsisted entirely on bread, about six pounds a day.

4 Jane Goodall, *Performance and Evolution in the Age of Darwin: Out of the Natural Order* (London: Routledge, 2002), 31. Traveling menageries in England kept attending fairs and remained common until the 1930s, but were doomed by zoos and by the movie industry, which emphasized education over sensationalism.

5 Kisling, *Zoo and Aquarium History*, 148.

6 *The Gentleman's Magazine* 17, November 1747.

7 Kisling, *Zoo and Aquarium History*, 58.

8 Laura Brown, *Homeless Dogs and Melancholy Apes: Humans and Other Animals in the Modern Literary Imagination* (Ithaca, NY: Cornell University Press, 2010), 67.

9 See John Berger's seminal essay "Why Look at Animals?" in *About Looking* (New York: Pantheon Books, 1980), 28.

10 Opel and Opel, *Eisbären*, 74.

11 Johanna Lutteroth, "König der Löwen: 100 Jahre Carl Hagenbeck," *Spiegel Online*, April 12, 2013, www.spiegel.de/einestages/tierpark-begruender-carl-hagenbeck-a-951096.html. Eric Ames, *Carl Hagenbeck's Empire of Entertainments* (Seattle: University of Washington Press, 2009). Carl Hagenbeck, *Beasts and Men: Being Experiences for Half a Century among Wild Animals* (Hard Press Publishing, 2013).

12 Susan Brownel, ed., *The 1904 Anthropology Days and Olympic Games: Sport, Race, and American Imperialism* (Lincoln: University of Nebraska Press, 2008), 141.

13 Thomas Patrick Doherty, *Pre-Code Hollywood: Sex, Immorality, and Insurrection in American Cinema, 1930–1934* (New York: Columbia University Press, 2013), 229, 245. Palle B. Petterson, *Cameras into the Wild: A History of Early Wildlife and Expedition Filmmaking* (Jefferson, NC: McFarland, 2011), 72. Probably the best critical overview is Gregg Mitman, *Reel Nature: America's Romance with Wildlife on Film* (Seattle: University of Washington Press, 2012).

14 Lutteroth, "König der Löwen."

15 Elizabeth Hanson, *Animal Attractions: Nature on Display in American Zoos* (Princeton, NJ: Princeton University Press, 2002), 142.

16 Tor Bomann-Larsen, *Roald Amundsen* (Stroud, Gloucestershire: History Press, 2011), 61–62. For a very anthropocentric account of the planned expedition from the point of view of a bear, see Hanna Astrup Larsen, "To Hunt the Pole with Polar Bears," *The San Francisco Sunday Call*, February 16, 1908.

17 Valerian Albanov, *In the Land of White Death: An Epic Story of Survival in the Siberian Arctic* (New York: Modern Library, 2000), 179.

18 "To the North Pole with Polar Bears," *The Inter Ocean*, November 10, 1907, 30.

19 Fridtjof Nansen, "The Race to the South Pole," *Scribner's Magazine* 51 (1912): 309.

20 Tor Bomann-Larsen, *Roald Amundsen*, 180.

21 Stratford F. Corbett, "Mushing with Bears in Alaska," *Popular Mechanics*, January 19, 1923.

22 SeaWorld Parks and Entertainment, http://seaworldparks.com/en/seaworldorlando/Attractions/Rides/Wild-Arctic (page discontinued).

23 *Le Petit Journal*, illustrated supplement, July 11, 1891. Inappropriately, after the guilty bear's death in 1903, some Frankfurt businessmen had postcards printed with the bear's obituary, which described him as an unrequited, ravenous lover of Karoline Wolf; he was so infatuated he "gobbled" her up. Zoologischer Garten der Stadt Frankfurt am Main, eds., *Hundertjähriger Zoo* (Frankfurt am Main: Zoologischer Garten der Stadt Frankfurt am Main, 1958), 44–45.

24 "Teacher Who Survived Polar Bear Mauling at Zoo 'Was Depressed over Job,'" *Daily Telegraph*, April 13, 2009.

25 James Barron, "Polar Bears Kill a Child at Prospect Park Zoo," *New York Times*, May 20, 1987. In typical tabloid style, the incident was also covered in an article headlined, "Playmates of Polar Bear Victim Heard His Final Cries for Help."

26 Because of the bears' preference for cold water, only the "people pool" of the facility is heated. Heading off visitor disappointment, the Cochrane Polar Bear Habitat website warns that "bears do not spend their whole day swimming, and may not be available for a photo-shoot." www.polarbearhabitat.ca/facility.

27 Katherine H. Adams and Michael L. Keene, *Women of the American Circus, 1880–1940*, (Jefferson, NC: McFarland, 2012), 5.

28 Ibid., 7. "Frank Bostock," University of Sheffield, National Fairground Archive, www.sheffield.ac.uk/nfa/projects/frankbostockbio.

29 William Bentley, *The Diary of William Bentley: 1793–1802* (Salem, MA: Essex Institute, 1907), 261. Museums are yet another rung down on the ladder of thrills—they are shrines, really, although modern ones try to liven up things with hands-on or automated displays. A similar "fatigue" affects audiences used to wildlife documentaries—in which animals continually fight, mate, flee, give birth, or kill—when they first encounter creaturely low-energy routines in nature (grazing or sleeping), or the animals' scarcity or reclusiveness, or no animals at all. On polar bear viewing tours, "with the possible exception of big males fighting, playful cubs are the ultimate 'get.'" Zac Unger, *Never Look a Polar Bear in the Eye* (Boston: Da Capo Press, 2013), 231.

30 Brenda Assael, *The Circus and Victorian Society* (Charlottesville: University of Virginia Press, 2005), 75. George Speaight, *A History of the Circus* (London: Tantivy Press, 1980), 38.

31 William Temple Hornaday, *Popular Official Guide to the New York Zoological Park* (New York: New York Zoological Society, 1911), 121.

32 George Speaight, *History of the Circus*, 80. Richard Reynolds, email message to author, June 26, 2013.

33 It can be confusing trying to pin down the number of polar bears in this Hagenbeck act—it is sometimes given as seventy, other times as seventy-five. Wilhelm stated in a magazine article that only seventy bears could perform tricks; the rest were just sitting around, "merely an ornament to the arena." Harold, "The Character of the Polar Bear," 303.

34 "A Herd of Polar Bears," *New Zealand Herald*, June 3, 1905, 2.

35 Susan Nance, *Entertaining Elephants: Animal Agency and the Business of the American Circus* (Baltimore, MD: Johns Hopkins University Press, 2013), 202. Al Stencell, "Frank Bostock in America."

36 "Frank Bostock," University of Sheffield, National Fairground Archive, www.sheffield.ac.uk/nfa/projects/frankbostockbio.

37 Jacob Smith, *The Thrill Makers: Celebrity, Masculinity, and Stunt Performance* (Berkeley: University of California Press, 2012), 94.

38 Katherine H. Adams and Michael L. Keene, *Women of the American Circus*, 163.

39 George Speaight, *History of the Circus*, 80.

40 Frank Charles Bostock, *The Training of Wild Animals* (New York: Century Co., 1903), 53.

41 "Polar Bears Bite? Never!" *New York Times*, August 4, 1905.

42 *Harrisburg Telegraph*, August 1, 1904, 9.

43 Opel and Opel, *Eisbären*, 91.

44 William Temple Hornaday, *The Minds and Manners of Wild Animals: A Book of Personal Observations* (New York: C. Scribner's Sons, 1922), 211. C. P. Fox, "Awesome Arctic Ice Bears," *Ringling Brothers and Barnum and Bailey Circus, 106th Edition Souvenir Program and Magazine*, 1977.

45 "Lions Drown Out 'Iris,'" *New York Times*, October 7, 1902.

46 George Speaight, *History of the Circus*, 87.

47 Ibid., 98.

48 Hornaday, *Minds and Manners*, 211. Opel and Opel, *Eisbären*, 92–93. A typical circus bear diet at the time included rice, noodles, fat meat, and "barrels of cod liver oil."

49 "An Awful Fight," *Virginia Citizen* 11, no. 12, December 20, 1901.

50 George Speaight, *History of the Circus*, 96–97.

51 "Polar Bear Kills Bonavita," *Variety*, March 23, 1917. Obituary, *Moving Picture World*, April 7, 1917. Q. David

Bowers, "Bonavita, Captain Jack," *Thanhouser Films: An Encyclopedia and History*, www.thanhouser.org/tcocd/Biography_Files/l96bjj.htm.

52 Bertram Mills' Circus and Menagerie program, 1931, in the Victoria and Albert Museum collection.

53 C. P. Fox, "Awesome Arctic Ice Bears." In the wilds, polar bear cubs do slide down snowy inclines in play, as do adults in their travels. According to the Russian polar bear expert Nikita Ovsyanikov, polar bear facial expressions really are "sufficiently well developed," but thick fur on the muzzle can make them hard to read. Nikita G. Ovsyanikov, "Behavior of Polar Bears in Coastal Congregations," *Zoological Journal* 84, no. 1 (2005): 94–103.

54 Hope B. Werness, *The Continuum Encyclopedia of Animal Symbolism in Art* (New York and London: Continuum, 2006), 33.

55 For my account of Böttcher (or Boettcher, as she spelled her name in the United States), I have drawn on Markus Maier, "Mein Leben mit den Eisbären," *Superillu.de*, April 10, 2007, www.superillu.de/show/ursula-boettcher-mein-leben-mit-den-eisbaeren-die-beruehmte-dompteurin-im-interview; Uta Keseling, "Die Nummer mit dem Todeskuss," *Berliner Morgenpost*, June 5, 2008; and Kerstin Decker, "Vor drei Wochen ging Ursula Böttchers weltberühmte Eisbären-Dressur zu Ende," *Der Tagesspiegel*, September 27, 1999. English speakers can find a good summary of Böttcher's life here: Dominique Jando and Christian Hamel, "Ursula Böttcher," *Circopedia*, www.circopedia.org/Ursula_Böttcher.

56 Mark Lavender, Dec. 28, 2008, comment on "Ursula Bottcher #4," *Buckles Blog*, Dec. 26, 2008, http://bucklesw.blogspot.com/2008/12/ursula-bottcher-4.html.

57 Katy Daigle, "Panting Polar Bears Getting Animal Advocates Steamed Up," *Los Angeles Times*, March 10, 2002. Animal Welfare Institute, "The Circus Is Coming to Town . . . with *No Polar Bears!*" *AWI Quarterly*, Spring 2002, https://awionline.org/content-types-orchid-legacy/awi-quarterly/circus-coming-town-no-polar-bears.

58 Opel and Opel, *Eisbären*, 77. The international studbook for the polar bear, kept and annually updated by the Rostock zoo, lists the provenance and pedigree of every polar bear in captivity, though some of the documentation can be hazy. For the nature of studbooks and downloads for the different species, see San Diego Zoo Global Library, "Studbooks," http://library.sandiegozoo.org/studbook.htm.

59 Megan A. Owen, Ronald R. Swaisgood, C. Slocomb, Steven C. Amstrup, George M. Durner, Kristin Simac, and A. P. Pessier, "An Experimental Investigation of Chemical Communication in the Polar Bear," *Journal of Zoology* 295, no. 1 (2015): 36–43.

60 "Los osos polares vuelven al circo," *Farodevigo.es*, August 9, 2009, www.farodevigo.es/comarcas/2009/08/09/osos-polares-vuelven-circo/356630.html.

HONORED GUEST AND TEN-LEGGED MENACE

1 Richard Nelson, *Shadow of the Hunter: Stories of Eskimo Life.* (Chicago: University of Chicago Press, 1980), 257–58.

2 Harry Brower Sr. and Karen Brewster, eds., *The Whales, They Give Themselves: Conversations with Harry Brower Sr.* (Fairbanks: University of Alaska Press, 2004), 104. In a scene in Robert Flaherty's classic 1922 ethnographic film *Nanook of the North*, Nanook teaches his son how to handle a bow and arrows by practicing on a small polar bear target made of snow.

3 University of Guelph, Canada, "Nanuq: Polar Bear," www.arctic.uoguelph.ca/cpl/Traditional/traditional/animals/polar_bear.htm. Also see Keith, *Inuit Knowledge of Polar Bears*, 92.

4 See Keith, *Inuit Knowledge of Polar Bears* and Moki Kokoris, "The Flying Bear Spirit, Part Two," Polar Bears International, www.polarbearsinternational.org/news-room/scientists-and-explorers-blog/flying-bear-spirit-part-two.

5 V. V. Pitul'ko and A. V. Kasparov, "Ancient Arctic Hunters: Material Cultural and Survival Strategy," *Arctic Anthropology* 33 (1996): 1–36.

6 Nikolai Nikolaevich Dikov, *Mysteries in the Rocks of Ancient Chukotka: Petroglyphs of Pegtymel'* (Washington, DC: U.S. Department of Interior, National Park Service, Shared Beringian Heritage Program, 1999). Also see Margarita Aleksandrovna Kiriyak, *Early Art of the Northern Far East: The Stone Age* (Washington, DC: U.S. Department of Interior, National Park Service, Shared Beringian Heritage Program, Government Printing Office, 2007).

7 John Muir, who in 1881 accompanied a party that landed on Wrangel Island and claimed it for the United States, commented on the rarity of polar bears in the Bering Strait region. Even under the best circumstances, Muir considered them "poor cattle to depend on for a living"—because there simply were not enough of them. John Muir, *The Writings of John Muir: The Cruise of the Corwin* (Boston and New York: Houghton Mifflin, 1918), 192.

8 Mareike Neuhaus, *That's Raven Talk: Holophrastic Readings of Contemporary Indigenous Literatures* (Regina, Saskatchewan: University of Regina Press, 2011), 81. Susan Georgette, *Brown Bears on the Northern Seward Peninsula, Alaska: Traditional Knowledge and Subsistence Uses in Deering and Shishmaref* (Juneau: State Department of Fish and Game, Division of Subsistence, 2001), 16.

9 Kochneva, *Polar Bear in Material and Spiritual Culture*,

13. Vatslav Seroshevskiy, *The Yakut: An Experiment in Ethnographic Study* (St. Petersburg: Imperial Russian Geographical Society, 1896), 139–40.

10 Kochneva, *Polar Bear in Material and Spiritual Culture*, 35, 62–66.

11 Inge Kleivan, *Iconography of Religions: Arctic Peoples: Eskimos, Greenland and Canada* (Leiden: Brill, 1985), 21.

12 Robert Brightman, *Grateful Prey: Rock Cree Human-Animal Relationships* (Berkeley: University of California Press, 1993), 92.

13 Laugrand and Oosten, "The Bear, a Fellow Hunter," 183, 204.

14 Keith, *Inuit Knowledge of Polar Bears*, 49.

15 Ronald H. Brower Sr., "Cultural Uses of Alaska Marine Animals, Part I" (1978), www.alaskool.org/projects/traditionalife/Brower/Brower-Pt1.htm.

16 Little information exists about the King Island Polar Bear Dance, and I have drawn on the best account: Sergei Bogojavlensky and Robert Fuller, "Polar Bears, Walrus Hides, and Social Solidarity," *The Alaska Journal* 3, no. 2 (1973): 66–76. Bogojavlensky and Fuller reconstructed the islanders' most significant ceremony from pre-WWII photographs and an account by Father Bernhard R. Hubbard, a Jesuit missionary and distinguished explorer and geologist.

17 Diana Haecker, "King Island Dance Group and Diomede Dancers Join to Keep Traditions Alive," *Nome Nugget*, December 20, 2012.

18 Jeff Rennicke, Charles Schwartz, Harry V. Reynolds, and Steven C. Armstrup, *Bears of Alaska in Life and Legend* (Boulder, CO: Roberts Rinehart, 1987), 87.

19 Asen Balikci, *The Netsilik Eskimo* (Garden City, NY: Natural History Press, 1970), 78. Kochneva, *Polar Bear in Material and Spiritual Culture*, 36. Opel and Opel, *Eisbären*, 112.

20 Ray Edinger, *Fury Beach: The Four-Year Odyssey of Captain John Ross and the Victory* (Berkeley: Berkeley Hardcover, 2003), 68. Kenn Harper, "Tulluahiu's Wooden Leg," *Nunatsiaq News Online*, March 25, 2011, www.nunatsiaqonline.ca/stories/article/taissumani_march_25/. Ross later heard that Tulluahiu was soon able to accompany other Inuit on a seal hunt again. He supposedly used a muskox skull on the bottom of the peg leg for deep-snow walking, with the skull acting much like a snowshoe.

21 B. G. Olsen and Mike Miller, eds., *Blood on the Arctic Snow* (Seattle: Superior Publishing Co., 1956), 93.

22 Keith, *Inuit Knowledge of Polar Bears*, 47–53.

23 Wenzel, "Inuit and Polar Bears," 94.

24 Rasmussen, *The Bear in the Ice Hole*, 2. Rasmussen, who at one time pursued an opera and acting career, was an

expert musher—the first European to travel the famed Northwest Passage by dogsled. In 1910, he established the Thule Trading Station at Cape York, together with Peter Freuchen, and later went on six exploratory and ethnographic journeys known as the Thule Expeditions. Born to a Danish missionary father and an Inuit-Danish mother, he was fluent in Kalaallisut, as he grew up working and playing with Native Greenlanders.

25 Ibid., 1–7.

26 Malaurie, "A Bear Hunt," 344.

27 Rasmussen, *The Bear in the Ice Hole*, 2.

28 H. Ostermann, ed., "Knud Rasmussen's Posthumous Notes on the Life and Doings of the East Greenlanders in the Olden Times," *Meddelser om Grønland* 109, no. 1 (1938): 195.

29 Rasmussen, *The Bear in the Ice Hole*, 3.

30 Malaurie, "A Bear Hunt," 343.

31 Ibid.

32 Waldemar Bogoras, *The Chukchee*, part 2, "Religion" (New York: G. E. Stechert and Co., 1909), 324–25.

33 Ibid. For a postmodern, non-Native take on such an encounter see Josh Medsker, "Qupqugiaq: An Alaskan Folk Tale Retold," *Brooklyn Rail*, May 4, 2011, www.brooklynrail.org/2011/05/express/qupqugiaq-an-alaskan-folk-tale-retold.

34 Vilhjalmur Stefansson, *The Stefánsson-Anderson Arctic Expedition of the American Museum, 1919*, vol. 14 (London: Forgotten Books, 2013), 202. Originally printed in *Anthropological Papers* 14, American Museum of Natural History, 1919.

35 Kochneva, *Polar Bear in Material and Spiritual Culture*, 20–21.

36 Madara Mason, "Blog 5 Ten-Legged Polar Bear, What?" *English 350: Literature of Alaska and the Yukon Territories* (blog), Department of English, University of Alaska Fairbanks, http://northernlit.community.uaf.edu/2012/10/.

A TASTE OF THE WILD

1 Sylvain Bonhommeau, Laurent Dubroca, Olivier Le Pape, Julien Barde, David M. Kaplan, Emmanuel Chassot, and Anne-Elise Nieblas, "Eating Up the World's Food Web and the Human Trophic Level," *Proceedings of the National Academy of Sciences of the United States of America* 110, no. 51 (2013): 20617–20.

2 Friedrich Martens and Isaac de La Peyrère, *A Collection of Documents on Spitzbergen and Greenland, Comprising a tr. from F. Martens' Voyage to Spitzbergen: A tr. from I. de la Peyrère's Histoire du Groenland: And God's Power and Providence in the Preservation of Eight Men* (London: Hakluyt Society, 1855), 279. Valerian Albanov, *In the Land of White Death: An Epic Story of Survival in the Siberian Arctic* (New York: Modern Library, 2000), 68.

3 "Exceedingly coarse": Constantine John Phipps, *A Voyage towards the North Pole: Undertaken by His Majesty's Command 1773* (London: W. Bowyer and J. Nichols, 1774), 185. "Strongly scented": Various authors, *Cooking Alaskan by Alaskans* (Seattle: Alaska Northwest Books, 1983), 234. "Passable, with a taste akin to lamp oil": Charles Francis Hall, *Life with the Esquimaux: The Narrative of Captain Charles Francis Hall of the Whaling Barque George Henry from the 29th May, 1860, to the 13th September, 1862* (Cambridge: Cambridge University Press, 2011), 107. "Very good flesh and better than our Venison": Friedrich Martens and Isaac de La Peyrère, *Collection of Documents*, 279.

4 Valerian Albanov, *In the Land of White Death*, 68.

5 Adolf Erik Nordenskiöld, *The Voyage of the Vega Round Asia and Europe*, vols. 1–2 (London: Macmillan and Co., 1881), 144.

6 William Scoresby, *An Account of the Arctic Regions: With a Description of the Northern Whale-Fisheries*, vol. 1 (Edinburgh: Archibald Constable & Co., 1820), 520.

7 Elisha Kent Kane, *Arctic Explorations: The Second and Last United States Grinnell Expedition in Search of Sir John Franklin* (Hartford, CT: R. W. Bliss, 1868), 396.

8 Majik Imaje, "Polar Bears!" *A Blog of Ice*, http://majikimaje.com/WordPress/tag/eat/.

9 Jeff Rennicke, *Bears of Alaska in Life and Legend* (Boulder, CO: Roberts Rinehart Publishers, 1987), 53.

10 Friedrich Martens and Isaac de La Peyrère, *Collection of Documents*, 81.

11 Valerian Albanov, *In the Land of White Death*, 69.

12 Kåre Rodahl, "The Toxic Effects of Polar Bear Liver," *Skrifter* 92 (1949), review in Guy Marier, "Recent Studies on Vitamins," *Arctic* 4, no. 1 (1951): 62–64.

13 Salomon August Andrée, Nils Strindberg, and Knud Fraenkel, *En ballon vers le pôle: Le drame de l'expédition Andrée d'après les notes et documents retrouvés à l'île Blanche publiés par la Société suédoise d'anthropologie et de géographie* (Paris: Librairie Plon, 1931), 138, 141. This book contains the edited journals and other documents of the expedition, published posthumously.

14 Ernst Adam Tryde, *De döda på Vitön: Sanningen om Andrée. [The Dead on White Island: The Truth about Andree]* (Stockholm: Bonniers förlag, 1952).

15 Alec Wilkinson, *The Ice Balloon: S. A. Andree and the Heroic Age of Arctic Exploration* (New York: Vintage, 2013), 72, 223. Bernhard Hantzsch and L. H. Neatby, *My Life among the Eskimos: Baffinland Journeys in the Years 1909 to 1911* (Saskatoon: University of Saskatchewan, 1977). To test the parasite's stamina, researchers deep-froze

polar bear meat for up to six years and still could not kill *Trichinella*, the roundworm responsible for the disease.

16   H. Ostermann, ed., "Knud Rasmussen's Posthumous Notes on the Life and Doings of the East Greenlanders in the Olden Times," *Meddelser om Grønland* 109, no. 1 (1938): 194.

17   Laugrand and Oosten, "The Bear, a Fellow Hunter," 194.

18   Kochneva, *Polar Bear in Material and Spiritual*, 55.

19   Ibid., 54.

20   Ibid., 55.

21   Flora Beardy and Robert Coutts, eds., *Voices from Hudson Bay: Cree Stories from York Factory* (Montreal and Kingston: McGill-Queen's University Press, 1996), 39–40.

22   Keith, *Inuit Knowledge of Polar Bears*, 63.

23   This feasting was part of a "work party": while children were playing and the men rehashed details of the hunt, women scraped the bearskin clean. This was an arduous job, which could take two or three women several hours. James W. Van Stone, *Point Hope, an Eskimo Village in Transition* (Seattle: University of Washington Press, 1962), 34.

24   Gwladys Fouché, "Bear Necessities," *The Guardian*, November 16, 2007.

25   Jeff Dyrek, email message to author, Nov. 25, 2014.

26   Nina Berglund, "Skiers Shot Polar Bear on Svalbard," *News in English*, April 19, 2013.

27   "Thanksgiving on the Bering Strait's Little Diomede Island," *Alaska Dispatch*, November 21, 2012.

THE TRANSFORMATIVE BEAR

1   Trott, "The Gender of the Bear," 17.

2   Tim Ingold, *The Perception of the Environment: Essays on Livelihood, Dwelling and Skill* (London and New York: Routledge, 2000), 125.

3   David Crantz, *The History of Greenland: Including an Account of the Mission Carried on by the United Brethren in That Country* (London: Longman, 1820), 196. Torngarsuk is also sometimes spelled "Tornarssuk."

4   Daniel Merkur, *Powers Which We Do Not Know: The Gods and Spirits of the Inuit* (Moscow: Idaho University Press, 1991), 232–33.

5   E. W. Hawkes, *The Labrador Eskimo* (Ottawa: Canada Department of Mines, 1916), 124–25. Knud Rasmussen, *Myths and Tales from Greenland* (Copenhagen, Christiania, Berlin, London: Nordisk Forlag, 1921), 96.

6   Benjamin Kohlmeister and George Kmoch, *Journal of a Voyage from Okkak, on the Coast of Labrador, to Ungava Bay, Westward of Cape Chudleigh* (London: W. McDowall, 1814), 50–51.

7   David Crantz, *The History of Greenland: Containing a Description of the Country, and Its Inhabitants and Particu-*

larly, a Relation of the Mission, Carried on for above These Thirty Years by the Unitas Fratrum, at New Herrnhuth and Lichtenfels, in That Country* (London: Brethren's Society for the Furtherance of the Gospel among the Heathen, 1767), 206.

8   Harrison Robertson Thornton, *Among the Eskimos of Wales, Alaska 1890–93* (Baltimore, MD: Johns Hopkins Press, 1931), 164.

9   Hans Egede, *A Description of Greenland* (London: T. and J. Allman, 1818), 191–92. Born in 1890, Andreassen became a talented portraitist after his conversion. In 1919, he met Knud Rasmussen and helped illustrate the Fourth Thule Expedition's report. His pencil drawings are the best graphic representations of Greenlandic shamanistic practices and beliefs.

10   Knud Rasmussen, "Intellectual Culture of the Iglulik Eskimos," *Report of the Fifth Thule Expedition, 1921-24*, vol. 7, no. 1 (Copenhagen: Nordisk Forlag, 1929), 38.

11   Daniel Merkur, *Becoming Half Hidden: Shamanism and Initiation Among the Inuit* (New York: Garland, 1992), 233–46.

12   Merete Demant Jakobsen, *Shamanism: Traditional and Contemporary Approaches to the Mastery of Spirits and Healing* (New York and Oxford: Berghahn Books, 1999), 54–55.

13   H. Ostermann, ed., "Knud Rasmussen's Posthumous Notes on the Life and Doings of the East Greenlanders in Olden Times," *Report of the Sixth and Seventh Thule Expedition, 1931–33*, vol. 109 (Copenhagen: C. A. Reitzel), 107.

14   Ibid., 95.

15   Patricia Sutherland, "Shamanism in the Iconography of Palaeo-Eskimo Art," in *The Archeology of Shamanism*, ed. Neil S. Price (London and New York: Routledge, 2002), 135–46. László Zsolt Zságer and Péter Pázmány, "Miniature Carvings in the Canadian Dorset Culture: The Dorset Belief 'System,'" *Freeside Europe Online*, 2012, www.kodolanyi.hu/freeside/issues/issue7.

16   Edmund Carpenter, ed., *Upside Down: Arctic Realities* (Houston: Menil Foundation, 2011), 49. G. LeMoine, J. W. Helmer, and D. Hanna, "Altered States: Human-Animal Transformational Images in Dorset Art," in *The Symbolic Role of Animals in Archaeology*, ed. K. Ryan and P. J. Crabtree (Philadelphia: University of Pennsylvania Museum, 1995), 38–49.

17   Edmund Carpenter, *Man and Art in the Arctic* (Browning, MT: Museum of the Plains Indian, 1964).

18   Knud Rasmussen, *Eskimo Folk-Tales* (Copenhagen and London: Gyldendal, 1921), 104–5.

19   Alexander B. Dolitsky and Henry N. Michael, *Fairy Tales and Myths of the Bering Strait Chukchi* (Juneau: Alaska-Siberia Research Center, 1997), 23.

20 Sutherland, "Shamanism in the Iconography of Palaeo-Eskimo Art," 140.

21 *Federal Register* 78, no. 232 (December 3, 2013): 72711–12.

22 Dolitsky and Michael, *Fairy Tales and Myths*, 19.

23 Daniel Merkur, *Powers Which We Do Not Know: The Gods and Spirits of the Inuit* (Moscow: University of Idaho Press, 1991), 125. Harold Seidelman and James Turner, *The Inuit Imagination* (New York: Thames and Hudson, 1994), 73–74.

24 Knud Rasmussen, *The People of the Polar North: A Record* (London: K. Paul, Trench, Trübner and Co., 1908), 176.

25 Ole Knudsen, *Inuit Star Lore* (Buffalo: Science First/Starlab, 2008), 19.

26 Regitze Margrethe Søby, "The Eskimo Animal Cult," *Folk* 11–12 (1969/1970): 45.

27 Maranda and Maranda, "Of Bears and Spouses," 109. Merkur, *Powers Which We Do Not Know*, 231.

28 Andrei A. Popov, "Tavgitsy," *Trudy Instituta antropologii i etnografii* 1, no. 5 (1936): 63–79.

29 Galina Nikolaevna Gracheva, "Nganasan Shaman Costume," in *Shamanism in Siberia*, ed. Vilmos Diószegi and Mihály Hoppál (Budapest: Akadémiai Kiadó, 1978).

30 Aado Lintrop, "The Incantations of Tubyaku," *Studies in Siberian Shamanism and Religions of the Uralic Peoples* (Tartu: Shamaaniraamat, 1995).

31 Waldemar Bogoras, *The Chukchee*, Memoirs of the American Museum of Natural History, vol. 11 (New York: Johnson Reprint Corporation, 1909), 256. Lars Krutak, "St. Lawrence Island Joint-Tattooing: Spiritual/Medicinal Functions and Intercontinental Possibilities," *Études/Inuit/Studies* 23, nos. 1–2 (1999): 229–52.

32 Krutak, "St. Lawrence Island Joint-Tattooing," 284. Bodil Kaalund, *The Art of Greenland: Sculpture, Crafts, Painting* (Berkeley: University of California Press, 1983), 23–26.

33 Henry Goddard Leach, *Angevin Britain and Scandinavia*, vol. 6 (Cambridge, MA: Harvard University Press, 1921), 212.

34 Jón Árnason, *Icelandic Legends*, vol. 2 (London: Longmans, Green, and Co., 1866), cxiii.

35 Adalheidur Gudmundsdóttir, "The Werewolf in Medieval Icelandic Literature," *Journal of English and Germanic Philology* 106, no. 3 (2007): 283.

36 Galway Kinnell, *Three Books: Body Rags; Mortal Acts, Mortal Words; The Past* (Boston: Houghton Mifflin Harcourt, 2002), 67–70. For a closer reading of the poem, see Cary Nelson, *Our Last First Poets: Vision and History in Contemporary American Poetry* (Champaign: University of Illinois Press, 1981), 71–76, available at "On the Porcupine and the Bear," *Modern American Poetry* (blog), www.english.illinois.edu/maps/poets/g_l/kinnell/bear.htm.

37 Erica Hill, "Animals as Agents: Hunting Ritual and Relational Ontologies in Pre-Historic Alaska and Chukotka," *Cambridge Archaeological Journal* 21, no. 3 (2011): 408. The poem's hunter uses an ingenious polar bear "death pill," a method described by an Inupiaq elder from Barrow. In this technique, a bowhead-baleen strip sharpened at both ends is bent and tied with sinew. This is wrapped with a thin layer of seal blubber and left to freeze. The weapon is then dropped at a sea-ice lead, where a bear might devour it. Stomach acids quickly digest the sinew, causing the snare to spring open and pierce the animal's stomach. See Ronald H. Brower Sr., "Cultural Uses of Alaska Marine Mammals, Part II" (1978), www.alaskool.org/projects/traditionalife/Brower/Brower-Pt2.htm.

38 "An Interview with Galway Kinnell, 2001," by Daniela Gioseffi, *Hayden's Ferry Review* 31 (Fall/Winter 2002–3), available at *Poets USA* (blog), www.poetsusa.com/kinnell_interview.html.

39 Raymond Ian Page, *Chronicles of the Vikings: Records, Memorials, and Myths* (Toronto: University of Toronto Press, 1995), 69.

40 Edmund Carpenter, ed., *Upside Down: Arctic Realities* (Houston: Menil Foundation, 2011), 16–17.

HELPER AND PROTECTOR

1 Piper Grosswendt, "Polar Bear Mascot Puts New Paw Forward," *The Bowdoin Orient* 138, no. 6 (2008), http://bowdoinorient.com/article/3813. Bowdoin's ice-hockey teams to this day are the Polar Bears—but my alma mater's Nanooks will kick their furry butts any day.

2 Patrick Delaforce, *The Polar Bears: Monty's Left Flank: From Normandy to the Relief of Holland with the 49th Division* (Stroud, Gloucestershire: Chancellor Press, 1995).

3 Hope B. Werness, *The Continuum Encyclopedia of Animal Symbolism in Art* (New York: Continuum, 2006), 213.

4 Office of the Prime Minister of Iceland, "A Brief History of the Icelandic Coat of Arms," http://eng.forsaetisraduneyti.is/state-symbols/icelandic-coat-of-arms/history/.

5 Kochneva, *Polar Bear in Material and Spiritual Culture*, 86; Avataq Cultural Institute, "Traditional Medicine," www.avataq.qc.ca/en/Nunavimmiuts/Traditional-Medicine/Illnesses/Skin-Problems. Halldór Hermannsson, "Jón Guðmundsson and His Natural History of Iceland," *Islandica* 15 (1924): 14–15. Emil Brass, *Aus dem Reiche der Pelze [The World of Furs]* (Berlin: Verlag der Neuen Pelzwaren-Zeitung und Kürschner-Zeitung, 1911), 543–58.

6 Kochneva, *Polar Bear in Material and Spiritual Culture*, 87.

7 Vladimir G. Bogoraz, *Chukchi Religion*, vol. 2 (Leningrad: Izdatel'stvo Instituta, 1939), 100–101. The Nanaits of the Amur region swallowed the eyes of brown bears whole, to improve vision.

8 Adolf Erik Nordenskiöld, *The Voyage of the Vega Round Asia and Europe* (London: Macmillon and Co., 1881), 284.

9 Alexander Leslie, *The Arctic Voyages of Adolf Erik Nordenskiöld, 1858–1879* (Cambridge: Cambridge University Press, 2011), 380.

10 Nordenskiöld, *Voyage of the Vega*, 507.

11 Kochneva, *Polar Bear in Material and Spiritual Culture*, 21, 80.

12 Knud Rasmussen, *The People of the Polar North: A Record* (London: K. Paul, Trench, Trübner and Co., 1908), 138. Bodil Kaalund, *The Art of Greenland: Sculpture, Crafts, Painting* (Berkeley: University of California Press, 1983), 16–19.

13 Ludwig Kumlien, "Fragmentary Notes on the Eskimo of Cumberland Gulf," *Bulletin of the United States National Museum* 14–15 (1879): 45–46.

14 Edward L. Keithahn and George Aden Ahgupuk, *Alaskan Igloo Tales* (Anchorage: Alaska Northwest Publishing Company, 1974), 11.

15 R. Jordan, "The University of Pennsylvania Museum Collection of Chipped Stone Amulets," *Anthropological Papers of the University of Alaska* 19, no. 2 (1980): 33–35.

16 Harrison Robertson Thornton, *Among the Eskimos of Wales, Alaska, 1890–93* (Baltimore, MD: Johns Hopkins Press, 1931), 227–28.

17 Martin Appelt, email message to author, Dec. 20, 2013. Knud Rasmussen, *Greenland, along the Polar Sea* (New York: Stokes, 1929), 156–58. Wilton Derek, Cynthia Colosimo, and Janet McNaughton, *The Polar Bear in the Rock: Two Windows on the World* (Happy Valley–Goose Bay, Newfoundland, Labrador: Institute of Memorial University, 2010).

18 Franz Boas, *The Central Eskimo*, Sixth Annual Report of the Bureau of Ethnology to the Secretary of the Smithsonian Institution, 1884–85 (Washington, DC: Government Printing Office, 1888), 639.

19 Kai Birket-Smith, *The Eskimos* (London: Methuen, 1959), 166.

20 Edwin S. Hall, *The Eskimo Storyteller: Folktales from Noatak, Alaska* (Knoxville: University of Tennessee Press, 1975), 262–63.

21 Sakiasi Qaunaq, *The Orphan and the Polar Bear* (Iqaluit, Nunavut: Inhabit Media, 2011).

22 Hall, *Eskimo Storyteller*, 179–80.

23 Norman Allee Chance, *The Iñupiat and Arctic Alaska: An Ethnography of Development* (Fort Worth: Holt, Rinehart and Winston, 1990), 119.

24 Jón Árnason, *Icelandic Legends*, vol. 2 (London: Longmans, Green, and Co., 1866), xxxi, xxix. The archetypal allure of the polar bear is also the subject of Sally Ruddy's painting *The Guardian* (1997), which depicts an enormous

alter ego that towers over but protects the nude and vulnerable female body, a self-portrait of the artist. Werness, *Continuum Encyclopedia*, 37.

25 Árnason, *Icelandic Legends*, cxiv.

26 The American surrealist illustrator and set and costume designer Edward Gorey felt differently about the baby on the rug. In one collection of gothic quatrains, a newborn acquires decidedly unpleasant aspects from his furry white mattress: "The Baby, lying meek and quiet / Upon the customary rug, / Has dreams about rampage and riot, / And will grow up to be a thug." Edward Gorey, *The Fatal Lozenge: An Alphabet* (New York: Ivan Obolensky, 1960).

27 Árnason, *Icelandic Legends*, 657–59.

28 T. J. Oleson, "Polar Bears in the Middle Ages," *Canadian Historical Review* 34 (1950): 49.

29 Aevar Petersen, email message to the author, Nov. 24, 2014.

30 Árnason, *Icelandic Legends*, cxiv.

31 Ibid., xxx. When strongly religious societies are under stress, accusations of witchcraft often mushroom, providing scapegoats and cathartic relief.

32 Jón Baldur Hlíðberg and Sigurður Ægisson, *Meeting with Monsters: An Illustrated Guide to the Monsters of Iceland* (Reykjavik: Forlagid, 2008), 10–13.

33 Walter William Skeat, *An Etymological Dictionary of the English Language* (London: Clarendon Press, 1910), 713.

34 Heinrich Heine, *Atta Troll* (New York: B. W. Huebsch, 1914), canto 8, www.gutenberg.org/files/31305/31305-h/31305-h.htm. For a critical assessment, see Ritchie Robertson, "The Last Mock Epic? Heine's *Atta Troll*," in *Mock-Epic Poetry from Pope to Heine* (Oxford: Oxford University Press, 2009).

35 Philip Pullman, *The Northern Lights* (London: Scholastic, 1995), 214. http://worldwildlife.org/partnerships/the-golden-compass.

36 Marshall University Libraries, "Banned Books: The Golden Compass," www.marshall.edu/library/bannedbooks/books/goldencompass.asp.

LOVER, SUPER-MALE, MATE

1 Michel Pastoureau, *The Bear: History of a Fallen King* (Cambridge, MA: Belknap Press, 2011), 68–78.

2 Francisque Michel, *Chroniques Anglo-normandes*, vol. 2 (Rouen: E. Frère, 1836), 104.

3 James Hogg, *The Surpassing Adventures of Allan Gordon*, ed. G. H. Hughes (Glasgow: James Hogg Society, 1987), 16. Sara Moss, "Romanticism on Ice: Coleridge, Hogg and the Eighteenth-Century Missions to Greenland," *Érudit* 45 (February 2007), www.erudit.org/revue/ron/2007/v/n45/015816ar.html. Hogg (1770–1835), born in rural

poverty, worked as a shepherd before becoming one of the most prolific Scottish writers of the nineteenth century.

4   Hogg, *Surpassing Adventures*, 47. Originally included in volume 1 of Hogg's *Tales and Sketches* (Glasgow: Blackie and Son, 1887), Gordon's adventure is missing from subsequent editions, perhaps because it was thought too "indelicate" for Victorian tastes.

5   Sick of *Elle*'s repetitive bear symbolism, one reviewer summed it up thus: "She gets plopped by a bear, sleeps in a [butchered] bear, eats bear, wears bear, dreams of bears, turns into a bear, sleeps with a bear, owns a bear, wants to be a bear . . ." John Hanson, March 26, 2014, comment on Goodreads, www.goodreads.com/book/show/867331 .Elle#other_reviews.

6   In yet another version, a Canadian historical novel from 1899, Marguerite kills a she–polar bear and, like Hogg's Allan Gordon, tames the orphan cub ("François") as a companion. Unlike Allen Gordon's bear, this one is a classic child substitute. Arthur Phillips Stabler, *The Legend of Marguerite de Roberval* (Pullman: Washington State University Press, 1972). Edward E. Leslie and Sterling Seagrave, *Desperate Journeys, Abandoned Souls: True Stories of Castaways and Other Survivors* (Boston: Houghton Mifflin Books, 1998).

7   Thomas Elsaesser and Michael Wedel, eds., *A Second Life: German Cinema's First Decades* (Amsterdam: Amsterdam University Press, 1996), 103.

8   *Le Petit Journal*, July 11, 1891. Pastoureau, *The Bear*, 184.

9   Mary McCarthy, *The Group* (Boston: Houghton Mifflin Harcourt, 1991), 165.

10 Ian McEwan, *Solar* (New York: Nan A. Talese, 2010), 104, 107.

11 Eva Olympia, March 2, 2008, comment on COSMiQ (author's translation), www.cosmiq.de/qa/show/718054/ Welche-Gedichte-sind-sehr-schoen-aber-gleichermassen-obszoen/.

12 Tanya Krzywinska, *Sex and the Cinema* (New York: Columbia University Press/Wallflower Press, 2006), 190. Sacher-Masoch's autobiographical novella, *Venus in Furs* (1870), is his best-known work. Present-day role-playing fans who slip into animal costumes (many of whom profess sexual attraction to such costumes) are called "furries." There also is "plushophilia," an erotic fetish for stuffed animals.

13 Audrey Schulman, *The Cage* (Chapel Hill, NC: Algonquin Books, 1994), 2, 7.

14 In yet another playful melding of sexual and species identities, a subset of male bisexual and gay North American men—large-framed, hirsute guys who project an image of rugged masculinity—self-identifies as "bears." In that community's slang, "polar bear" refers to an older, graying, or white-haired gay man. The bear gay community has its own flag, an equivalent of the rainbow flag. The International Bear Brotherhood Flag is striped in various hues that represent the fur colors of the world's bear species and, naturally, includes a white stripe.

15 Monte Reel, *Between Man and Beast: An Unlikely Explorer and the African Adventure that Took the Victorian World by Storm* (New York: Anchor Books, 2013), 352.

16 Derocher, *Polar Bears*, 210. Ted Alvarez, "We Are Literally Breaking Polar Bear Penises Now," *Grist*, http://grist.org/ list/we-are-literally-breaking-polar-bear-penises-now/. Christian Sonne, Markus Dyck, Frank F. Rigét, Jens-Erik Beck Jensen, Lars Hyldstrup, Robert J. Letcher, et al., "Penile Density and Globally Used Chemicals in Canadian and Greenland Polar Bears," *Environmental Research* 137 (February 2015): 287–91.

17 Tim Moore, *Frost on My Moustache: The Arctic Exploits of a Lord and a Loafer* (New York: St. Martin's Press, 2001), 236.

18 Y. Makhovskiy, *Fireball: Legends, Beliefs, Folk Tales of Eskimos*, trans. S. Tel'nyuk (Magadan), 319, quoted in Kochneva, *Polar Bear in Material and Spiritual Culture*, 9.

19 Saladin d'Anglure, "Nanook, Super-Male," 187.

20 Trott, "The Gender of the Bear," 20.

21 Malaurie, "A Bear Hunt," 344.

22 Some cultural anthropologists associate shamanism in general with schizophrenia, though not without controversy; see Richard Noll, "Shamanism and Schizophrenia: A State-Specific Approach to the 'Schizophrenia Metaphor' of Shamanic States," *American Ethnologist* 10, no. 3 (Aug. 1983): 443–59. Saladin d'Anglure, "Nanook, Super-Male," 192.

23 Ibid., 189.

ARCHETYPE, ROLE MODEL, ECO AMBASSADOR

1   Rob Waugh, "Nature at Its Most Savage," *Daily Mail Online*, December 9, 2011, www.dailymail.co.uk/sciencetech/ article-2071638/Polar-bears-Cannibal-pictures-prove-theyll-eat-bear-cubs.html. Female zoo polar bears that abandon or eat their cubs defy the caring-mother image. Such infanticides could be similar to obsessive pacing or the biting of cage bars, "stereotypic" behavior triggered by boredom or stress; or they could result from lack of a mother bear's proper nurturing as a cub. Laura Barton, "Our Soft Spot for the Serial Killer of the Arctic," *The Guardian*, January 9, 2008.

2   Gerrit de Veer, *The Three Voyages of William Barents to the Arctic Regions (1594, 1595, and 1596)* (London: Hakluyt Society, 1853), 207.

3 Gary A. Polis and Christopher A. Myers, "A Survey of Intraspecific Predation among Reptiles and Amphibians," *Journal of Herpetology* 19, no. 1 (1985): 99–107.

4 James W. Brooks, *North to Wolf Country: My Life Among the Creatures of Alaska* (Fairbanks: Epicenter Press, 2004), 218.

5 Marla Cone, *Silent Snow: The Slow Poisoning of the Arctic* (New York: Grove Press, 2005), 207.

6 "Fur and Skin," Polar Bears International, www .polarbearsinternational.org/about-polar-bears/essentials/ fur-and-skin. Seton, "Polar Bear, White Bear, Sea-Bear," 196.

7 *The Portsmouth Herald*, August 20, 1941. Opel and Opel, *Eisbären*, 93. Heinrich Lomer, *Der Rauchwaarenhandel [The Furrier Trade]* (Leipzig: Preußisches Handels-Archiv, 1864), 77–80. Karla Dutton, "Being Proactive for Polar Bears," *Defenders of Wildlife* (blog), www.defendersblog .org/2013/09/being-proactive-for-polar-bears/.

8 Mya Frazier, "Should the Polar Bear Still Sell Coca-Cola?" *The New Yorker*, Nov. 6, 2014. Mike Esterl, "A Frosty Reception for Coca-Cola's White Christmas Cans," *Wall Street Journal*, December 1, 2011. Just a reminder of some collateral costs of sugar-laden soft drinks: Nonrecycled aluminum cans (about 45 percent of the total sold) last up to five centuries before they decompose. They take up landfill space, and energy is needed to produce, ship, col- lect, and recycle them. Aluminum is refined from bauxite, the mining of which also impacts the environment.

9 Alexis Schwarzenbach, *Saving the World's Wildlife: The WWF's First Fifty Years* (London: Profile Books, 2011), 271. "A Shellish Faux Pas," *Earth Island Journal* 12, no. 3 (2011): 17.

10 A. K. Greaves, R. J. Letcher, C. Sonne, and R. Dietz, "Brain Region Distribution and Patterns of Bioaccumulative Per- fluoroalkyl Carboxylates and Sulfonates in East Greenland Polar Bears (*Ursus maritimus*)," *Environmental Toxicology and Chemistry* 32, no. 3 (2013): 713–22.

11 In 2008, Gwich'in Indian hunters near Fort Yukon, Alaska shot such a climate refugee: a polar bear they initially mis- took for an albino or frost-covered grizzly. It was feeding on a lynx carcass, 250 miles inland from the Arctic Ocean. Fort Yukon's oldest resident had just died at the age of 102. "She must have some powerful medicine to bring a polar bear to us," one of the townspeople said, as the Gwich'in live well outside the animal's range.

12 Shel Silverstein's "Bear in There" is a song that also cir- culates in printed, illustrated form. For unfriendly bears in present-day children's literature, one needs to turn to Scandinavians, especially Icelanders, or to earlier times. Jón Sveinsson's *Nonni og Manni* [*Nonni and Manni*], which was adapted to a TV series in the 1980s, features

a monstrous polar bear that threatens to tear apart the young protagonists, but is killed at the last minute. Jón Sveinsson, *Nonni og Manni* (Reykjavík: Arnason, 1925).

13 Sally Carrighar, *Icebound Summer* (Lanham and New York: Derrydale Press, 2000), 49.

14 "Adopt a Polar Bear," Polar Bears International, www .polarbearsinternational.org/adopt.

15 Irus Braverman, *Zooland: The Institution of Captivity* (Stanford: Stanford Law Books, 2013), 57.

16 Andrew E. Derocher, Jon Aars, Steven C. Amstrup, Amy Cutting, Nick J. Lunn, Péter K. Molnár, et al., "Rapid Ecosystem Change and Polar Bear Conservation," *Conser- vation Letters*, February 15, 2013, http://onlinelibrary.wiley .com/doi/10.1111/conl.12009/full.

17 Steven Chase, "Beavers Can't Cut It as National Emblem, but Polar Bears Can, Senator Says," *The Globe and Mail*, October 27, 2011. Jules Verne, *Works of Jules Verne*, ed. Charles F. Horne, vol. 9 (London/New York: Vincent Parke and Company, 1911), 230. Louis Auguste Gustave Doré, *Histoire pittoresque, dramatique et caricaturale de la Sainte-Russie* (Paris: Bry, 1854), 3.

18 Mowat, "White Ghost," 96.

19 Damian Carrington, "U.S. and Russia Unite in Bid to Strengthen Protection for Polar Bear," *The Guardian*, March 5, 2013.

20 Damian Carrington, "Bid to Halt Polar Bear Trade Fails," *The Guardian*, March 7, 2013.

21 Ibid.

22 Bryndís Snæbjörnsdóttir and Mark Wilson, "*Matrix* to Be Part of Polar Lab Exhibition in Anchorage Museum, Alaska," http://snaebjornsdottirwilson.com/matrix/.

23 Heather Ackroyd and Dan Harvey, "Polar Diamond," Ackroyd & Harvey, www.ackroydandharvey.com/polar- diamond/.

24 Olivia Williams, "Life-Size Sculpture of a Polar Bear's Skeleton Which Was Taken on a Tour around the World Is Stolen from a Wiltshire Garden," *Daily Mail*, June 29, 2013.

25 "Climate-Change Messages Visible from Outer Space," *New Scientist*, November 29, 2010, www .newscientist.com/gallery/climate-change-messages- visible-from-space/2.

26 "Westfjords Polar Bear Shot," *Ice News*, May 2, 2011, www .icenews.is/2011/05/02/westfjords-polar-bear-shot/.

27 "Evidence of the Socio-Economic Importance of Polar Bears for Canada," ÉcoRessources Consultants, 2011, www.motherjones.com/files/value_of_polar_bears_in_ canada.pdf.

28 Sherry Simpson, *Dominion of Bears: Living with Wildlife in Alaska* (Lawrence: University Press of Kansas, 2013), 308.

29 Geoff Manaugh and Nicola Twilley, "How the Polar Bear Lost Its Power, and Other Animal Tales," *The Atlantic*, August 1, 2013, www.theatlantic.com/technology/archive/2013/08/how-the-polar-bear-lost-its-power-and-other-animal-tales/278281/.

30 Jon Mooallem, *Wild Ones: A Sometimes Dismaying, Weirdly Reassuring Story about Looking at People Looking at Animals in America* (New York: Penguin, 2013), 22.

31 It has to do more with Lorenz, because he ferreted out the dynamics between market forces and ecological catastrophes (outlined in his 1973 book *Civilized Man's Eight Deadly Sins*); with McLuhan, because he realized how the medium shapes the message; and with Piaget, because he stressed learning from the past and teaching our children well. I prefer these three figures to Barnum, because better promotion of the polar bear will only get us so far. What really is needed is a drastic restructuring of our society, or at least, our economic system.

ANOTHER SEASIDE ATTRACTION

1 "For Hudson Bay Polar Bears, the End Is Already in Sight." *Yale Environment 360*, July 8, 2010, http://e360.yale.edu/feature/for_hudson_bay_polar_bears_the_end_is_already_in_sight/2293/. Jon Mooallem, *Wild Ones: A Sometimes Dismaying, Weirdly Reassuring Story about Looking at People Looking at Animals in America* (New York: Penguin, 2013), 28–29.

2 "Good, but Not for Everyone," online review on *Trip Advisor*, www.tripadvisor.com/ShowUserReviews-g154952-d1228094-r185640015-Great_White_Bear_Tours-Churchill_Manitoba.html.

3 Geoffrey Peake, "From the Glowing Teepee, Thanks," Canoe Onriver Online: Winisk to the Bay, www.canoe.ca/winiskriver/aug15_gpeake.html.

4 Aldo Leopold, "Conservation Esthetic," *Bird-Lore* 40, no. 2 (1938): 101–9. Aldo Leopold, *A Sand County Almanac with Essays on Conservation from Round River* (New York: Ballantine Books, 1966), 284.

5 Unger, *Never Look a Polar Bear in the Eye*, 42. For social status and other reasons for watching polar bears, also see Lemelin and Wiersma, "Gazing upon Nanuk."

6 Mooallem, *Wild Ones*, 71.

7 John Berger, *About Looking* (New York: Vintage, 1992), 4–5.

8 Barry Holstun Lopez, *Arctic Dreams: Imagination and Desire in a Northern Landscape* (New York: Scribner, 1986), 73.

9 Kelsey Eliason, email message to the author, Jan. 12, 2014.

10 David A. Fennell, *Ecotourism* (London: Routledge, 2007), 41. Lemelin and Wiersma "Gazing upon Nanuk," 47–50.

11 Mark Neumann, *On the Rim: Looking for the Grand Canyon* (Minneapolis: University of Minnesota Press, 2001), 22.

12 Harvey Lemelin, Jackie Dawson, Emma J. Stewart, Pat Maher, and Michael Lueck, "Last-Chance Tourism: The Boom, Doom, and Gloom of Visiting Vanishing Destinations," *Current Issues in Tourism* 13, no. 5 (2010): 477–93.

13 Thomas B. Lawrence, Deborah Wickins, and Nelson Phillips, "Managing Legitimacy in Ecotourism," *Tourism Management* 18, no. 5 (1997): 307.

14 Arthur Calder-Marshall, *The Innocent Eye: The Life of Robert J. Flaherty* (New York: Harcourt, Brace and World, 1963), 86.

15 Carl M. Dunrud, *Let's Go! Eighty-five Years of Adventure* (Cody, WY: Words Worth, 1998). While trophy hunting accounts for only a small fraction of all polar bear kills, I examine it at some length for its rich symbolic connotations and contrast with Native hunting.

16 Garry Marvin, "Perpetuating Polar Bears: The Cultural Life of Dead Animals," draft of chapter from Snæbjörnsdóttir and Wilson, eds., *nanoq: flat out and bluesome*, 10.

17 On their westbound journey, Lewis and Clark killed dozens of grizzlies, often for scientific purposes. One that they brought back served as the type specimen for the species' formal description and naming. Paul A. Johnsgard, *Lewis and Clark on the Great Plains: A Natural History* (Lincoln: University of Nebraska Press, 2003), 45.

18 "Taxidermists Profits Mount," *Miami News*, March 14, 1966.

19 Irving C. Rosse, "The First Landing on Wrangel Island, with Some Remarks on the Northern Inhabitants," *Journal of the American Geographical Society of New York* 15 (1883): 168.

20 Ernest William Hawkes, *The Labrador Eskimo* (Ottawa: Government Printing Bureau, 1916), 83.

21 Lew Freedman, "For Some Big-Game Hunters, Polar Bears Offer a Shot at a Dream," *Chicago Tribune*, March 28, 2004. The author of this article, admittedly a journalist not a hunter, calls the bears "predatory pests." Henry Charles Howard, *The Encyclopedia of Sport* (London: Lawrence and Bullen, 1900), 88.

22 Sarkis Atamian, *The Bears of Manley: Adventures of an Alaskan Trophy Hunter in Search of the Ultimate Symbol* (Anchorage: Publication Consultants, 1995), 75–76.

23 John Berger, *About Looking*, 6.

24 Rick Herscher, "Join Us," Polar Bear, www.polarbearhunting.net.

25 Milton M. R. Freeman and George W. Wenzel, "The Nature and Significance of Polar Bear Conservation Hunting in the Canadian Arctic," *Arctic* 59, no. 1 (2005): 21–30.

26 Megan Waters, Naomi Rose, and Paul Todd, *The Economics of Polar Bear Hunting in Canada* (Washington, DC,

and Yarmouth Port, ME: Humane Society International and International Fund for Animal Welfare, 2009), 1–20.

27   Ian Stirling, "Polar Bears and Seals in the Eastern Beaufort Sea and Amundsen Gulf: A Synthesis of Population Trends and Ecological Relationships over Three Decades," *Arctic* 55, Supplement 1 (2002): 70.

28   "Custom Taxidermy Mounting Price List," Wildlife Taxidermy Studios, www.wildlifetaxidermy.info/Custom-Taxi-price-list-info-1.html.

29   *Life*, May 4, 1962; Bill Miller, "Arthur Dubs: Rogue Valley Hunter," *Mail Tribune*, www.mailtribune.com/article/20130630/News/306300334. The bear was exhibited at the Seattle World's Fair of 1962, but its present whereabouts are unknown. A producer and director of 1970s documentary films, Dubs supposedly was location scouting when he first sighted his trophy. Ironically, one of his films is titled *Vanishing Wilderness* (1974). In the Disneyesque style of the times, the trailer's voiceover offers "wholesome family entertainment," asking viewers to "see this wilderness paradise before civilization sweeps it away forever." Vicariously, audiences also "face the terrifying wrath of the Queen of the North," as a female polar bear defends her cubs against a sled dog—was it provoked for good footage? Heinz Sielman and Arthur R. Dubs, prod. and dir., www.amazon.com/Vanishing-Wilderness-Rex-Allen/dp/B00BP4VPWC/ref=sr_1_3?s=movies-tv&ie=UTF8&qid=1453225048&sr=1-3&keywords=vanishing+wilderness%5B%5Bthis.

30   Robert E. Peary, *The North Pole: Its Discovery in 1909 under the auspices of the Peary Arctic Club* (New York: Frederick A. Stokes Co., 1910), 130, 175.

31   Melissa Milgrom, *Still Life: Adventures in Taxidermy* (Boston and New York: Houghton Mifflin Harcourt, 2011), 6–7.

32   William T. Hornaday, *Taxidermy and Zoological Collecting: A Complete Handbook for the Amateur Taxidermist, Collector, Osteologist, Museum-Builder, Sportsman, and Traveller* (New York: Charles Scribner's Sons, 1894), viii. Gregory J. Dehler, *The Most Defiant Devil: William Temple Hornaday and His Controversial Crusade to Save American Wildlife* (Charlottesville: University of Virginia Press, 2013).

33   Philip C. Ritterbush, "Art and Science as Influences on the Early Development of Natural History Collections," *Proceedings of the Biological Society of Washington* 82 (1969): 568. Werner Paravicini, "Tiere aus dem Norden," *Deutsches Archiv für die Erforschung des Mittelalters* 59, no. 2 (2003): 578–79.

34   H. D. Schepelern, "The Museum Wormianum: A Note on the Illustration of 1655," *Journal of the History of Collections* 2, no.1 (1990): 81–85.

35   Mark Wilson, email message to the author, Jan. 24, 2014.

36   Museum curator Rachel Poliquin coined this term for the practice of taxidermy in general. Rachel Poliquin, *The Breathless Zoo: Taxidermy and the Cultures of Longing* (University Park: Pennsylvania State University Press, 2012), 1–10.

37   I lifted this quote from an entertaining article that in fact is about dragons: Philip Hoare's "From Smaug to the Clangers: A Brief History of Dragons," *The Guardian*, September 9, 2013.

38   Lopez, *Arctic Dreams*, 79.

Crest of Barentsburg, at latitude
78 degrees north. The name of this
Svalbard town, which is administered
by Norway but largely inhabited by
Russian miners, commemorates the
Dutch explorer Willem Barentsz.
The peaceable bears holding flags
symbolize friendship between the
two nations. Courtesy of Wikimedia
Commons.

ASSOCIATIONS AND WEBSITES

For readers interested in the biology of polar bears, their management, and conservation efforts related to them, as well as some of the art and history discussed in this book, I suggest the following websites, which have been helpful to me:

ALASKA NANUUQ COMMISSION
www.thealaskananuuqcommission.org

BRYNDÍS SNÆBJÖRNSDÓTTIR AND MARK WILSON
www.snaebjornsdottirwilson.com
www.radioanimal.org

EISBÄREN IM ZOO—POLAR BEARS IN ZOOS
ullijseisbaeren.wordpress.com

GREAT BEAR FOUNDATION
www.greatbear.org

INTERNATIONAL ASSOCIATION FOR BEAR RESEARCH AND MANAGEMENT
www.bearbiology.com

NORTH AMERICAN BEAR CENTER
www.bear.org/website/bear-pages/polar-bear/22-/70-polar-bear-facts.html

POLAR BEAR ALLEY
www.polarbearalley.com

POLAR BEARS INTERNATIONAL
www.polarbearsinternational.org

POLAR BEAR PROGRAMME (RUSSIAN ACADEMY OF SCIENCES)
programmes.putin.kremlin.ru/en/bear/program

POLAR BEAR SPECIALIST GROUP OF THE INTERNATIONAL UNION
FOR CONSERVATION OF NATURE (IUCN) SPECIES SURVIVAL COMMISSION
pbsg.npolar.no/en

Polar bear burglarizing a house
in Churchill, Manitoba, the
mecca of polar bear viewing.
Scavenging bears have become a
problem, and the town closed its
dump and now keeps garbage in
a bear-proof concrete building.
Photo by Marc Gadoury.

SELECTED BIBLIOGRAPHY

Audubon, John James, John Woodhouse Audubon, and John Bachman. *The Viviparous Quadrupeds of North America*, Vol. 2, 281–92. New York: Wiley and Putnam, 1851.

Auger, Emily E. "Dorset and Thule Traditions in Canada." In *The Way of Inuit Art: Aesthetics and History in and Beyond the Arctic*, 67–100. Jefferson, NC: McFarland, 2005.

Bogojavlensky, Sergei, and Robert Fuller. "Polar Bears, Walrus Hides and Social Solidarity." *The Alaska Journal* 3, no. 2 (1973): 66–76.

Collins, Henry. "The Okvik Figurine: Madonna or Bear Mother?" *Folk* 17, no. 2 (1976): 125–32.

Derocher, Andrew E. *Polar Bears: A Complete Guide to Their Biology and Behavior.* Baltimore: Johns Hopkins University Press, 2012.

Dion, Mark. *Polar Bear (Ursus Maritimus).* Köln: Walther König, 2003.

Dittrich, Sigrid. "Geschichte der Eisbären in Menschenhand." *Der Zoofreund*, no. 82 (1991). Available at *Eisbären im Zoo* (blog), https://ullijseisbaeren.wordpress.com/haltungen-enclosures/geschichte-der-eisbaeren-in-menschenhand/.

Ellis, Richard. *On Thin Ice: The Changing World of the Polar Bear.* New York: Knopf, 2009.

Feazel, Charles T. *White Bear: Encounters with the Master of the Arctic Ice.* New York: Ballantine Books, 1990.

Hallowell, A. Irving. "Bear Ceremonialism in the Northern Hemisphere." *American Anthropologist* 28, no. 1 (1926): 1–175.

Harington, C. R. "The Bear behind the Paw." *The Beaver* (Autumn 1966): 14–15.

Harold, Arthur. "The Character of the Polar Bear." *The Strand Magazine*, no. 35 (1908): 302–6.

Ingólfsson, Ólafur, and Øystein Wiig. "Late Pleistocene Fossil Find in Svalbard: The Oldest Remains of a Polar Bear (*Ursus maritimus Phipps*, 1744) Ever Discovered." *Polar Research* 28, no. 3 (2008): 455–62.

Kazlowski, Steven. *The Last Polar Bear: Facing the Truth of a Warming World.* Seattle: Mountaineers Books, 2008.

Keith, Darren E., ed. *Inuit Knowledge of Polar Bears [Inuit Qaujimaningit Nanurnut]: A Project of the Gjoa Haven Hunters' and Trappers' Organization.* Nunavut, Canada: Canadian Circumpolar Institute (CCI) Press, 2005.

Klumbies, Anneliese. *Knut: Der Bär, die Stadt und der Zoo: Eine Berliner Geschichte.* Berlin: Anneliese Klumbies, 2013.

Kochneva, Svetlana. *Polar Bear in Material and Spiritual Culture of the Native Peoples of Chukotka.* Anadyr and Nome: Association of Traditional Marine Mammal Hunters of Chukotka and Alaska Nanuuq Commission, 2007.

Kurtén, Björn. "The Evolution of the Polar Bear, *Ursus maritimus (Phipps)*." *Acta Zoologica Fennica* 108 (1964): 1–26.

Larsen, Helge. "Some Examples of Bear Cult among the Eskimo and Other Northern Peoples." *Folk* 11–12 (1969/1970): 27–42.

Larsen, Thor. *The World of the Polar Bear.* London and New York: Hamlyn, 1978.

Laugrand, Frédéric, and Jarich Oosten. "The Bear, a Fellow Hunter." In *Hunters, Predators and Prey: Inuit Perceptions of Animals*, edited by Frédéric Laugrand and Jarich Oosten, 179–208. New York and Oxford: Berghahn Books, 2015.

Lemelin, Raynald H., and Elaine C. Wiersma. "Gazing upon Nanuk, the Polar Bear: The Social and Visual Dimensions of the Wildlife Gaze in Churchill, Manitoba." *Polar Geography* 30, nos. 1–2 (2007): 37–53.

Lewis-Jones, Huw W. G. "Nelson and the Bear: The Making of an Arctic Myth." *Polar Record* 41, no. 4 (2005): 335–53.

Lønø, Odd. *The Polar Bear in the Svalbard Area.* Oslo: Norsk Polarinstitutt, 1970.

Malaurie, Jean. "A Bear Hunt." In *The Last Kings of Thule: With the Polar Eskimos, as They Face Their Destiny*, 341–46. New York: E. P. Dutton, 1982.

Maranda, Elli Köngäs, and Pierre Maranda. "Of Bears and Spouses: Transformational Analysis of a Myth." In *Structural Models in Folklore and Transformational Essays*, 98–115. The Hague and Paris: Mouton, 1971.

Marvin, Garry. "Perpetuating Polar Bears: The Cultural Life of Dead Animals." In *nanoq: flat out and bluesome: A Cultural Life of Polar Bears*, edited by Bryndís Snæbjörnsdóttir and Mark Wilson, 157–65. London: Black Dog Publishing, 2006.

Maurer, Konrad von. "Waldbär und Wasserbär." *Anzeiger für Kunde der deutschen Vorzeit* 10, no. 11 (1863): 396–400.

Merkur, Daniel. "*Tornarssuk*, the Polar Bear Spirit." In *Powers Which We Do Not Know: The Gods and Spirits of the Inuit*, 227–41. Moscow: Idaho University Press, 1991.

Miller, William Ian. *Audun and the Polar Bear: Luck, Law, and Largesse in a Medieval Tale of Risky Business*. Leiden: Brill, 2008.

Mills, William. *Bears and Men: A Gathering*. Chapel Hill, NC: Algonquin Books, 1986.

Mooallem, Jon. "Bears." In *Wild Ones: A Sometimes Dismaying, Weirdly Reassuring Story about Looking at People Looking at Animals in America*, 13–102. New York: Penguin, 2013.

Mowat, Farley. "White Ghost." In *Sea of Slaughter*, 79–97. Mechanicsburg, PA: Stackpole Books, 2004.

Myers, Steven Lee. "Russia Tries to Save Polar Bears with Legal Hunt." *The New York Times*, April 16, 2007.

Oleson, T. J. "Polar Bears in the Middle Ages." *Canadian Historical Review* 31, no. 1 (1950): 47–55.

Opel, Mechtild, and Wolfgang Opel. *Eisbären: Wanderer auf dünnem Eis*. Berlin: Mana Verlag, 2014.

Ovsyanikov, Nikita. *Polar Bears: Living with the White Bear*. Minneapolis: Voyageur Press, 1996.

Packard, Alpheus Spring. "The Former Southern Limits of the White or Polar Bear." *The American Naturalist* 20 (1886): 655–59.

Perry, Richard. *The World of the Polar Bear*. London: Cassell, 1966.

Randa, Vladimir. *L'ours polaire et les inuit*. Paris: Société d'êtudes linguistiques et anthropologiques de France, 1986.

Rasmussen, Knud. *The Bear in the Ice Hole*. Copenhagen: Royal Danish Ministry of Foreign Affairs, 1962.

Ravelhofer, Barbara. "'Beasts of Recreacion': Henslowe's White Bears." *English Literary Renaissance* 32, no. 2 (2002): 287–23.

Russell, John C. *Nanuq: Cultural Significance and Traditional Knowledge among Alaska Natives*. Nome: Alaska Nanuuq Commission, 2005.

Saladin d'Anglure, Bernard. "Nanook, Super-Male: The Polar Bear in the Imaginary Space and Social Time of the Inuit of the Canadian Arctic." In *Signifying Animals: Human Meaning in the Natural World*, edited by Roy Willis, 178–95. London: Routledge, 1994.

Schimek, Michael. "Der Foto-Eisbär: Ein ungewöhnlicher Erinnerungsträger an schöne Augenblicke." In *Die Macht der Dinge: Symbolische Kommunikation und kulturelles Handeln*, edited by Andreas Hartmann, Peter Höher, Christiane Cantauw, Uwe Meiners, and Silke Meyer, 429–40. Münster: Waxmann Verlag, 2011.

Scoresby, William. "*Ursus Maritimus*: Polar or Greenland Bear." In *An Account of the Arctic Regions, with a Description of the North Whale-Fisheries*, Vol. 1, 517–26. Edinburgh: Archibald Constable and Co., 1820.

Seton, Ernest Thompson. "Polar Bear, White Bear, Sea-Bear, Water-bear, Greenland Bear, Ice Bear, Ice-king, Ice-tiger, Brownie, Nahnook." In *Lives of Game Animals*, 196–228. Boston: Charles T. Branford, 1953.

Shadbolt, Tanya, Geoff York, and Ernest W. T. Cooper. *Icon on Ice: International Trade and Management of Polar Bears*. Vancouver: TRAFFIC North America and WWF Canada, 2012.

Simpson, Sherry. "The Disappearing Ice Bear." In *Dominion of Bears: Living with Wildlife in Alaska*, 203–38. Lawrence: University Press of Kansas, 2013.

Smelcer, John. "The Ten-Footed Polar Bear." In *Last New Land: Stories of Alaska Past and Present*, edited by Wayne Mergler, 413–15. Seattle: Alaska Northwest Books, 2009.

Snæbjörnsdóttir, Bryndís, and Mark Wilson, eds. *nanoq: flat out and bluesome: A Cultural Life of Polar Bears*. London: Black Dog Publishing, 2006.

Søby, Regitze Margrethe. "The Eskimo Animal Cult." *Folk* 11–12 (1969/70): 43–78.

Stirling, Ian. *Polar Bears: A Natural History of a Threatened Species*. Markham, Ontario: Fitzhenry and Whiteside, 2011.

Struzik, Edward. *Arctic Icons: How the Town of Churchill Learned to Love Its Polar Bears*. Markham, Ontario: Fitzhenry and Whiteside, 2014.

Trott, Christopher G. "The Gender of the Bear." *Etudes/Inuit/Studies* 30, no.1 (2006): 89–109.

Unger, Zac. *Never Look a Polar Bear in the Eye: A Family Field Trip to the Arctic's Edge in Search of Adventure, Truth, and Mini-Marshmallows*. New York: Da Capo Press, 2013.

Wenzel, George. "Inuit and Polar Bears: Cultural Observations from a Hunt near Resolute Bay, N.W.T." *Arctic Institute of North America* 36, no. 1 (1983): 90–94.

Wenzel, George W., and A. L. Foote. "Conservation Hunting Concepts, Canada's Inuit, and Polar Bear Hunting." In *Tourism and the Consumption of Wildlife: Hunting, Shooting and Sport Fishing*, edited by B. Lovelock, 115–28. London: Routledge, 2008.

INDEX

Page numbers with fig. may refer to
either illustration or caption.

D

E

ABOUT THE AUTHOR

TUTI MINONDO

Michael Engelhard is the author of two essay collections, *Where the Rain Children Sleep* and *American Wild*, and the editor of four anthologies, including *Wild Moments: Adventures with Animals of the North*. His writing has appeared in *Sierra, Outside, National Wildlife,* the *San Francisco Chronicle, High Country News,* and other publications. Trained as a cultural anthropologist at the University of Alaska Fairbanks, he has participated in fieldwork north of the Arctic Circle. He now guides wilderness trips in Gates of the Arctic National Park and the Arctic National Wildlife Refuge, his favorite places in the world. Moving frequently, he has lived in Nome, at the southern limit of the White Bear's range but these days calls Fairbanks his home.